Improving Learning through Consulting Pupils

D0165353

Pupil consultation can lead to a transformation of teacher-pupil relationships, to significant improvements in teachers' practices, and to pupils having a new sense of themselves as members of a community of learners. In England, pupil involvement is at the heart of current government education policy and is a key dimension of both citizenship education and personalised learning.

Drawing on research carried out as part of the Teaching and Learning Research Programme, *Improving Learning through Consulting Pupils* discusses the potential of consultation as a strategy for signalling a more partnership-oriented relationship in teaching and learning. It also examines the challenges of introducing and sustaining consultative practices. Topics covered include:

- the centrality of consultation about teaching and learning in relation to broader school level concerns;
- teaching approaches that pupils believe help them to learn and those that obstruct their learning;
- teachers' responses to pupil consultation - what they learn from it, the changes they can make to their practice and the difficulties they can face;
- the things that can get in the way of pupils trusting in consultation as something that can make a positive difference.

While consultation is flourishing in many primary schools, the focus here is on secondary schools where the difficulties of introducing and sustaining consultation are often more daunting, but where the benefits of doing so can be substantial. This innovative book will be of interest to all those concerned with improving classroom learning.

Jean Rudduck and **Donald McIntyre** were both Professors of Education at the Faculty of Education, University of Cambridge, UK. Both of them retired in 2004, but continued to work. Sadly, Jean Rudduck died on 28 March 2007, shortly after completing this book, and Donald McIntyre died on 16 October 2007, just before it was published.

Improving Learning TLRP

Series Editor: Andrew Pollard, Director of the ESRC Teaching and Learning Programme.

Improving Learning How to Learn: classrooms, schools and networks
Mary James, Paul Black, Patrick Carmichael, Mary-Jane Drummond, Alison Fox, Leslie Honour, John MacBeath, Robert McCormick, Bethan Marshall, David Pedder, Richard Procter, Sue Swaffield, Joanna Swann and Dylan Wiliam.

Improving Literacy by Teaching Morphemes
Terezinha Nunes and Peter Bryant

Improving Schools, Developing Inclusion
Mel Ainscow, Alan Dyson and Tony Booth

Improving Subject Teaching: lessons from research in science education
John Leach, Robin Millar, Jonathan Osborne and Mary Radcliffe

Improving Workplace Learning
Karen Evans, Phil Hodkinson, Helen Rainbird and Lorna Unwin

Improving Learning Cultures in Further Education: understanding how students learn
David James and Gert Biesta

Improving Learning through Consulting Pupils
Jean Rudduck and Donald McIntyre

Improving Learning through Consulting Pupils

Jean Rudduck and Donald McIntyre
on behalf of theTLRP Consulting
Pupils Project Team

Routledge
Taylor & Francis Group
LONDON AND NEW YORK

DOWLING GREEN STATE
UNIVERSITY LIBRARY

First published 2007
by Routledge
2 Park Square, Milton Park, Abingdon, Oxon OX14 4RN

Simultaneously published in the USA and Canada
by Routledge
270 Madison Ave, New York, NY 10016

Routledge is an imprint of the Taylor & Francis Group, an informa business

© 2007 Jean Rudduck and Donald McIntyre

Typeset in Charter ITC and Stone Sans
by Keystroke, 28 High Street, Tettenhall, Wolverhampton
Printed and bound in Great Britain by
Tj International Ltd, Padstow, Cornwall

All rights reserved. No part of this book may be reprinted or
reproduced or utilised in any form or by any electronic, mechanical,
or other means, now known or hereafter invented, including
photocopying and recording, or in any information storage or
retrieval system, without permission in writing from the publishers.

Library of Congress Cataloging in Publication Data
McIntyre, Donald, 1937–
Improving learning through consulting pupils / Jean Rudduck and
Donald McIntyre.
p. cm.
Includes bibliographical references and index.
1. Teacher–student relationships—Great Britain. 2. Student participation
in administration—Great Britain. 3. Communication in education—
Great Britain.
I. Rudduck, Jean. II. Title.
LB1033.M345 2007
371.102'3—dc22
2007017234

ISBN 10: 0–415–41615–9 (hbk)
ISBN 10: 0–415–41616–7 (pbk)
ISBN 10: 0–203–93532–2 (ebk)

ISBN 13: 978–0–415–41615–3 (hbk)
ISBN 13: 978–0–415–41616–0 (pbk)
ISBN 13: 978–0–203–93532–3 (ebk)

Contents

Series editor's preface   vii
Acknowledgements   ix

PART I
What are the issues?   **1**

1 **Pupil voice: changing contexts**   **3**

PART II
What does the research tell us?   **23**

2 **Strategies for consulting pupils about teaching
   and learning**   **25**

3 **What pupils say about teachers and
   teacher–pupil relationships**   **46**

4 **What pupils say about classroom teaching and
   learning**   **57**

5 **What pupils say about their own teachers'
   teaching**   **74**

6 **What pupils say about conditions for their
   learning**   **85**

7 **What pupils say about being consulted**   **103**

8 Teachers' responses to what pupils say   118

9 The impact of pupil consultation on pupils
   and teachers   139

10 Reservations, anxieties and constraints   154

11 Conditions for developing consultation   168

PART III
What are the overall implications?   181

12 Summary: what have we learned?   183

13 The development of consultation and its
   transformative potential   192

   Appendix 1   202
   Appendix 2   206
   References   210
   Index   217

Series editor's preface

The Improving Learning series showcases findings from projects within the Economic and Social Research Council's Teaching and Learning Research Programme (TLRP), the UK's largest ever co-ordinated educational research initiative.

Books in the Improving Learning series are explicitly designed to support 'evidence-informed' decisions in educational practice and policy-making. In particular, they combine rigorous social and educational science with high awareness of the significance of the issues being researched.

Working closely with practitioners, organisations and agencies covering all educational sectors, the program has supported many of the UK's best researchers to work on the direct improvement of policy and practice to support learning. Over seventy projects have been supported, covering many issues across the life course. We are proud to present the results of this work through books in the Improving Learning series.

Each book provides a concise, accessible and definitive overview of innovative findings from a TLRP investment. If more advanced information is required, the books may be used as a gateway to academic journals, monographs, websites, etc. On the other hand, shorter summaries and research briefings on key findings are also available via the programme's website at http://www.tlrp.org.

We hope that you will find the analysis and findings presented in this book helpful to you in your work on improving outcomes for learners.

Andrew Pollard
Director, TLRP
Institute of Education, University of London

Acknowledgements

We want to thank all the many teachers and pupils who contributed to the Consulting Pupils about Teaching and Learning Project by sharing their thoughts with researchers.

Our thanks too to all our academic colleagues on whose work this book focuses. First among these, of course, are the members of the Consulting Pupils team: Madeleine Arnot, Sara Bragg, Nick Brown, Helen Demetriou, Michael Fielding, Julia Flutter, John MacBeath, Kate Myers, David Pedder, Diane Reay and Beth Wang. We are also especially grateful to members of linked projects who have allowed us to draw on their work: Lesley Hendy, Bethan Morgan and Elaine Wilson.

We appreciate too the support and patience of Mary James and Andrew Pollard as editors of this series and directors of the TLRP programme.

Neither the project nor the book would have been possible without the work of Nichola Daily, Ann Curtis (the project) and Theresa Daly (the book), who, with great good humour and kindness, efficiently administered and communicated for us and kept us organised. We are most grateful.

Part I

What are the issues?

Chapter 1 discusses the different 'surges' of interests in pupil* voice since the 1970s and speculates about the reasons for the present level of interest. It outlines the TLRP Consulting Pupils about Teaching and Learning Project and some linked projects that provide the focus for the book and affirms the project's commitment to exploring the potential of *consultation in the classroom*.

Chapter 1 also outlines the issues that the TLRP Project team became aware of during the project and that have remained prominent:

1   the tension between 'participation' (which has a broader remit and need not involve pupil voices) and 'consultation', and the danger that the complexities of developing consultation about teaching and learning could lead to a focus outside rather than inside the classroom;

2   the tension, for researchers and practitioners interested in pupil voices, between the government's general encouragement of listening to pupils and the lack of practical support offered, especially in relation to finding time for consultation in the context of the sustained prioritisation of 'performance';

3   the extent to which citizenship education is seen as teaching *about* politics, democracy and power in the community beyond school rather than as learning about citizenship through experiencing and reflecting on democratic structures within the community of the school – the latter tying in more closely with the consultation agenda;

4   the feeling, among people without recent and close experience of consulting pupils about teaching and learning, that it is nothing new and the consequent need to communicate a fuller understanding of both its procedures and potential.

* Throughout the book we have used the word 'pupil' rather than 'student' even though the latter is gaining ground; we decided to do so in order to be consistent with the title of the TLRP Project.

Chapter 1

Pupil voice

Changing contexts

> This book is about pupil voice in the classroom and reports what we learned from our research project on consulting pupils about teaching and learning.
>
> Why a project on pupil voice? There is nothing new about seeking to hear and to represent pupil perspectives. But in the present climate of unprecedented national and international support for the idea of listening to young people it is important to understand consultation's potential for strengthening learning and improving the conditions of learning.
>
> In this chapter we look at the development of pupil voice and go on to discuss the trend whereby consultation about teaching and learning is giving way to consultation about broader school-level concerns and more global issues. We also describe the project that provides the main focus for the book, together with some of the smaller projects that followed in its wake.

The growth and diversity of interest in pupil perspectives

There was vigorous pursuit of pupil voice by educational researchers in the late 1960s and 1970s. Their commitment to exploring pupil perspectives was driven by the desire to build a fuller understanding of life in classrooms and schools; rounding out the picture meant eliciting and valuing pupils' accounts of experience. Prominent among the pupil voice researchers was Peter Woods. Despite his already substantial collection of writing about pupils, the publishers of his 1980 book still felt it necessary to explain to readers that 'there are remarkably few studies that take the pupils' perspectives and reconstruct experience from their points of view'. Two years earlier, Roland Meighan was building a special issue of *Educational Review* around the pupil perspective. He presented it, tellingly, as a minority practice in educational research:

> There are only a few studies of schooling from the point of view of the learners . . . This special edition attempts to focus on this neglected aspect of educational writing . . . by bringing together contributions from a number of current researchers interested in the various aspects of the pupils' viewpoint.
>
> (Meighan, 1978: 91, Editorial)

The articles in the special issue reported on studies where the external researchers went into schools, talked to pupils, wrote up what they had to say and made their accounts available through publications. The tradition is an important one: it rests on the analytic expertise of the professional researcher who must also, of course, be skilful in talking and listening to young people. But in none of the articles in the special issue was there evidence of *the school itself* being committed to what we would now call 'pupil voice'. And although such research provides a legitimate space for pupils to talk about their learning, there has usually been no attempt to feed back the outcomes of the enquiry to the pupils involved, and no guarantee that the opportunity for pupils to talk about their experiences as learners will be kept open.

Again, there has been a recognisable tradition of consultation within particular subjects, the most obvious being constructivist approaches in science where teachers find out from pupils what their present state of understanding is and try to build from that. But where this strategy is primarily about subject knowledge, ours engages directly with pedagogic experience and the teaching strategies that pupils find more or less helpful for their learning.

In the 1970s there were also concerns with democratic principles and for young people's rights which prefigured the interest of the 1990s. It was in the 1970s, at a time when pupil unrest in higher education was hitting the headlines internationally, that the secondary school wing (NUSS) of the National Union of Students (NUS) drew up a list of twenty-seven 'articles'. Their policy statement has been described by Wagg (1996: 14–15) as 'one of the most uncompromising and idealistic statements of liberation philosophy ever seen in British educational politics'; although now, in the midst of the present wave of interest in pupil voice, the things they called for seem less radical (see Rudduck and Flutter, 2004: 107–10). The student wing had a short life but in 2004 a new organisation was set up – a possible reincarnation of the NUSS – the English Secondary Students' Association (ESSA).

During the 1990s and the early 2000s there was evidence of a steadily increasing interest in young people's voices and involvement. Government interest, it is said, was largely shaped by two impulses: the desire to be seen to be responding positively, if slowly, to the United Nations Convention on the Rights of the Child; and concern about political apathy among young voters. One response has been to emphasise the importance of citizenship education – in the hope, perhaps, that a habit of involvement might be established in school and sustained beyond it. In relation to taking seriously the articles of the 1989 Convention (ratified in 1992), Lynn Davies reported that the UK lags well behind other European countries in terms of its acceptance of pupil voice and its understanding of the effectiveness of involving pupils in educational decision-making. In Denmark, she reported, pupils are required to be represented on school boards; in the two participating Länder of Germany pupils must be represented on the Scholkonferenz with – as in Denmark – the actual numbers of pupil representatives predetermined. In the Netherlands every secondary school must have a participation council with pupil representatives. In Sweden older pupils must participate in the same number as teachers in meetings about teaching, learning and the curriculum (see Davies, 2001).

The UK is now moving faster to keep up with the European Joneses: it has encouraged government departments, non-government agencies and other bodies, such as local education authorities, to ensure that young people's views are canvassed on issues that affect them. In 2004 it also established a Children's Commissioner, and it backed the idea of a Youth Parliament. An influential DfES publication, *Every Child Matters* (2003), highlights the importance of young people being able to participate in decision-making on issues that are important to them and to make a positive contribution to their community, both in and out of school. Not much of this activity, however, was about learning in the classroom.

Interestingly, inspectors from the Office for Standards in Education (Ofsted) have now lent their considerable weight to pupil voice: they have carried the logic of pupil involvement into their enquiries by formally asking pupils about aspects of schooling – including teaching

– and they must now also report back to pupils as a separate con-
stituency in the school. While the principle of inclusion and of respecting
pupils' accounts of their experience is a good one, there have been some
objections (*TES*, 18.11.05) to the feedback procedure: the staff of one
school saw feedback as inspectors repeating their criticisms of teachers
in a letter sent to pupils and thereby potentially undermining teachers'
authority and professional competence in pupils' eyes. The attempt to
be inclusive can, unless carefully handled, prove divisive.

Alongside government and Ofsted endorsement of pupil involvement
came the interest and support of a large number of other agencies and
organisations which had a remit to work with young people. The reasons
why different agencies – governmental and non-governmental – have
taken up the banner of young people's participation in school vary, but
together they make appeal to the following:

- *the principle of democracy in school* as a way of preparing young
  people for their role in society;
- *the principle of young people's rights*, including their rights as
  members of the school community;
- *the idea that schools need to be more inclusive* and to offer more
  opportunities of involvement to students as the main stakeholder
  group;
- *concern for students' personal and social development* which, it is
  argued, would be nurtured by the respect and confidence that being
  consulted can offer;
- *the possibility of enhanced commitment to learning* in that pupils
  could help define a practical agenda for improvement that they
  themselves would endorse and of which they would feel some
  ownership.

So, although the reasons for supporting the pupil voice movement
may be different for different agencies, all are contributing, in their own
ways, to a widespread if somewhat confusing awareness of the
importance of listening to young people.

Competing agendas and the implications for consultation in the classroom

By the end of 2004 it seemed that pupil voice was in danger of turning
away from the classroom before its full potential had been documented

and understood. There were several reasons for thinking that this might be the case. One was a generalising trend whereby the broader concept of participation came to be seen as more accessible than the more specific – and more demanding – concept of consultation. Another reason was the ambiguity of the government's interest in and support for consultation: it was strong on rhetoric but less forthcoming in terms of practical support. A third reason was the formalising trend whereby citizenship education came to be defined in ways that prioritised 'teaching about' government, and while there was space for different forms of participation, the contribution of consultation was less clear. The fourth reason, a protective response to an awareness of the challenge of consultation, was the claim that good teachers had always consulted pupils anyway, so there was really nothing new in it. We discuss each of these in turn below.

Consultation and participation

We saw *consultation* as talking with pupils about things that matter to them in the classroom and school and that affect their learning. Ideally consultation is a conversation that builds a habit of easy discussion between teacher and pupil about learning. Pupils may want to talk about their experiences of learning in a particular lesson or subject and explain what they find engaging, stimulating, satisfying, bewildering, difficult or off-putting. Teachers may want to learn what pupils have to say about, for instance, a new teaching strategy or a new way of assessing learning, or about the way that homework is currently set or feedback given, or the system of incentives and rewards used by teachers to motivate pupils and recognise their progress. And of course pupils and teachers may have shared concerns – for instance, how to deal with constant low levels of noise in the classroom that get in the way of teaching and learning. Pupils involved in consultation know that their views are being sought because it is expected that they will have something useful to contribute.

Participation may or may not involve pupil commentary. It is about involving pupils in the school's work through, for example, at school level

- a wider range of roles and responsibilities;
- membership of committees and working parties that are focusing on events, problems, possibilities that are important to pupils as well as to teachers.

At the classroom level participation may involve

- opportunities for decision-making;
- understanding your own learning styles and your weaknesses and strengths in learning and managing priorities for focusing your efforts towards improvement.

This is a rather conventional interpretation of participation. It falls midway between the bottom-line definition (participation as 'bums on seats') and the elaborated, community-oriented ideal discussed by Ruth Berry (2006: 494–5) which, in its emphasis on the intersection of social relationships and academic achievement, comes closer to the dynamic of consultation and is potentially 'transformative for both individual and context' (*ibid.*: 494, quoting Lave and Wenger, 1991). However, Berry concludes that 'participation as a construct is greatly underdefined and underexamined'; we would add that the relationship of participation and consultation also merits review.

In 2003–4 the DfES was preparing draft guidance notes on pupil participation with admirable but ambitious aspirations expressed in the title: *Working Together: Giving Children and Young People a Say*. The guidance was designed to help schools and LEAs organise opportunities for the development of pupils' 'skills as active citizens' (DfES, 2004: iii), and for involvement in decision-making processes. Consultation is not explicitly included but the document talks about involving pupils more actively in their education and 'in the evaluation process and review of lessons learned' (*ibid.*: 7) and also about pupils learning 'how to make a difference from an early age'. The concern with 'active pupil participation' is explained in terms of a commitment to recognise 'children and young people as major stakeholders in society with important contributions to make to the design and delivery of services they receive, including education' (*ibid.*: 3). Our criticism is that the legitimation and guidance schools need to prioritise such aims for the here-and-now community of the school are underplayed.

The tension between consultation and participation was sharpened by the stance of the Children's Commissioner, who argued in public lectures in 2005 that consultation is not democratically acceptable because it implies that teachers are controlling young people's right to speak and setting the boundaries of what they might discuss. But there may be some aspects of teaching and learning that teachers are curious about and have every right to explore through consulting their pupils. And we would add that in many schools consultation may well have to start as a teacher initiative but that the balance of power will change as teachers and pupils learn to trust each other. Thus, with one sweeping statement pupil consultation and all that it offers to teachers and achieves for pupils could be diminished. You can, of course, have participation without consultation, but you cannot have consultation without participation: the latter is implicit in the former.

Compared with participation, consulting pupils about teaching and learning is altogether more risky and difficult to manage: its capacity for destabilising habitual ways of behaving and familiar patterns of expectation – about power issues in teacher–pupil relationships, for instance – is obvious. As McQuillan notes, after following through the development of pupil voice in one high school, 'disequilibrium seems unavoidable given that student empowerment contradicts what many students, teachers, administrators and parents believe students and schools should do' (2005: 664).

The ambiguity of government interest and support

Developing consultation is seen by many teachers as in competition with the government's all-powerful performance agenda for the scarce resource of curriculum time; moreover, although government, in the wake of the 1989 Convention on the Rights of the Child, had explicitly supported the idea of listening to pupils, and at some levels continues to do so, it has offered little practical guidance on and support for the very real problems of implementing consultation in classrooms (see above). The issue of time remains unresolved and is closely tied up with achievement issues: teachers are uneasy about spending time on introducing and sustaining something as complex and demanding as consulting pupils about teaching and learning when they know that the priority for government is performance and, consequently, that the priority for teachers is preparing pupils for high-stakes tests and examinations. The irony of course is that being consulted can, albeit indirectly, strengthen pupils' interest in the school's learning purposes and their commitment to doing well. But government failed fundamentally to develop a research agenda around – or to appear interested in – the key issue of the impact of consultation on pupils' learning and on their commitment to learning.

Within our research, consultation was seen as a pathway to school improvement, but by 'school improvement' we meant much more than a narrow focus on grades. For teachers, it was about learning from their pupils ways in which classroom teaching and learning can become not only more effective, more meaningful and more enjoyable but a task that teachers and pupils can undertake collaboratively. For pupils, it was about their development individually and in groups as they come better to understand their own learning and take control of their work, and as they come to believe that they can contribute to improving the conditions of learning in school. So the direct benefits for pupils include the confidence that comes from knowing that your ideas are taken seriously and confidence in being able to express your view. As one pupil said, '[Now] I can put across my views even to posh people.' Moreover, a growing body of evidence from other projects and education systems (see Chapter 12) suggests that the experience of being consulted supports the development of pupils' confidence as learners and that this in turn can positively affect their commitment to learning. In short, consultation should not be seen as in conflict with the achievement agenda and competing with it for time and resources but recognised as supporting it while at the same time securing a range of social and personal outcomes that pupils see as important but that tend to be marginalised by the present narrow boundaries of the performance agenda.

The uncertain relationship between citizenship education and consultation

The government's youth agenda is related to New Labour's love affair with the three Cs – consumerism, choice and community: it backs young people's involvement in pupil councils, youth committees and citizenship education. But despite its launch of the personalised learning agenda (which remains poorly defined) it is tentative in recognising and recommending the pedagogic potential of consultation. This tentativeness was noticed by Lynn Davies: 'While it is seen as acceptable and indeed desirable to centralise and legislate the curriculum and assessment – and even teaching methods in the literacy and numeracy hours – when it comes to pupil involvement in decisions on their own learning we revert to a neo-liberal ideology which upholds the freedom of schools to decide their own affairs' (2001: 3).

At national level, then, government seems unable to perceive or certainly to give attention to unravelling what Davies called the 'bizarre contradictions' in its stance on pupil voice. It has been publicly supportive but has done little to help teachers deal with the dilemma of prioritisation within the curriculum. One way out of this dilemma was for citizenship education (which has been compulsory in secondary schools in England since 2002) to be endorsed as the proper site for consultation and participation. However, this is not an entirely secure refuge for consultation in that the focus for citizenship education is being tightened in ways that leave little space for consultation: 'citizenship is educating children about public institutions, power, politics and community and "equipping them to engage effectively as informed citizens"'. Moreover, citizenship education is, it seems, having to take on an additional aim: 'the government's determination [is] to make citizenship lessons a key weapon in the fight against extremism, the education watchdog Ofsted warns today'. The article goes on to say that inspectors are making it clear that 'more room will have to be found for citizenship' – but not, it seems, for consultation, despite its potential for strengthening pupils' learning as well as their social skills and sensitivities (Meikle, 2006).

The emphasis on citizenship education as teaching about 'public institutions, power, politics' is at odds with the findings of the National Foundation for Educational Research's review of citizenship education conducted for the DfES and published in May 2006. The report (Ireland et al., 2006: v, viii) indicates that 'most young people were keen to make an active and responsible contribution to the communities to which they belong, particularly the school community'. Within that community 'young people believed that they should have a voice on matters that affect them [and] they were keen to show that they can use their voice, both individually and collectively, in a responsible manner'. The report concluded that 'there are a number of measures that schools can take to develop a sense of belonging for students within the school community' including:

- giving students a voice;
- creating a climate for mutual respect between teachers and students;
- ensuring that there is equality of opportunity for all students;
- dividing the school community into smaller communities;
- improving the quality of the school buildings and facilities that students use.

The report also suggested that schools need to do more to help students to:

- understand why having a voice is important;
- use their voice effectively;

- understand the mechanisms and processes of influencing policy and change;
- believe that their voice will be heard, taken seriously and acted upon.

In short, the NFER report, based on interviews with young people in schools, places much more emphasis on pupil voice as a key component of citizenship education and on the school as offering an experience of community where they can learn about the give and take of 'membership'. It takes us back to the various statements (from Dent in the 1930s) about the importance of pupils learning about democracy through its enactment in the daily life of the school. Dent's recommendation was terse and to the point: 'Before you can have an educated democracy you must offer your democracy an education that is likely to make it one' (1930: 14).

'There's nothing new about consultation'

It is, of course, all too easy to step back from consultation, claiming that it is merely an easy extension of what good teachers do anyway rather than something that most teachers would experience as novel and complex. Indeed, during our research there were always some sceptical voices challenging us to explain what was so special about our project. And, aware that Giroux (1981: 150) had once said that what went under the name of educational innovation was often little more than the recycling and repackaging of old ways of doing things, we tried to explain what was, potentially, new about consultation:

- students are more explicitly invited to comment not just on their own learning but on frameworks for learning, including teaching strategies and other conditions of learning;
- students have a more consciously analytic and responsible stance, knowing that they are contributing to school improvement and that their voices can make a difference;
- students' expertise as insightful commentators on teaching and learning is recognised;
- the status of students is enhanced through this recognition of their capacity to contribute to school improvement through informed commentary.

In the context of a widespread interest in young people, we saw our research project as investigating a more transformative potential in terms of teacher–pupil relationships and of the way young people are seen and valued in schools. And we recommended – as we would for any challenging and important initiative – that teachers, before rushing into it, should ask some serious questions. These are about the early stages of implementation:

- Why they are interested in it (i.e., they need to understand the basis of their own commitment and know what they expect from consultation)?
- What resources are available to support its development?
- How will the idea of consulting pupils be legitimised as a worthwhile educational strategy?
- Will the values that underpin consultation be in harmony with the current values of the school and the other initiatives that the school is pursuing?

And then there are the questions that define an important research agenda that teachers should hold on to throughout their work on consultation:

- Does the experience of consultation contribute to pupils' learning? If so, what is the process by which it does so?
- What is the impact on pupils and, if it is beneficial, are all pupils able to benefit?
- What is the impact on teachers' pedagogic practices and on teacher–pupil relationships?

Consulting pupils about teaching and learning proved to be difficult for pupils, teachers and schools to manage. We have already mentioned the issue of time; there were also attitudinal difficulties and it was apparent that consultation could generate personal and interpersonal insecurities. For instance, schools may subscribe to a traditional view of pupils and their role in school which is shaped by what Gerald Grace (1995: 201) calls 'an ideology of immaturity': he suggests that 'the idea that school pupils are too immature to participate in responsible decision making in [classrooms] . . . is a useful argument for the maintenance of adult and professional hegemony'. But, of course, as many teachers have found, it is not until you invite pupils to talk about their experiences of teaching and learning that you can understand how insightful their comments are. Then teachers may feel more comfortable with whole-class delivery and ill-prepared for the more reflective discussions that consultation usually entails. And teachers may be nervous about relinquishing the security of their traditional authority by putting their teaching on the line (as they sometimes see it) for pupils to discuss.

As this chapter has tried to make clear, we became particularly aware that consultation about teaching and learning in the classroom was in danger of being dumbed down or sidelined before its potential had been fully understood. And its potential, as our project demonstrates, is considerable.

The ESRC TLRP Consulting Pupils about Teaching and Learning (CPTL) Project

The Consulting Pupils Project was a major development and research project funded by the ESRC with the Teaching and Learning Research Programme (TLRP). It built on two earlier ESRC projects: Jean Rudduck *et al.*'s Pupils' Experiences of Teaching and Learning and Donald McIntyre and Paul Cooper's Teachers' and Pupils' Perceptions of Effective Classroom Learning. Both of these projects foregrounded pupil perspectives, confirming that pupils can be a rich source of information about the relationship between teaching and learning. However, in both pupils were interviewed by members of the project research teams and there was no explicit intention to support teachers in developing consultation practices that they could manage themselves. The TLRP Project therefore had a different agenda but drew on our earlier experience of talking with pupils about teaching and learning. The research and development was carried out between 2000 and 2003.

The Consulting Pupils about Teaching and Learning Project

Most members of the project team[1] had worked on aspects of pupil voice before, and it was our sustained interest in the topic that brought us together. We already shared the view that young people have a lot to offer to school improvement and that the relevance of their insights should not be underestimated. Our proposal for a programme of work on consulting pupils about teaching and learning reflected both the 'animation' and the uncertainty in the system in 2000 in relation to pupil voice. Our main concerns, given that the idea of consulting pupils was for many teachers a new and somewhat scary venture, were to

- map the territory and potential of consulting pupils;
- respond to teachers' needs for basic guidance;
- identify key issues in its development and implementation, including constraints.

These concerns were more formally articulated as five aims:

- to understand and document *the process* whereby giving attention to pupil perspective and participation in schools can contribute to enhanced pupil engagement and achievement;
- to understand and document *the conditions* in school in which pupil perspective and participation can be constructively used to enhance pupil engagement and achievement;
- to offer *support to teachers* who want to develop ways of enhancing pupil engagement and achievement through consulting pupils and increasing opportunities for participation;
- to ensure that the growing interest in pupil consultation is grounded in *worthwhile and defensible educational principles and practices*;
- to integrate a *theory of teaching, learning and attainment with a theory of pupil consultation and participation.*

We pursued these aims through six constituent projects, which in this book we shall refer to as 'enquiries' in order to distinguish them from the overall project (see Appendix 1 for details):

- CPTL1 How teachers respond to pupils' ideas on improving teaching and learning in different subjects.
- CPTL2 Ways of consulting pupils about teaching and learning.
- CPTL3 The potential of pupils to act as (co-)researchers into the process of teaching and learning.
- CPTL4 Pupil perspectives and consultation: starting and sustaining the process.
- CPTL5 What pupils can tell us about how the conditions of learning in the classroom affect the identity and participation of different groups of pupils.
- CPTL6 Breaking new ground: innovative initiatives involving pupil consultation.

These were the projects, their directors (d) and their team members: each has a code for quick reference later; where a passage quoted comes from a published account, both the enquiry's code and the publication details are given. Across the six enquiries, teachers and pupils from forty-eight primary and secondary schools were involved. The key concerns of each enquiry are summarised below.

CPTL1   How teachers respond to pupils' ideas on improving teaching and learning (Donald McIntyre [d] and David Pedder)

Although we knew a good deal about the quality of the ideas that pupils can offer about improving classroom teaching and learning (e.g., Cooper and McIntyre, 1996) we knew much less about how teachers respond to and use such ideas.

We wanted to find out whether, if teachers were offered in-depth commentaries on their teaching from different pupils in the same class,

- they would find these ideas valuable in offering sensible ways in which they might change their classroom practices;
- they would actually change their practices, both in the short term and in the longer term;
- the experience would persuade teachers to build pupil consultation procedures into their normal practice; and
- constraints might limit their use of pupil ideas.

Teachers and pupils from six Year 8 classes (two each of English, Maths and Science) in three East Anglian secondary schools were involved.

CPTL2   Ways of consulting pupils about teaching and learning (John MacBeath [d], Kate Myers and Helen Demetriou)

Social science researchers, educational psychologists and other education professionals have considerable experience of using questionnaires, diaries, interviews, group discussion and visual means of eliciting young people's accounts of experience, feelings and views. However, we were less confident in our understanding of how teachers can manage consultation in the time-constrained conditions of the classroom, what they see as the benefits of such consultation and what they see as the key issues.

The project was designed to respond to these questions. Its key purposes were:

- to develop, in partnership with teachers, tools for consulting pupils about their learning;
- to support schools in embedding these in classroom practice;
- to evaluate the impact on pupils.

The project team worked with seven secondary and two primary schools in England, Wales and Scotland.

CPTL3   The potential of pupils to act as (co-)researchers into the processes of teaching and learning (Michael Fielding [d] and Sara Bragg)

The idea of pupils acting as researchers or co-researchers with their teachers was relatively new in the UK and its potential, especially in relation to teaching and learning, was unexamined.

The aims were:

- to document the potential for involving pupils as 'researchers' in the task of improving teaching and learning;
- to gather data about the process and its impact and outcomes from pupils involved as researchers, from pupils not involved directly in the research and from teachers;
- to identify factors that affect the success of such initiatives.

The core working group consisted of seven schools, two primary and five secondary, in the South of England, but the team had close contact with a number of other schools engaged in similar work and this additional resource enabled us to test the robustness of our findings and extend our understanding.

CPTL4   Pupil perspectives and consultation: starting and sustaining the process (Michael Fielding [d] and Sara Bragg)

It is widely recognised now that school reform efforts have consistently underestimated the difficulty of sustaining innovations, especially when they reflect the enthusiasm of individual teachers. The task is particularly difficult in relation to pupil consultation which challenges the power base of existing teacher–pupil relationships and requires, if something more than superficial is attempted, a transformation of mutual perceptions. The literature on pupil voice had, by 2000, said little on these issues.

The aims were:

- to collect data on schools at different stages in the process of giving attention to pupil perspectives and to document the issues involved in both starting and sustaining that process;
- to generate materials that would be helpful to other schools in assessing their own contexts and considering how best to begin this process themselves.

The team gathered data in seven primary and secondary schools in the South East.

CPTL5   What pupils can tell us about how the conditions of learning in the classroom affect the identity and participation of different groups of pupils (Madeleine Arnot [d], Diane Reay [d] and Beth Wang)

Most of the project's six enquiries focused on building the confidence of teachers in managing consultation in their own classrooms and schools. However, we also wanted, realistically, to signal the existence of situations where pupils might not be prepared to open up to their teachers and where their concerns might otherwise go unheard and unheeded. Following the tradition of earlier pupil voice research, the agency of an external researcher was chosen as a useful strategy for eliciting pupils' views and, with permission from pupils, making them accessible to teachers.

The particular focus of the project was the social conditions of learning in particular classrooms. The aims were:

- to collect data from pupils on the ways in which the social conditions of learning affect learning identities and experiences;
- to explore the potential of pupil commentaries for
  - improving communication strategies between teachers and pupils
  - creating effective learning environments for lower-achieving pupils.

Pupil consultation was organised through group discussions with Year 8 and Year 4 classes in two secondary and two feeder primary schools, one pair in Cambridgeshire and one pair in London. (Only the secondary school data are discussed in this book; the primary school data are being analysed separately.)

CPTL6   Breaking new ground: innovative initiatives involving pupil consultation (Julia Flutter [d], Nick Brown and Elaine Wilson)

This was a two-year initiative which supported schools in investigating what were, for them, new investments in pupil consultation.

Whereas in the other projects the broad focus was identified by the network team, here we wanted to see what issues teachers would choose to pursue in their own classrooms and school contexts. Interested schools had to apply for a small grant, submitting an outline proposal. We advertised the opportunity in the project newsletters and also wrote directly to groups of schools we had worked with in the past. There were two rounds of applications; on both occasions a panel of researchers and a deputy headteacher read the proposals. Five infant/primary schools and twelve secondary schools were successful in their bids for a small grant (one proposal included a cluster of schools). Support was provided through a 'link researcher' – Nick Brown, Elaine Wilson or Julia Flutter (the latter also coordinated the project). These link researchers helped with data gathering and offered guidance on interpreting data and managing the evaluation.

Linked pupil voice projects

Pupil voice projects directed by members of the team but which were completed before the start of the TLRP Project are referred to by their full name and/or through reference to their published outcomes. These included: the two projects directed by Jean Rudduck (Pupils' Experiences of Teaching and Learning) and Donald McIntyre (Teachers' and Pupils' Perceptions of Effective Classroom Learning), and the West Sussex project coordinated by Jean Rudduck and involving Nick Brown and Lesley Hendy (Learning about Improvement) in which pupil perspectives were a distinctive feature.

Then there were some linked projects, directed or supervised by members of the project team, which overlapped with, or followed closely on the heels of, the TLRP Project. The two main ones are summarised below; each of these will be referred to in the text by its code – LP (for 'linked project') and number.

LP1   Personalised Learning and Pupil Voice (Jean Rudduck,
Nick Brown and Lesley Hendy)

This project set out to explore what the idea of personalised learning could usefully offer schools.

The framework for action had two non-negotiables:

- 'every child matters' was to be the overarching principle;
- consultation would be the means of accessing pupils' thinking (i.e., talking to pupils about their learning in school and taking seriously what they had to say).

Schools wanted ideas that they could work on in response to their own needs and unique contexts. The topics that the schools chose to work on were these:

- making sure that every child feels he or she matters in school;
- helping pupils understand how to improve their own learning;
- enabling pupils to contribute to the school improvement agenda;
- developing teaching and learning strategies that are engaging and participatory;
- promoting opportunities for choice, relevance and ownership;
- building positive and collaborative teacher–pupil and pupil–pupil relationships.

The project's first phase ended in July 2005. Phase 2 was end-on and finished in July 2006. The purpose was to look at strategies for 'scaling up'. The data, from both phases, included recorded and transcribed conversations and discussions with pupils and teachers; information from the learning logs that some groups of pupils kept; short written reports and poster presentations prepared by the participating schools for the termly cross-school conferences; and summaries of observations and issues prepared by members of the research team.[2]

LP2   Consulting Pupils about Classroom Teaching and
Learning: Policy, Practice and Response in One School
(Bethan Morgan, Donald McIntyre and David Pedder)

Bethan Morgan completed two projects linked to the TLRP Project, and her M.Phil. thesis (Morgan, 2000) was designed to extend the work of CPTL1 and she adopted a similar approach to it, working in the English department of a separate school.

She later went on to investigate pupil consultation (Morgan, 2007) based on a recognition that nowhere in the literature was there a detailed research account of teachers consulting pupils about teaching and learning except with the support of researchers. She wanted to know how, for what purposes, with what support and with what outcomes, teachers would consult their own pupils without such support from researchers. She therefore identified a secondary school with a strong reputation for pupil consultation and studied four teachers' consultation, each of one class, for a year. In the course of the year she observed the teachers' engagement in consultation, and interviewed each of them on several occasions about their consultation and the use that they made of it. She also explored the school's consultation policies and practices with senior and middle management staff, and the views of the pupils in the four classes.[3]

Summary

Chapter 1 tracks the development of interest in pupil voice since the 1970s. In the 1970s/1980s researchers explored pupil perspectives on the world of school but there was no general expectation, as there is now, that the data would be fed back to teachers and pupils as a basis for informed action. Nor was there any expectation that the episode would serve to open up dialogue, on a regular basis, between pupils and their teachers. Nevertheless, these earlier enquiries yielded valuable insights into the social world of the school, and persuasive evidence that pupils had things to say that were worth hearing.

The chapter identified some initiatives that have helped foster a more widespread interest in young people's voices, including the United Nations Convention on the Rights of the Child in 1989. Other landmarks in this country were the appointment of a Children's Commissioner, the increasingly high profile of school councils, of citizenship education and of personalised learning, and the extension of inspection criteria to include pupils' testimony as evidence of a school's commitment to the principles of pupil voice. At the same time there appears to be some ambiguity in the government's position, especially in relation to practical support, and in its failure to recognise the challenges to innovation posed by the performance agenda.

continued

One of the book's key themes is that, for various reasons, and before its full potential has been documented, consultation seems to be giving way to a broader interest in participation; as a consequence, the focus on teaching and learning is in danger of being weakened. The chapter identified some serious questions that teachers should ask themselves before starting the process of consultation and again as a way of monitoring direction and impact during the period of implementation.

Finally in this chapter we outlined the Consulting Pupils about Teaching and Learning Project, on which this book is largely based.

Overall, this introductory chapter indicates the changing contexts of work on pupil voice during the last forty years and the events that have influenced its direction.

Notes

1   Members of the project team: Madeleine Arnot, Sara Bragg, Nick Brown, Helen Demetriou, Michael Fielding, Julia Flutter, John MacBeath, Donald McIntyre, Kate Myers, David Pedder, Diane Reay, Jean Rudduck and Beth Wang. The project was coordinated by Jean Rudduck. Nichola Daily and Ann Curtis provided administrative and secretarial support throughout the project's period of funding. Associate members who contributed to its programme of seminars and helped in other ways: Lynn Davies, Derry Hannam, Victoria Morrow, Audrey Osler, Andrew Pollard, Iram Siraj Blatchford, Chris Watkins and Mike Wyness. Elaine Wilson helped with a school-based initiative in Enquiry 6 and Isobel Urquart helped out in Enquiry 5 during maternity cover.
2   Data from Phase 2 offer penetrating insights into the way young people are experiencing – and thinking about – aspects of schooling, and we are grateful to Nick Brown for allowing us to draw on the project transcripts – and also to Lesley and Nick for permission to quote the Phase 1 transcripts.
3   We draw on Bethan Morgan's evidence at a number of points in the book. But her work in exploring pupils' views on consultation is especially and uniquely rich, and we have gratefully drawn heavily on it in Chapter 7.

Part II

What does the research tell us?

In Part II we aim to give a fairly comprehensive and balanced picture of the problems and possibilities of developing consultation in the classroom. First we focus on what consultation can look like in the classroom and then, in four chapters, what pupils tend to comment on when consulted about their experiences of teaching and learning. Another chapter reports pupils' perceptions of consultation as an opportunity for them and for their teachers. In the last four chapters of Part II we step back and look at how teachers respond to what their pupils have said, including the criteria they use to determine which comments should be followed up, and the impact of consultation on pupils' learning and sense of self-as-learner and on teachers. Finally, we review some of the difficulties and tensions of developing consultation in the classroom and the conditions under which it can begin to flourish.

There are ten chapters in Part II:

- **What consultation looks like in the classroom**

  - Chapter 2: Strategies for consulting pupils about teaching and learning

- **What pupils say when they are consulted**

  - Chapter 3: What pupils say about teachers and teacher–pupil relationships
  - Chapter 4: What pupils say about classroom teaching and learning
  - Chapter 5: What pupils say about their own teachers' teaching
  - Chapter 6: What pupils say about the conditions for their learning

- **Pupils talk about the practice and potential of consultation**

  – Chapter 7: What pupils say about being consulted

- **The impact of consultation**

  – Chapter 8: Teachers' responses to what pupils say
  – Chapter 9: The impact of pupil consultation on pupils and teachers

- **Reviewing the problems of consultation**

  – Chapter 10: Reservations, anxieties and constraints
  – Chapter 11: Conditions for developing consultation

Chapter 2

Strategies for consulting pupils about teaching and learning

One of the aims of our TLRP Project was to support teachers in developing consultation by identifying, documenting and disseminating manageable and appropriate strategies for consulting pupils, together with principles of procedure. In this chapter we report what we have learned in relation to that aim. We look at the claims made for 'informal consultation' and go on to suggest three questions that would help teachers to think *why* they might want to consult pupils. The chapter offers a set of 'guiding principles' for initiating consultation and ends with a discussion of strategies for encouraging pupils to talk about their teaching and learning.

A simple but very important starting point is that we should be clear in respect of what we are consulting pupils about. The kind of explicit pupil consultation to which schools are most accustomed is consultation of pupils by senior management about aspects of school life other than classroom teaching and learning, such as meals, uniforms, cloakrooms, toilets and break-times. Our concern, however, is exclusively with pupil consultation by classroom teachers about teaching and learning in their classrooms. At least for the present, the main work of schools is classroom teaching and learning, and it is in classrooms that pupils spend most of their time in school. What schools do for their pupils can be significantly enhanced through listening to pupil voices only if these voices influence what happens in classrooms.

Such a focus is too narrow for some. For example, Noyes (2005: 539–40) has commented on some of the work of this project that 'for pupil voice research's transformative potential to be more fully realised, the limited focus on improved teaching and learning needs to be complemented by explicit intentions of developing participatory citizenship, democratic partnerships and challenging powerful assumptions and practices that maintain educational hierarchies and social injustice'. Similarly, Fielding and McGregor (2005: 9–10, 12, 13) suggest that the title of our project, 'Consulting Pupils about Teaching and Learning' is a sinister reflection of what, to them, is the unacceptable 'dominant script' of a 'neo-liberal hegemony' characterised by 'atomistic, market-oriented reductionism'. While we are in complete agreement about the importance of citizenship, democracy and social justice, and of 'the role of collective or communal voice', we are unapologetic about focusing our concern here on the benefits that pupils and teachers can gain through the latter consulting the former about classroom teaching and learning. So long as young people are obliged to spend so much of their time in schools, largely in classrooms, optimising the quality of classroom teaching and learning for all of them has to be a priority concern. Moreover, the 'transformative potential' of pupil voice in schools will certainly not be realised unless pupils are enabled and encouraged to voice their ideas about teaching and learning in their individual classrooms.

Our focus is limited furthermore to teachers consulting pupils with the purpose of learning from pupils about classroom teaching and learning. We distinguish this from consultation with the primary purpose of checking on how well teachers are doing. That latter purpose is an obvious one in a world where 'performance' and 'accountability' are key words. As we have already noted (see Chapter 1), Ofsted are among those who have recognised that pupils are very well informed about their teachers' teaching and have concluded that pupils might be useful collaborators in helping them to judge teachers' performances. Similarly, since teachers in England have to prepare themselves for annual 'performance reviews', thoughtful senior management teams have suggested that teachers might find it helpful to gather evidence from their pupils; and some have developed procedures that teachers could use to gather such evidence (see Flutter and Rudduck, 2004: 52–4). Our own evidence (McIntyre et al., 2005) suggests that when pupils are asked about their teachers' teaching, they generally have a great deal to say that should be reassuring for the teachers. So it seems entirely appropriate for teachers themselves to ask their pupils to help them in reviewing their performance; and there is no doubt that performance review can lead to learning. But, as both pupils and teachers are well aware, questions about how well teachers are doing are primarily asked in order to check on the adequacy of present or past performance. They are not well suited to helping teachers to gain new insights from their pupils, which is our concern here. We shall not, therefore, be giving further attention in this book to consulting pupils for accountability or performance review purposes.

Informal consultation

It is easy for teachers to see consultation as something that is already embedded in their practice. And it is certainly true that teachers constantly consult their pupils. Among the core tasks of teaching are, for example, finding out whether pupils understand what they are being asked to do, whether they are working appropriately, whether they understand what they have been taught, whether they have completed tasks and whether their interest in a topic or their attention to a task is beginning to waver. All of these involve elements of consulting pupils: 'Is there anything you don't understand?'; 'Is that clear?'; 'Do you want me to go over that again?' In addition, many teachers teach interactively, responding to the interests and understandings that pupils reveal, or allow pupils choice in the tasks that they undertake; and such teaching may be seen as involving implicit consultation of pupils.

So normal classroom teaching does involve considerable consultation. However, this consultation is not generally *about teaching and learning*. It does not involve asking pupils their views about which of their teachers' practices are helpful or unhelpful and why, nor about what characterises the classroom activities or choices that they find motivating or productive. That is the kind of consultation with which we are concerned here.

It is, however, true that some teachers do quite frequently consult their pupils informally about teaching and learning, perhaps as they leave the classroom, asking them whether they enjoyed particular activities, found particular tasks easy or difficult, or found particular experiences helpful for their learning. Such informal consultation is surely valuable. Among its strengths are:

- teachers can engage in informal consultation at any convenient time, when they and any of their pupils have a few moments together;
- teachers can focus informal consultation on whatever concerns them at a particular time, or in relation to a particular pupil, easily

guiding the conversation so as to find out what they want to know;

- informal consultation is likely to contribute to good relationships between teachers and pupils, through teachers' evident and frequent desire to listen to what pupils have to say;
- informal consultation can fit easily into the rhythms of school life, especially for teachers, who are accustomed to snatching a few moments between other activities in order to seek or to share information.

Given these strengths of informal pupil consultation, many teachers may not only value it but feel that they learn enough from it to make any more systematic kind of consultation of pupils about teaching and learning superfluous. At least two of Morgan's (2007) four case study teachers seemed to take this view. Even teachers who have experienced the benefits of using in-depth pupil consultation to improve the quality of their teaching, like Catharine and Richard (two teachers involved in our Enquiry 1 study), can conclude that informal 'chatting' is a good, realistic, 'normal' way of consulting pupils.

However, while the very informality of informal consultation makes it difficult to evaluate, it does seem likely to have some important limitations:

- being neither carefully planned nor pursued at any length, informal consultation may not get to the heart of the issues under discussion;
- when informally consulted, pupils may not have the opportunity to reflect in any depth on the issues under discussion and so may present only rather superficial views;
- informal consultation may tend to be concerned with specific or immediate concerns of teachers or of particular pupils, and so may not give teachers access to pupils' broader perspectives on teaching and learning in their classrooms;
- it seems likely that pupils who like talking with teachers will be those most frequently involved in informal consultation, while other pupils may be very rarely involved, and there is a consequent danger that teachers may be misled by the unrepresentative views that they hear;
- the informality of informal consultation may mean that pupils do not recognise that they are being consulted, and so the benefits that can follow from such recognition may be lost.

While we are in no doubt then about the potential value of informal consultation, we seriously doubt its adequacy as a means of consulting pupils. Our focus, therefore, will be on more *strategic* approaches, by which we mean *more deliberate, broader and more explicit* kinds of pupil consultation. We shall argue that the more carefully teachers plan consultation, the more helpful it can be to them; that, at its most useful, consultation involves a *broader* invitation to pupils to comment generally and openly on their classroom experience, and is not limited to asking about particular activities or topics; and that consultation is most powerful when it is *explicit*, so that it is clear to pupils that their views are being sought, with the clear implication that these views are valued and will be taken seriously. This kind of explicit, open consultation, inviting pupils to reflect on their classroom experiences and to share their reflections with teachers, has, until recently, been rare in British schools.

What do we hope to learn by consulting pupils?

The first decisions necessary in planning a strategy for consulting pupils are about what we hope to learn from the consultation. This question breaks down into at least three major sub-questions, all of them quite complex and none of them with simple right answers. These three questions are:

- How general or specific is the learning that we want from pupil consultation?
- How open-ended do we want our learning from pupils to be?
- Which pupils do we want to learn from?

How general or specific is the learning that we want from pupil consultation?

There are at least three possible levels of generality in what teachers might hope to learn from pupil consultation:

- What do pupils in general find helpful?
- What do pupils in a particular class find helpful from their particular teacher?
- What do particular pupils find helpful for their learning?

It is easiest to find what kinds of teaching and learning activities pupils generally regard as helpful in the classroom. This is because teachers need only read the findings of other people's investigations (as, for example, summarised in Chapters 3 and 4 of this book). It is also useful because there seems to be quite a high degree of consistency across schools, subjects and teachers about what is helpful from pupils' perspectives.

Valuable and easily accessible as such information can be, it does neglect one important aspect of teaching: its very personal nature. So any teacher might reasonably decide that, interesting as such generalised learning from the research literature might be, it is too remote and generalised to be of immediate help to them personally. For that immediate personal help, it would be necessary for such a teacher to consult his or her own pupils, to answer such questions as: 'What is helpful and unhelpful for them in *my* classroom?' and 'What kinds of modifications to *my* lessons, to *my* ways of managing their learning, would make learning more attractive, easier, more effective for them?' Consultation of their own pupils about their learning experiences can give teachers far richer and more directly relevant ideas with which they can reflect upon their own practice and how it might be improved (as exemplified in Chapter 5). And, of course, where teachers do value their own pupils' perspectives on life and learning in their classrooms, they need to work out how best they themselves can consult their pupils, with all the considerations of practicality, authenticity and obligations to treat pupils' views respectfully that this entails.

Learning, like teaching, is also very personal. Some of our project's research (outlined in Chapter 6) has emphasised how different the social conditions for learning in school classrooms are for different pupils. For example, differences among pupils in gender, in ethnicity, in social class and in their previous school attainments can be associated with very different classroom experiences. So while most pupils tend to agree with one another about the kinds of teaching approach that they find helpful, in other respects they have very different perspectives on classroom learning. Teachers might therefore want to learn about pupils' views regarding the social conditions of learning that would help each of them individually to learn and to succeed in their schoolwork. This would be the most ambitious and challenging aspiration that teachers might have for learning from pupil consultation, raising new questions both about the practicality of accessing and responding to individual pupils' personal perspectives and about the demanding conditions of mutual trust that such an enterprise would require. We have hardly any evidence of teachers undertaking such an ambitious enterprise, with or without the help of researchers.

How open-ended do we want our learning from pupils to be?

Another necessary consideration concerns the extent to which, in consulting pupils, we want to leave the agenda open. Experienced teachers know what it is like to be on the other end of consultation exercises, when governments 'consult' the profession about initiatives that they plan to take. It is common for those doing the consulting to set a very tight agenda, not only through specifying the questions to be answered but through specifying the choice of possible answers. Similarly, it is possible for teachers to keep total control when consulting pupils, for example through using closed-choice questionnaires. This has some considerable advantages, because it allows teachers to focus precisely on those things on which they want pupils' views, and because it minimises the amount of work necessary in analysing pupils' responses.

The use of such closed-choice questionnaires is, however, just one end of a spectrum of possibilities for giving pupils varied degrees of opportunity to participate in setting the agenda. Some of these possibilities, with increasing pupil influence on the agenda, are:

- teacher-constructed questionnaires with closed-choice questions to be answered by pupils;
- teacher-constructed questionnaires with open questions for pupils;
- semi-structured interviews or group discussions with pupils, in which they can influence the direction and substance of the conversation;
- the use of researchers or other intermediaries to conduct such interviews or discussions, thus avoiding the initially potentially inhibiting effect of the teacher's presence;
- pupils as co-enquirers, participating in decisions about the questions to be investigated;
- pupils as researchers, determining the agenda to be investigated.

As one moves along this spectrum, control over the agenda gradually shifts from teachers to pupils. It seems likely that one implication is that increasingly complex and time-consuming practical arrangements will be necessary in order to ensure that such more pupil-controlled consultation can be conducted effectively. It also means, however, that the information generated will increasingly reveal what pupils care about, and will be construed in pupils' terms and expressed in their language. Other things being equal, increasingly authentic pupil voices will be articulated so that teachers can listen to them, and the opportunities for teachers to learn will be correspondingly enhanced. On the other hand, that may mean increased challenges to teachers' own established ways of thinking and acting, and therefore increased difficulties for them in being responsive while dealing with the many constraints that school and government policies and requirements impose upon them. The greater control pupils have over the terms on which they are consulted, the greater the opportunities there are likely to be for useful teacher learning, but also the more demanding the tasks for teachers, both at the level of effective practical arrangements and at the more fundamental level of being constructively responsive to what pupils have to say.

Furthermore, the more independent pupils are in setting the agenda, the greater the danger that their agenda will be of no interest to teachers. Unilateral control of the agenda either by pupils or by teachers may undermine effective dialogue between them, and the transformed teacher–pupil relationships that such dialogue would imply. Many different considerations are necessary in determining what point on the spectrum is most desirable in a specific context.

Sometimes, of course, teachers want to conduct consultation exercises on relatively specific issues, such as classroom seating arrangements, noise in the classroom or collaboration with peers in learning. In such circumstances, the teachers are setting the broad agenda for consultation. None the less, within such broad frameworks, the same issues arise, with the same spectrum of possibilities, from tight teacher specification of the agenda to support for pupils construing the agenda as they see fit.

From which pupils do we want to learn?

A third consideration in thinking about what teachers might hope to learn by consulting pupils has to focus on which pupils should be consulted. Should all pupils in all classes be consulted? That is clearly necessary if the purpose is to understand each pupil's thinking about what helps or hinders his or her individual learning. But if the purpose is to understand what pupils find or would find helpful in individual teachers' teaching, then important decisions have to be made about the benefits and disadvantages of consulting only samples of pupils. In particular, where it is considered that more time-consuming procedures, such as individual interviewing, should be used, the practicality of this may seem to depend on limiting consultation to only a sample of pupils. And then the decision has to be made: which pupils?

A teacher might be especially concerned at a particular time with the classroom experiences and concerns of a particular sub-group of pupils (e.g., the girls, the boys, the quiet ones, the noisy ones, members of a particular cultural or religious group) and in that case these pupils select themselves. But decisions are not always so easy.

We have found that this issue leaves teachers with a number of dilemmas. One is about whether it is only older pupils who are mature enough to be worth consulting. The evidence is very clear, we think, in showing that children and young people of all ages have very useful insights to offer teachers when they are thoughtfully consulted. Another dilemma is about whether to reserve consultation for year groups that are not under any immediate pressure from important tests or examinations, with Year 8, for example, being a popular choice. But that makes sense only when one is exploring the potential of pupil consultation, not if one has decided that it should be an important element in the work of schools. Another common dilemma is about whether to concentrate on consultation of the more academically successful pupils or classes. They are sometimes the most enthusiastic about being consulted, and the most ready to volunteer. They may also have thought more about what helps their learning, and be more articulate about what they find helpful, and so apparently be likely to make consultation a more productive exercise. (These are tendencies that we have found in some contexts, though not in all.) But these benefits are a direct consequence of these pupils tending to be more on the same wavelength as teachers than are others, which also means that teachers tend to be already more on *their* wavelength, and so in general have less to learn from them. Teachers have more to learn from those pupils who have been relatively unsuccessful in school, who may not have learned to treat successful learning as a high personal priority, and who may not be at all keen to talk about what helps their learning. These pupils may well have had bad experiences of school, not be inclined to identify with the school or with teachers and have no great interest in helping teachers to improve their practice (see Silva, 2001). Persuading such pupils to reflect on what characterises those classroom activities that most motivate and facilitate their learning, and helping and encouraging them to articulate their ideas on such matters, can be uphill work; but it is from them that teachers are most likely to learn things that might make the biggest differences to their teaching and to their pupils' commitment to learning.

If teachers want to choose samples in order to consult their pupils generally about teaching and learning in their classrooms, they need to consider carefully how to choose a sample which best represents the diverse characteristics of all their pupils, and who are also trusted by the other pupils to be representative of them all. Yet even here there are dilemmas. One teacher with whom we worked took great care to choose, in consultation with her class, six pupils who were agreed to be representative. Over a period of weeks each of these pupils was interviewed several times by a researcher about what helped or would help their learning in this teacher's class. The teacher was greatly impressed by the insights of these six pupils and asked them to help her in planning an innovative unit of work in response to their suggestions. But here she ran into big problems. Over the short period of a few weeks, the trusted class representatives had come to be seen by their peers as an elite little group who were much too full of themselves. Being representative is clearly a temporary and vulnerable attribute!

We have sought to argue in this section that some of the important decisions in choosing strategies for pupil consultation are about what it is that one wants to learn. Our concern in this book is with classroom teaching and learning, and with what teachers can learn from their pupils that may help them to help their pupils to learn. But within that framework, there are choices to be made about whether to look for pupil perspectives on teaching and learning in general, on teaching and learning in a particular teacher's own classroom, or on what does and does not help particular pupils' individual learning. Choices also need to be made about what part teachers and pupils are each going to play in setting the consultation agenda, and in addition about which pupils are to be consulted. There are no right answers to these questions, and what it is sensible for any teacher or group of teachers to attempt will probably depend considerably on the techniques, resources and support available to them. But knowing what one wants to learn is an important starting point for choosing a consultation strategy.

Guiding principles for the planning of strategies for consulting pupils

Having a general idea of what we want to learn and from whom, we can then think about the best way of going about it. Perhaps the next most important issue to think about when choosing a strategy is that pupil consultation does not occur in a vacuum. Instead, it happens as part of the complex ongoing work together of teachers and their pupils. So there are many ways in which that ongoing work is going to be affected by engaging in pupil consultation. For one thing, the more time a teacher devotes to consulting pupils in a class, the less time there will be for other things. More fundamentally, pupil consultation has the potential to make not only the teacher's work but the pupils' classroom lives and the relationship between teacher and pupils more satisfying and fruitful if, but only if, teachers engage in it thoughtfully and with commitment. Bearing in mind such wider implications, a number of key guiding principles may be formulated for the planning of an appropriate strategy. The following principles are derived largely from the TLRP Project investigations by MacBeath *et al.* (2003) and Fielding and Bragg (2003), and from the linked New Zealand study by Kane and Maw (2005).

Teachers should embark on pupil consultation only if they have a genuine desire to hear what pupils have to say and a firm commitment to try to use what pupils say to improve teaching and learning in their classrooms

In proposing to consult pupils about classroom teaching and learning, a teacher will probably seem to the pupils to be embarking on a significantly different relationship with them from the teacher–pupil relationships to which they have been accustomed. This promise of a new relationship, in which pupils' views are apparently to be taken seriously, will be highly attractive to pupils. Significant benefits are likely if the promise is kept. But if teachers show a lack of commitment to keeping the promise, significant disillusionment and undermining of trust can easily follow.

Teachers should explain clearly to pupils the purpose and focus of their consultation, making clear how, and why if appropriate, they were selected for consultation and what will happen to what they say, including the teachers' own willingness to be influenced by what pupils say as well as by other necessary considerations

For consultation to be effective, pupils need to understand why they are being consulted. The account given to them should be such as to persuade them that it is worthwhile for them to engage with the consultation seriously and wholeheartedly, but it should accurately explain both the extent and the limits of the influence that pupils may be able to exert on the teacher's practices. Pupils are generally well able to understand the multiplicity of considerations to which teachers have to attend, and it is important that they should not have unrealistic expectations about the outcomes of consultation.

For the consultation process to be productive, we need to create conditions of dialogue in which we listen to and learn from each other in new ways

It is necessary but not enough that pupils should understand the consultation process clearly, that their participation should be by informed consent and that they should feel comfortable and safe. Effective consultation also depends on all pupils feeling that they are being accepted by their teacher and by each other as partners in the work of classroom teaching and learning. They all need to feel that their views – whatever they may be – count for something and that they are valued as active collaborators who have useful contributions to make to thinking about what does and should happen in the classroom. Noyes (2005: 536) puts the point bluntly: 'when teachers consult pupils on how to improve teaching and learning within existing curriculum and assessment regimes, an implicit assumption is made that pupils share these interests. This is evidently not the case and so the power differentials between teacher and pupil require careful negotiation and critique in order to allow pupils to shape such dialogues.' Above all, pupils need to feel that they are trusted and respected by their teacher and equally that they can trust their teacher. As Pedder and McIntyre (2006) have noted, this kind of inclusive solidarity cannot be taken for granted in British classrooms. However, as they also indicate, thoughtful use of pupil consultation is one way in which teachers can effectively build up mutual trust and respect between themselves and their pupils.

The methods of consultation used should be chosen to deepen teachers' understanding of pupils' experiences of teaching and learning in their classrooms

Teachers are not likely to find pupil consultation fruitful unless they engage in it with the intention to understand better what classroom life is like for their pupils. While teachers sometimes find that pupils can see aspects of classroom life in reassuringly predictable ways, the main value of consultation for teachers is in the new insights that it brings for them. This has implications for the methods chosen. For example, finding out how pupils respond to closed questions formulated by teachers is not on its own likely to lead to such deepened understanding, although it may be a useful start. Such understanding is likely to come only from *a process of dialogue* through which pupils are helped to reflect on their experiences and to articulate their ideas while at the same time teachers are helped to question and modify their preconceptions.

After consultation, pupils need feedback on how what they have said has been understood and on how it will influence or has influenced teacher planning and actions

Pupils need to know that their efforts to formulate and to express their views and their readiness to trust their teacher have been justified by the attention given by the teacher to their views. They need first of all to know how far their individual views have been the same as those expressed by other pupils. They need to know too that the teacher has treated the things they have said seriously and has thought about them. Finally, they need to be persuasively made aware of actions that the teacher has taken or plans to take as a result of what they have said, and to be equally persuasively told why the teacher has not felt able to act on other suggestions that they have made.

Pupil consultation needs to be planned realistically from the beginning, with particular attention to the time and energy needed for all phases of it

Every phase of pupil consultation can be time and energy consuming: preparing procedures, recruiting pupils and explaining to them what will be involved, doing the consultation, analysing the collected evidence, reflecting on its meaning and implications, deciding what to do in response to it, giving feedback to the pupils and, most of all, working to change the classroom practices that one has decided to change. To have to give up halfway through because of lack of time or energy would not only be a waste of everything done up to that point but could lead to a damaging undermining of pupils' hopes. So it is very important to be realistic and to make sure from the beginning that the necessary time is going to be available.

These principles provide a framework within which specific pupil consultation strategies for particular contexts can be developed. Among the contextual issues that need consideration are the nature of the pupil population, including most obviously their age, but also their confidence in expressing their views, in writing or in speech, about teaching and learning, and possibly distinctive concerns or interests related to their culture or gender.

Other important contextual issues, considered in later chapters, relate to school policy and the resources available to teachers.

Methods of consultation

In view of the considerations we have discussed and of the above principles of procedure, what manageable and appropriate strategies can we suggest for consulting pupils? Other publications from our TLRP Project (especially MacBeath *et al.*, 2003; Fielding and Bragg, 2003; Flutter and Rudduck, 2004) have given clear practical guidance on, and rich exemplification of, procedures for pupil consultation. Rather than offering what would necessarily be only a pale reflection of that guidance, we shall continue to focus only on what seem to be the most important strategic decisions.

Among the fundamental practical decisions that teachers have to make, in the light of the contexts in which they are working, are whether they are able and prepared to do the consultation themselves, whether it is possible and acceptable to delegate the process of consultation to an intermediary, or finally whether they see it as attractive and possible to enable pupils themselves to take the initiative. Our discussion will therefore be framed in terms of these three broad strategic approaches.

Methods for teachers themselves to use in consulting pupils

There are many different methods that teachers themselves can use for consulting pupils. MacBeath *et al.* (2003) distinguish three broad types:

- *Direct consultation*, where pupils are asked directly about their experiences or views, through questionnaires, interviews, discussions, logs, or posting views in boxes;
- *Prompted consultation*, where pupils are 'prompted' to express their views through the use of a stimulus, such as a particular very recent lesson, data from completed questionnaires or video replay of extracts from a lesson;
- *Mediated consultation*, where pupils who are unaccustomed to being consulted, or to reflecting on what helps their learning, are helped to formulate and express their views through, for example, drawings, posters or making a video, and then to talk about what they wanted to communicate.

MacBeath *et al.* (*ibid.*: 13) suggest two principles that need to be weighed against each other:

In selecting the best tool for the job, there are two important principles: economy and power. Economy is about simplicity, accessibility and ease of use. Complex questionnaires, too sophisticated a technology, too much planning or analysis present obstacles for teachers and for pupils. But tools need also to be powerful, that is, capable of generating insights which deepen understanding and inform practice.

One element in getting the balance right between these two principles is the question of how open-ended the methods that are used allow the consultation to be. In our experience teachers frequently feel obliged to emphasise economy, for example using closed-choice questionnaires, when they would ideally prefer to use much more open methods, such as individual semi-structured interviews.

MacBeath *et al.* (*ibid.*: 3) also describe and give detailed and helpful guidance on the use of 'a selection of approaches that we know schools have found useful and that do not make excessive demands on time and resources', a selection 'designed to help teachers develop a repertoire of consultation approaches'.

The use of intermediaries

In planning Enquiry 1 of our TLRP Project, we adopted, purely for research purposes, the strategy of using a researcher to interview pupils about their classroom experiences and to seek their suggestions about how their teaching and learning could be improved. The researcher passed on transcripts of the pupil interviews to the teachers and subsequently explored with the teachers their responses to the pupils' ideas. As a research strategy, this seemed to work well, and we have used and adapted it in subsequent projects, such as the East Sussex Project, where small groups of pupils were interviewed by a linked researcher. Increasingly, however, we have come to think of this as not just a research strategy but as a very practical strategy that teachers could profitably use for pupil consultation.

The primary advantage of this strategy is that it offers a very satisfactory way of resolving the tension discussed above between economy and power. Any approach to consultation requires teachers to work out what they want to consult pupils about, to consider pupil ideas, to decide how and how much to take account of these ideas, to implement these plans and to provide feedback to pupils. All that involves a considerable use of time and energy; so it should not be surprising to find that teachers who consult pupils themselves generally feel obliged to use the least time-consuming methods for the consultation process itself, even when they recognise that these methods are relatively lacking in power. Delegating the task of consulting pupils to others is, however, an even more effective way of being economical with teachers' time, and imposes no restrictions on the power of the consultation methods used.

Another advantage of this strategy is that pupils in our experience tend to be less inhibited in expressing views about their classroom experiences when they are addressing a third party rather than their teacher. The third party need not be a professional researcher; for example, one or more teaching assistants in a school, chosen because they are manifestly good at establishing empathetic relationships with pupils, could be trained as specialist assistants, available to interview pupils individually or in small groups on behalf of teachers. This strategy is in our view a very valuable one for the early stages, when teachers and pupils are unaccustomed to consultation. Once the importance of pupil consultation has been established in a school, when pupils have become confident in talking openly to teachers, and when the time and energy that teachers need to invest in consultation are recognised as essential investments, this kind of strategy will become superfluous.

Pupils as researchers

Perhaps the most radical approach to pupil consultation is the 'pupils/ students as researchers' approach, which involves not only consulting pupils but enabling them to determine, at least in part, the nature of the consultation. The central rationale for this approach is that the more pupils are enabled to ask and to answer their own questions about teaching and learning, the more fully teachers will be able to learn from the different perspectives that pupils can bring. Fielding and Bragg (2003: 5) suggest that:

> Students as Researchers rests on a number of beliefs and observations:
>
> • Young people and adults often have quite different views of what is significant or important in their experience of and hopes for learning
> • Even when they identify similar issues as important, they can mean quite different things by them
> • These differences are potentially a source of creativity rather than a source of conflict
> • If we start from students' questions (as well as, or even instead of, teachers' questions) and support their capacity to pursue their enquiries, we often find that new knowledge emerges about learning, about teaching and about ourselves as teachers and learners
> • For this process to be productive and engaging, we need to create conditions of dialogue in which we listen to and learn from each other in new ways for new purposes.

Fielding and Bragg (*ibid.*: 15–18) suggest that this approach also offers distinctive benefits for pupils, including their development of 'a positive sense of self and agency . . . enquiring minds . . . new skills

. . . new social competences and new relationships . . . [and] a chance to be active and creative'; and they discuss (*ibid*.: 25–42) in some detail the processes involved.

A possible limitation of the 'pupils as researchers' approach is that it has tended to be directed most frequently to issues outside the class-room, with the result that the general implications of its use by teachers and pupils in classrooms are not yet very clear. Its fruitfulness in the classroom context will depend not only on the efficiency and effec-tiveness with which pupils are able to formulate and investigate their research questions, but perhaps even more crucially on the processes of teacher–pupil dialogue involved in and following from these investigations.

Another potential limitation of this approach is that it can be difficult to plan for *all* pupils to have the opportunity to conduct investigations into teaching and learning; and that the effects of allowing and encouraging only some pupils to be researchers can be deeply divisive and so can seriously undermine the benefits to be gained. In our view it is important to decide on the key benefits for pupils for which this approach is being chosen, and then to concentrate on ensuring that these benefits are realised for all pupils. This is likely to involve finding ways for all pupils to engage in open and creative dialogue with teachers and with each other about the questions to be asked and about answers to these questions. That may mean that notions of 'research' need to be replaced by more modest ideas of 'enquiry' and by a priority emphasis on inclusive dialogue; and it should at all costs ensure that this approach to consultation is not seen as being appropriate only for 'able', 'sensible' or 'volunteer' pupils.

Conclusion

Many different approaches are possible to pupil consultation, depending on what we want to learn and achieve. Different approaches might be preferable depending on whether a teacher's main purpose is to learn from his or her pupils or to give pupils a stronger sense of their own importance as members of the classroom community. In most circumstances, teachers will want to achieve both these purposes. But there are other big decisions to be made, especially about *what* we want to learn and about how much time and energy we are prepared to invest. These two primary decisions need to be considered together, because the most ambitious learning will generally require the biggest investment.

There are many different things that teachers might want to learn. For example, we have highlighted the contrast between finding out about pupils' preferred teaching and learning activities and approaches and, on the other hand, finding out about individual pupils' differing classroom experiences and concerns. One thing that we have learned is that it is important to try to plan realistically in advance, since both the processes of consultation and, even more, teachers' use of what they learn from consultation can be more time-consuming than is initially assumed, and also because pupils' trust in their teachers can be severely damaged if consultation seems to be abandoned mid-stream or to lead nowhere.

This exemplifies a consideration that is of central importance when developing a strategy for consulting pupils. If approached thoughtfully and in a principled way, consultation can do a great deal to enhance teacher–pupil relationships and especially the level of mutual trust and respect between teacher and pupils. But a thoughtless approach to consultation can have the opposite effect. Two major conclusions seem to follow from this. First, it may be wise for teachers to develop consultation procedures gradually, for example at early stages using intermediaries to do the consulting or using structured questionnaires, before later moving towards a more direct dialogic relationship between teacher and pupils. Second, since consultation is perhaps both more complex and more risky than it can initially seem, there is much to be said for the senior managements of schools developing both guidelines and support mechanisms so that individual teachers do not have to take risks in isolation.

Summary

This chapter reaffirms and justifies the project's concern with consultation that focuses on teaching and learning in the classroom. It starts by considering the strengths and limitations of 'informal' consultation which teachers have practised for many years and compares it with the more deliberate and more explicit approach of the project.

We learned that in order to be able to decide which consultation strategies would suit their purposes, teachers (who, in the early stages of consultation tend to be the initiators) need to be clear about what their expectations of consultation are and what issues it

continued

might illuminate. Teachers will also have to think about how open the process of consultation is to be and the extent to which the agenda will be controlled by them or by their students, or by both (the agenda needs to be one in which both teachers and pupils are interested). Another issue is from which pupils teachers want to hear. Again, responses to this question will determine the approach adopted – a whole class, samples of pupils from one class or several classes, selected individuals. In short, the chapter underlines the importance of knowing what one wants to learn as a starting point for choosing a consultation strategy.

We also learned that authenticity is an important condition for developing consultation practices. Authenticity is reflected in three things: the importance of teachers genuinely wanting to hear what pupils have to say in order to improve teaching and learning in their classrooms; the importance of teachers explaining and discussing the purpose and procedures to pupils so that they feel assured about what will happen to the data and have some sense of partnership; the importance of creating conditions for dialogue which will allow teachers and pupils to listen to and learn from each other in new ways.

The chapter ends with a discussion of different methods of consultation used by project teachers and researchers. We identified three broad methods: direct consultation, where pupils are asked to talk about their experiences or perspectives in interviews or discussions or to write about them in questionnaires or in learning logs; prompted consultation, where a stimulus is used to elicit pupil responses, such as a video of part of a lesson; mediated consultation, where pupils who are less articulate or less confident can express their views initially through another medium, such as drawing, and then explain what the drawing is about.

While it was evident from project data that classroom teachers can benefit greatly from consulting their pupils about teaching and learning, we also learned that classroom consultation is not something to be undertaken lightly. The time and energy that teachers need to invest in order to reap rewards from it are sub-stantial. Furthermore, considerable thought needs to go into ensuring that pupils' rights and dignity are respected and that all pupils benefit from, and are not damagingly disappointed by, their investment in the exercise. It seems to us especially important to recognise the tension between MacBeath *et al.*'s (2003) concepts of economy and power. While hard-pressed individual teachers must inevitably and properly prioritise economy in any additional enterprise that they undertake, there seems little doubt that the full benefits of pupil consultation are likely to be gained only when methods other than the most economical are used.

Two tentative implications follow from this. The first of these, relevant for individual teachers, for subject departments and for whole schools, is that it would seem necessary to adopt long-term but flexible strategies through which expertise, trust and commitment are gradually developed on all sides. Initial procedures could be relatively economical, but if clear, realistic, limited expectations about the benefits of these are realised, this can provide a platform for more informed, more committed and more ambitious further planning.

The second implication, primarily for whole schools and their senior managements, is that it is realistic to expect classroom teachers to develop effective classroom consultation only if very well-conceived whole-school strategies are in place to encourage and to support them in doing so.

Chapter 3

What pupils say about teachers and teacher–pupil relationships

Since the 1960s, an extensive ethnographic literature about the lives of school pupils, in England especially, has profoundly influenced our understanding of what schooling means in the lives of young people. The vivid accounts provided by Hargreaves (1967), Lacey (1970) and their many successors have greatly enhanced our understanding of young people's lives at school. At first sight, however, they seem to have little to say to us as we seek to consult pupils about classroom teaching and learning: little of this literature is about pupils' efforts to learn, or about things done by their teachers or their peers to facilitate their learning. On the contrary, much of it is about conflict between mutually disrespectful groups of young people, about resistance to the demands of schools and teachers, and at best about the negotiation of acceptable compromises. Yet we will do well to start from it because it is much the richest body of available scholarly literature representing pupils' perspectives on school life. In the main part of the chapter we look at what pupils from our TLRP Project have said about the qualities they look for in a teacher and in a good teacher–pupil relationship.

Woods (1990: 158) provides a helpful synthesis of the strong tradition of ethnographic studies of the late 1960s and beyond. He notes that 'pupils' approach to schoolwork has been less commonly researched. In what few studies we have, all concerned with small groups in individual schools, "school" is not an organizing principle in their lives.' The ethnographers, he is suggesting, have rightly focused their attention on those things to which the young people themselves attach meaning and importance in their lives. These accounts reveal that the people the pupils meet in schools, including the teachers, are consistently important for them; and it is especially the teachers *as people who relate to pupils* who are important. Being 'human' therefore takes pride of place in these accounts as an attractive characteristic of teachers, something that includes 'respecting' pupils (especially if teachers wish the respect to be returned) and whether teachers are able and prepared to 'have a laugh with you'. 'Fairness' and 'not being picked on' are also seen as important, and 'fairness also involves consistency and predictability' (*ibid.*: 17–19, 23).

Humanity and justice are then widely seen as important qualities for teachers, but Woods (*ibid.*: 17) is quick to note that other 'most important attributes of good teachers' for pupils 'are that they should . . . be able to "teach" and make you "work", and keep control'. He notes a pervasive preference for 'strict' teachers who get you to work rather than 'soft' teachers who are incapable of doing so and, while emphasising that the strictness must be tempered with humanity and respect, and should not be taken to mean rigid authoritarianism, he concluded that many pupils accepted the need to be 'made to work' (*ibid.*: 164). While research in this tradition does not offer us insight into the nature of learning activities or teaching strategies that pupils find helpful, at a broader level it helps us to consider the assumptions that pupils bring to 'school as work'.

Woods (*ibid.*: 158) found little evidence that pupils studied by ethnographers showed much tendency to find their school learning tasks intrinsically motivating or even that they saw the academic success goals offered by schools as instrumentally worthwhile. Rather, he found that the significance pupils attached to work tended consistently to depend on 'two main items in their view of work within the school – the school's own distinctions among forms of work, and the quality of the teacher'. On the first of these criteria, 'unless the work "counts" (from the perspective of the school and its staff), nothing can redeem it'. Work that was not for examinations, for example, tended to be little valued. When, on the other hand, schoolwork was treated seriously by the school and its staff, then the way that pupils responded to that work would depend on how their own teacher negotiated it with them. 'If it does count, the teacher can transform it into either something felt to be enjoyable, constructive and rewarding on the one hand, or something painful, inhibiting and onerous on the other.'

We need to be quite cautious in seeking to learn from these ethnographic studies, both because they were very varied and mostly small scale, and because the lives and concerns of these young people twenty and more years ago, in and out of school, may differ in many ways from those of young people today. None the less, some conclusions can be drawn that are both general and may well have stood the test of time. One consistent conclusion appears to be that whether or not schoolwork becomes worthwhile for pupils depends on how much value the school attaches to that work. In more recent times, this is reflected in the frequency of research reports of schools concentrating their resources on the years in which there are external examinations and on the sets likely to affect the headline statistics, and in the corresponding lack of motivation of pupils in other year groups and 'lower' sets. Other potentially generalisable conclusions all seem to be about the qualities of teachers and teacher–pupil relations: good teachers 'make you work' and are the main determinants of whether work is interesting and engaging or boring and burdensome. But the clearest and probably most important conclusion seems to be that it is how teachers relate to their pupils that is most crucial. While interesting lessons are much valued, that is not the most important thing: 'Some teachers can make the lesson interesting but that don't mean you are going to work. They've got to sort of treat you like human beings – you know, listen to what you want to say, not treat you like kids' ('Kathleen' in *ibid*.: 166). As Woods himself concludes (*ibid*.: 168), 'motivation for these pupils was not to come from socialisation into a work ethic, nor from an appeal to instrumentalism, but from the school's own valuation of work, and above all, the relationships with the teacher'.

What kind of people do pupils want teachers to be?

Given the importance of teachers to pupils, it should not surprise us that researchers have asked pupils at intervals over the last century for their views about good teachers, nor that pupils have been ready to respond (e.g., Taylor, 1962; Meighan, 1977; Wragg and Wood, 1984). We have been among such researchers. For example, Brown and McIntyre (1993) asked pupils in the first two years of a Scottish second-ary school to write briefly about what it was that each of 'the three teachers they thought were best' over these two years had done that was good. The hundreds of responses were sorted into ten categories:

- creation of a relaxed and enjoyable atmosphere in the classroom;
- retention of control in the classroom;

- presentation of work in a way that interests and motivates pupils;
- making sure that pupils understand the work;
- making clear what pupils are to do and achieve;
- judging what can be expected of a pupil;
- helping pupils with difficulties;
- encouragement of pupils to raise their expectations of themselves;
- development of personal, mature relationships with pupils;
- teachers' personal talents (subject-related or other).

Here, as in all such pupil lists of desired teacher qualities, are the two priority criteria that Woods found so prominent in the ethnographic studies: 'development of a personal, mature, relationship with pupils' and 'retention of control in the classroom'. In addition, the pupils wanted their teachers to take the lead in making classroom life and work pleasant and enjoyable, interesting, clear and comprehensible. They also wanted their teachers to be demanding but sensitive in their expectations of them, and to support them when they were having difficulties.

A first and continuing reaction to such a list must surely be to admire the collective judgement of these pupils as eminently sensible and balanced. What they have identified are surely the qualities that they are right to want in a teacher if their classroom life is to be pleasant, civilised, rewarding and productive. A second reaction, when one has read other such pupil lists, is to note how consistent pupils generally are, even across decades and continents, in their balanced appraisal of what makes a good teacher.

Our next example, which is much fuller, is taken from Rudduck and Flutter (2004: 76), who describe how it was generated:

> Our original summary of the qualities of a good teacher was based on a series of interviews with secondary school pupils in three schools in the north of England [see Rudduck, Day and Wallace, 1996: 86]. We went on to ask similar questions of pupils in other schools in different parts of the country – including ten schools participating in our *Learning about Improvement Project* in West Sussex. There was remarkable consistency across pupils in the different schools.

Their list is in four sections (Rudduck and Flutter, 2004: 77–8), each relating to one central assertion:

Good teachers are human, accessible, reliable and consistent. They

- are fair
- are people you can talk to
- don't give up on you
- don't just remember the bad things you have done
- are consistent in their mood
- are calm and have a sense of humour
- understand students and treat them 'like an equal'
- know what it is like to be young and a teenager
- have common sense
- are not petty over silly things
- don't take things personally
- can admit they have made a mistake.

Good teachers are respectful of students and sensitive to their difficulties. They

- don't go on about things (like how much better other classes are)
- don't shout
- don't make fun of you or humiliate you in front of others
- are not sarcastic or vindictive
- do not speak to you in an irritating tone of voice
- don't assume students have not listened when help is asked for
- respect students so that students can respect teachers
- will let pupils have a say and will listen to them
- explain things and will go through things you don't understand without making you feel small
- believe students when students tell them something
- treat students as individuals rather than just one of the mass.

Good teachers are positive and enthusiastic. They

- enjoy being a teacher
- enjoy teaching a subject
- enjoy teaching us
- give praise more than punishment
- make you think you can do well
- don't put red lines all through things you have worked hard on

- don't say 'I would rather not be teaching you'
- don't say 'You're the worst class I have ever taught.'

Good teachers are professionally skilled. They

- make the lesson interesting and link it to life outside school
- will have a laugh but know how to keep order
- are knowledgeable in their subject but know how to explain
- find out who needs help and give it
- vary the way they teach to suit the students in their classes
- allow some input from the students
- find ways of giving students choices.

Given the consistency that these researchers noted in their findings across schools, it comes as no surprise that their list incorporates everything that was on the shorter earlier list. It is interesting, however, to note what the additional items are. Most striking are the large number of negative items. Pupils' identification of such a multiplicity of things that good teachers *don't* do clearly suggests that they feel oppressed by the amount of teacher negativity that they encounter, as does their identification of 'positive and enthusiastic' attitudes as among the most desirable of teacher qualities. Second, as in the ethnographic studies synthesised by Woods (1990), there is an especially strong emphasis on the humanity, respect and sensitivity with which teachers relate to pupils. It might indeed be noted that the two first and longer sub-lists, concerned with these qualities, do not seem to be distinctively about teacher–pupil relationships at all, but could be about any human relationships in which one set of people has power over others. The broadly human nature of teacher–pupil relationships is further highlighted by the fact that only the last and shortest of the four sub-lists is identified as including elements of teachers' professional expertise. As with research of an ethnographic kind, research into pupils' views of the characteristics of good teachers leads to conclusions about the centrality of teachers' human relationships with pupils.

What do pupils value in their relationships with teachers?

I think it's quite important to get a good relation with the teacher cos then they talk to you more. We get on well with our teacher cos she talks to us more, not as in 'Oh, you're a pupil', more as in 'I'm working with you'. Obviously you don't want it to be so you can get away with anything but I think it's the interaction between the teacher and the student that helps.

(LP1)

In our more recent research, we find no change in the priority that pupils attach to the human relationships that they want to have with teachers. In the East Sussex Personalised Learning Project, for example, a recurring theme in Year 8, 9, 10 and 11 pupils' discussions of teaching and learning concerned the importance of such relationships:

> A lot of the time with teachers it's like they're addressing the class as a whole but when they talk individually as well, it works so much better.

> It's easy to lose your identity, just become one of the many, the masses . . . I think it's very easy for a teacher just to fall into that as well because it must be hard for them if they get more personal with the students because then they have to deal with people's feelings and stuff but if you just treat it as statistics then you don't have to get involved in all that. It can be a lot easier for them, I'm sure.

> Teachers throughout the whole school are very personal on the whole and can help you individually. There's a good bond between pupils and teachers.

(LP1)

A Year 10 discussion on motivation, which started by comparing the practices of different departments, quickly focused on teachers:

> It completely depends on the teacher. I don't think we can argue this point.

> It all comes back to the classroom experience. If you have confidence in what a teacher is teaching you and what they're saying to you and how they deal with the class, then you're going to have more confidence in the feedback you get from them.

> I do think that teachers being honest and . . . well, being personal with you and honest and . . . using humour and stuff . . . and it

completely gives you confidence in them when you know you can talk to them and they talk to you individually like . . . Teacher X and Teacher Y. They use humour, they use personal skills like you would with someone who wasn't your teacher whereas a lot of teachers do the typical . . . stereotypical teacher thing where they talk to you as a class and they won't talk to you individually properly.

If they could just talk to you about . . . your brother or something like that. Well, perhaps not your brother! But just anything, just talk to you a bit more personally.

So imagine they asked you what you were doing tonight and you said, 'Oh, the cinema.' And next day they said to you, 'Was the film OK?' So they realised you were an individual.

Those are the kind of teachers you feel you would be able to go to and talk to about something that wasn't necessarily work related.

(LP1)

These pupils recognise that teachers have a role to fulfil in teaching *subjects* ('*what* a teacher is teaching you') to *classes*, but within that framework they want to be recognised and treated as *people*. Among the recurring indicators that they use for telling whether teachers are prepared to have a human relationship with them as people is whether teachers reveal 'a sense of humour':

I think I have a good range of teachers because they all have a sense of humour and if something funny happens, they're not telling you off about it, they're laughing with you. And I have this one teacher and I just feel I can be so open with her. That gives me confidence to just be myself and not be huddling in the corner. . . .

Kids like to have a laugh and joke with their friends and talk but if teachers take it all seriously then they're not going to get nowhere [*sic*] because the kids are just going to ignore them. So teachers need to have a sense of humour and understand. There are teachers who understand what you go through as a teenager so they try and help you through school.

(LP1)

Having a more personal relationship with teachers is not, however, enough. Teacher–pupil relationships have to be *respectful*, and the respect must be in both directions:

In my old school, the student–teacher relationship was very different. Here it's a much more personal relationship though in my old school students respected teachers a lot more, whereas here people aren't worried about what they say to teachers and how they behave at school. In some ways that's a good thing because it means it's not so hard to come to school, but in other ways it's bad because it means some students are very disrespectful and it can be disruptive.

If I respect a teacher and they respect me, there's no problem. They treat me nicely and do as much as they can for me and that makes me like them as a person.

I think we get more respect now that we're senior pupils. As well as the teachers respecting us I think we respect them a bit more so we've got a better relationship with them.

(LP1)

This emphasis on reciprocity in the way pupils talk about mutual respect also extends to their thinking about other aspects of the relationship:

Some teachers, you look at the work they've put into these smart-board presentations, you look at it . . . and you think to yourself 'Well, they're trying as hard as they can to make this lesson fun, we should try our hardest to co-operate with the teacher and do what they're asking and just keep it nice.'

(LP1)

There are also recurring concerns with teachers' fairness in their treatment of pupils and with the importance of trusting relationships:

[A good classroom relationship with a teacher is] when a teacher gives an equal amount of time to every student and is open to them but not getting the pupil down; they can say where they're going wrong, but they can also say where they are going right . . . a happy open relationship.

There's only individual teachers that I feel I can talk to. It's just who people get along with really – that's what it boils down to – certain people who pupils trust.

(LP1)

Conclusion

Pupils, then, consistently emphasise teacher–pupil relationships as being of central importance for the quality of their lives in classrooms; and, as we have noted, aspects of teachers' professional expertise, while appreciated, tend to come a poor second to teachers being the kind of people who relate well to pupils.

How are we to understand this? One of the most challenging features of pupil consultation is the need to recognise that things often look different from the perspectives of pupils. Confident as we are of the validity of these findings, it is unlikely that simple 'teacher characteristics' reflect nothing more than teachers' 'natural' characteristics or their simple personal preferences about how to relate to pupils. On the contrary, for teachers to act, for example, 'consistently', 'respectfully', 'with a sense of humour' and 'knowing what it is like to be young and a teenager', in what are likely to be demanding and stressful situations, depends on them having developed sophisticated professional expertise. Acting in ways that seem desirable to pupils has to be combined with whatever else the teacher was aiming to do; and only the teacher could know the possibilities and the problems involved. Thus, what may well seem to pupils a matter of having a pleasant personality is likely to be for the teacher a complex professional task, probably mastered only through long experience, reflection and hard work.

That, however, is at best only half the story. For surely pupils are right to assert that schools and classrooms should be places characterised by trusting human relationships, where people treat each other with respect, fairness and consistency, and where pupils are treated as 'persons', not as 'statistics'. It should be a priority for all human institutions, including workplaces, that they should be characterised by such human relationships. Furthermore, just as pupils assert is the case in schools, purposeful productivity can be enhanced, and certainly need not be undermined, by such relationships. And if we want such relationships to be valued for civilisation in general, is it not of paramount importance that young people should be educated in schools where priority value is placed on such relationships? Pupils may be wrong in their tendency to equate such civilised values with the personality characteristics of their preferred teachers, but they are right in a far more fundamental sense to value the human and the personal in the work of schools, and reciprocated respect, trust and fairness in teacher–pupil relationships.

Perhaps the first lesson that we can learn, then, from research on consulting pupils is that pupils can generally be relied upon to assert the importance of civilised human relationships in the work of schools. Few teachers would dissent from such values, but they are values that can easily be forgotten when schools feel themselves under constant pressure to do whatever is expedient to improve examination results. It is of some relevance therefore that pupils themselves care about their examination results and more generally about the quality of their learning in schools; and that their views about teacher–pupil relationships are linked to their views about classroom teaching and learning as a whole. It is on pupils' views about desirable kinds of classroom teaching and learning that we focus in the next chapter.

Summary

This chapter reveals the high value placed by pupils on having a 'good relationship' with their teachers and the qualities in teachers that help to define such a relationship. Pupils want to feel that they are trusted and respected and this in turn helps them to sustain their respect for and trust in teachers. Other qualities that pupils identify as helping build such a relationship are fairness and consistency. Good teacher–pupil relationships enable the 'partners' to be sensitive to each other's perspectives on a situation and to be willing to look at situations through the eyes of the other.

The chapter ends with a note of caution, for although the values that are prized in good teacher–pupil relationships are likely to be widely endorsed by schools and teachers, they can nevertheless be easily overlooked if teachers feel that they are under pressure to do whatever is expedient to improve examination results.

Chapter 4

What pupils say about classroom teaching and learning

In this chapter we move from looking at pupils' visions of a good teacher and a good teacher–pupil relationship to what they say about teaching approaches that help them to learn and those that get in the way of their learning. Consensus across the bodies of evidence from different studies enables us to be fairly confident about the findings. We identify four criteria that appear repeatedly in the consultation transcripts; discussion of these criteria constitutes the main content of the chapter.

There are close connections between asking pupils about the qualities of a good teacher and about teacher–pupil relationships and exploring with them questions about what teachers do that is helpful or unhelpful to them in influencing their engagement and their success with classroom learning. When pupils are asked these latter questions, their answers still emphasise teacher humanity. 'We found', Wallace (1996b: 39) reports, 'that time and again pupils emphasised the importance of interpersonal relationships with understanding teachers who were prepared to listen.' In answer to these more contextualised questions about classroom practice, however, pupils' concerns with teachers' humanity and sensitivity cannot easily be disentangled from their reliance on teachers' professional abilities and judgements. This is epitomised by Kershner's (1996: 79) finding that 'value [was] placed on individualised and fine-tuned support from teachers, which was most welcome when it had been sought and received at the right time during a lesson, and preferably discreetly'.

Just as for conceptions of a good teacher, so there seems to be a similar wide-ranging consensus across different pupil populations about the classroom teaching and learning activities that pupils most value. Repeatedly, researchers comment on such consensus as an important feature of their findings. Rudduck and Flutter (2004: 79), for example, comment on the 'striking . . . consistency across schools . . . in pupils' judgements of what makes a good lesson'. Pedder and McIntyre (2004: 9) similarly conclude that 'one of our most striking findings was that there was a high degree of consensus among pupils, irrespective of teacher, subject, school, or the pupil's previous level of academic success, about what helped them to learn'. Equally, the findings of different studies are highly similar.

It is also tempting to conclude that pupils see things in simpler and more straightforward terms than is possible for teachers. Cooper and McIntyre (1996: 100–1), comparing the 'classroom craft knowledge' of teachers and pupils, came to that conclusion:

> Both teachers and pupils were deeply concerned with the means by which learning was facilitated in the classroom. There were strong agreements between teachers and pupils about the range of most effective strategies and techniques . . . However, while many pupils favoured certain of these methods . . . as particularly powerful learning aids, the teachers tended not to see these as distinctive. Rather, the teachers tended to take a more contextualised view, seeing different methods as being appropriate for different learning tasks, and being appropriate for reasons relating to prevailing conditions (such as time, nature and availability of resources, perceptions of the class, classroom management considerations, their view of the nature of the subject). The important point to be made here is that pupils had preferred ways of engaging with and acquiring new knowledge and understanding, and these preferences were perceived by them to relate to the success of the learning experience; for teachers, on the other hand, the choice of teaching method was governed by a range of sometimes conflicting considerations, which may or may not relate to pupils' preferred approaches to learning.

This suggestion – that while both teachers and pupils are concerned with effective pupil learning, teachers have to take account of many other considerations – seems quite valid. While Pedder and McIntyre (2004) found that some pupils were ready and able spontaneously to consider the different perspectives of teachers and indeed of other pupils, most of the preferences expressed by pupils to researchers have related almost exclusively to their personal classroom experiences. None the less, pupils' thinking has its own quite considerable complexity. To elucidate that complexity, we may start by recalling the strong impression given by the ethnographic studies synthesised by Woods (1990) that school learning was a relatively unimportant concern for most of the pupils studied. This stands in sharp contrast with Cooper and McIntyre's (1996) implication that pupils' preferences among classroom activities were based almost exclusively on their perceptions of the effectiveness of these activities for their learning. This contrast in the importance that pupils seem to give to learning could stem from the choice of pupil samples or even from historical changes. However, a more plausible explanation – and one that is supported by the evidence we have reviewed from several investigations – is that pupil preferences are rarely comprehensible in terms of a single rationale. Learning may be more or less important to different pupils, but there are always other concerns that are quite properly of importance to them.

That pupils generally have a multiplicity of concerns is obvious. Perhaps less obvious is that we can generally best understand their expressed preferences among classroom learning activities, or even their claims about the kinds of activity that help them to learn, in terms of such a multiplicity of concerns. The evidence that we have reviewed suggests that the kinds of classroom activity for which pupils recurrently express preferences tend to have multiple rationales, with the facilitation of learning often being the most important but rarely the only rationale. One consequence of this is that pupils with varying degrees of enthusiasm for school learning often tend to express preferences for similar classroom activities. And it may be because of this that the findings about pupil preferences are so remarkably stable both within and across studies.

Four criteria seem to be used recurrently by pupils across studies to explain their views of what makes for good lessons or helps their classroom learning:

- the avoidance of tedium;
- the pursuit of meaningful learning;
- the need for togetherness;
- the aspiration to be autonomous.

The avoidance of tedium

The most basic of pupil concerns is that the twenty-five or more hours that they are obliged to spend in classrooms each week should not be 'boring'. Common sources of boredom are sedentary activities in which there is no scope either for physical activity or mental initiative, such as long periods of listening to the teacher, copying or completing unimaginative worksheets. The content of lessons can also contribute to boredom.

> And she rambles on a bit and that makes us lose concentration . . . she talks and talks and talks and talks and she doesn't stop. And that goes on for ages. We just get so bored that we lose concentration and start talking to our friends.
>
> (Pedder and McIntyre, 2004: 11, Year 8 pupil)

> If we're doing practicals, we get on with the work because we enjoy doing the practicals, but if she's talking we get bored and start talking to each other.
>
> (Wallace, 1996a: 60, Year 9 pupil)

> Sometimes they give you a textbook and say you have to read it and answer the questions – that's even worse than being read to. You switch off. If someone's reading to you, you switch off anyway but if you have to read it yourself, it's more energy.
>
> (LP1, Year 9 pupil)

> He did a few poems with us but they were not interesting poems – they were sort of more adult . . . we want something that's more teenage, more interesting for us cos we're basically just sitting in our seats just falling asleep and he's just reading this out and we're just not interested.
>
> (Morgan, 2000: 56, Year 8 pupil)

Much the most commonly prescribed antidotes to boredom are activity and variety. If the teacher cannot think of something that is going to make the lesson interesting or fun, then the least that pupils hope for, but often apparently do not get, is *doing* something or doing something *different*:

> I like lessons where we have to do something, not just read, write and listen.
>
> (Rudduck and Flutter, 2004: 81)

Do something different – a different activity, not just sitting down all the time.

> (LP1, Year 9 pupil)

Not just read from a book. Reading from a textbook isn't that much fun. Things need to be fun. We haven't grown up that much.

> (LP1, Year 11 pupil)

Avoiding boredom is a rather negative and unambitious concern, one that becomes important only when boredom is frequently experienced. It is likely to become a dominant concern only if pupils do not find themselves able to pursue other concerns effectively. It certainly seems to have been a dominant concern in the classroom lives of many of the pupils in the ethnographic studies synthesised by Woods (1990) and it remains a recurrent theme today. Since the quality of teacher–pupil relationships is heavily dependent on pupils not feeling that boring regimes are being imposed on them, it is in teachers' interests to avoid pupil boredom. Fortunately, classroom activities that are effective in pupils' eyes for pursuing more positive goals also tend to be effective in avoiding boredom.

The pursuit of meaningful learning

Since research studies in recent years have often asked pupils explicitly about what helps their learning, it is about this that we have fullest information. The richness of that information and its frequent validation against observed classroom practice leaves us in little doubt about its authenticity.

Learning can take many forms and can be seen in many ways. Types of learning are most commonly differentiated according to the complexity of the cognitive processes required. On this kind of dimension, there seems to have been a clear historical shift in the kinds of learning that researchers have presented as being interesting to pupils. Thus, in so far as pupils were reported as being interested in learning at all in the ethnographic studies reviewed by Woods (1990), it tended to be learning of a very minimal kind. Furlong (1976: 179) was unusual in suggesting that 'how much they could learn in class was extremely important' to the fourth year (Year 10) girls he studied, but went on to say that 'in fact the word learning was somewhat ambiguously used, for it not only referred to situations where the girls actually understood something new . . . but also where they simply worked, they carried out the tasks set by the teachers . . . learning as new understanding seemed a fairly rare experience'. More generally, Woods (1990: 24) suggests that, from a pupil perspective, '"understanding" may represent the high point of learning'.

Most of these ethnographic studies, however, focused on pupils who were relatively unenthusiastic about school. The findings of more recent studies, which have not had such a focus and which have been more specifically concerned with pupil perspectives on learning, have in sharp contrast suggested that it is the *meaningfulness* of the learning that they are asked to do that is of most concern to most pupils. This concern is reflected in comments such as:

> You're doing work which you don't really understand, which doesn't exactly fill you with enthusiasm and then people start messing around and so no one works.
>
> (Wallace, 1996a: 61, Year 9 pupil)

Scrutiny of the evidence from several studies during the last fifteen years offers no indication at all of pupils valuing work or learning of a simple mechanistic kind, but instead suggests consistently that, for pupils, understanding what they are doing and learning is of central importance. Pupils do vary in how challenging they like learning tasks to be, but recent evidence suggests little variation in their concern that schoolwork should be meaningful.

Pupils' accounts suggest a wide variety of methods through which meaningfulness can be achieved. Many of these suggestions can be grouped in three broad categories: clear and thoughtful explanation; active pupil participation; and relating abstract ideas to concrete experience.

Clear and thoughtful explanation

Most simply, meaningful learning is facilitated by clear and coherent explanations from teachers. 'She explained it in a way that we could understand' is a regularly repeated comment. Explicit structuring and linkage, advance organisers, use of visual aids, good examples and analogies, links to personal experience, clear summaries, and assessment of pupils with individual feedback on their understanding are all well-established aspects of good explaining that pupils mention frequently.

It does seem, however, that in discussing pupils' perspectives on clear explanation, we need to take account of different kinds of meaning that learners may seek. There are some quite strong indications of a tendency for *personal* or learner-centred meaningfulness to be all-important for younger learners in secondary schools, but for an *instrumental* meaningfulness to become more important – though certainly not to take over entirely – as learners get older, or at least as they are increasingly obliged to face up to the importance of examinations. Wallace (1996a: 65) contrasts Woods's (1993) idea of 'child-meaningful' engagement, which 'is reflected in our evidence from Years 7, 8 and 9', with the concept of 'psychological investment' (Wehlage *et al.*, 1989), where meaning relates to future grades, which seemed increasingly relevant in Years 10 and 11. Similarly, while Cooper and McIntyre (1996: 106), in their study of Year 7 pupils, found that meaningfulness depended primarily on pupils being able to 'forge connections between their past or present experience and teacher input', in many of the older pupils' comments about meaningful learning in the East Sussex study the meaning seems to be sought primarily from the ways in which different elements of the subject content are interconnected or from ways in which specific tasks are shown to relate to wider understandings of the subject.

Younger pupils' comments suggest that explanations can be made clear in various ways which all seem to depend on making appropriate connections. Pedder and McIntyre (2004: 14–15) report that

> pupils told us that work became more appropriately contextualised if there were evident connections between the task at hand and their current knowledge and understanding. The connections that pupils seemed to find helpful were sometimes achieved through their teacher's introduction of materials, objects and images that were already familiar to them.

Cooper and McIntyre (1996: 105) highlight pupils' descriptions of 'the use of story telling and visual stimuli as teaching aids. In both cases these were seen to have a powerful effect on pupils' learning and understanding, and this effect seems to be related to the powerful imaginative impact of these stimuli.' They go on to discuss how the vivid structures embodied in pictures or stories 'often seemed to provide pupils with a framework by which they were able to reinstate information', enabling them both to make sense of the learning material and to recall it later. Some pupils are clearly sensitive to the implication that explanations for whole classes will need to make different connections for different members of the class:

> I like the different things that she did in class. Like, with a stick and with doing it on the board and we were telling her and so it's just lots of different ways of showing you and trying to get it across . . . Some people look at things different to other people. So some people might understand when she shows us with the pole and other people might not get that at all.
>
> (Pedder and McIntyre, 2004: 11, Year 8 pupil)

Such personal meaningfulness seems to be important for older pupils too:

> Original ways to show you something, like when we were doing medicine we were doing the times when they used to drink urine, we had big glasses of . . . like, apple juice and stuff.
>
> (LP1, Year 11 pupil)

> It's good when they bring stuff in . . . and [you can] dress up.
>
> (LP1, Year 11 pupil)

More often, however, their comments emphasise connections in, or clarity about, what they are being asked to learn:

> If we're starting a new topic we generally go over it before we expand on it so she knows we're OK with it. It's more structured. We do go through topics quite quickly but they sort of link with each other.
>
> (LP1, Year 10 pupil)

> He is quite confusing. He doesn't really use the board at all. He just sits at his desk and talks to us . . . we do more discussion, but it's not structured.
>
> (LP1, Year 10 pupil)

> Our teacher takes us through the mark scheme so we know exactly what we have to do to get the better marks. And she writes little notes in your books saying things like 'You need to explain this in greater detail to get the higher mark.'
>
> (LP1, Year 11 pupil)

[What's most helpful] is the advice she's given me because then you know how to improve.

(LP1, Year 10 pupil)

Active pupil participation

Meaningful learning, pupils report with great frequency, is much facilitated by pupils' active participation and engagement in classroom events. Active participation involves having the opportunity to make a distinctive contribution to the intended learning process, and can take many forms, including collecting evidence from source books or the Internet, class discussion, personal investigations or projects of any kind. Pupils frequently contrast such active participation with listening, reading and writing. Collaboration between teacher and pupil(s) is frequently seen to be important to meaningful learning, as in this pupil's account of her teacher's good teaching:

> She helps you with your ideas. She helps you make ideas matter if that makes sense . . . It helps if you know that somebody else knows your idea and they understand your idea and your idea isn't gobbledygook . . . because somebody else says 'That idea's really good, you should . . .' And then you think 'Yeah, it's good. Somebody else has told me it's good. I can go into that idea.' And if it didn't make sense she might say 'I don't really understand that. Maybe you could explain it more to me.' And then I did.
>
> (Pedder and McIntyre, 2004: 13)

Cooper and McIntyre (1996: 103) reported that

> Pupils recalled more readily lesson activities that they associate with a relatively high level of arousal. Pupils' accounts of their own most effective learning were associated with these same events. Invariably pupils describe a high degree of constructive participation in the events recalled. Accounts of such participation often revealed important links between the activities engaged in and pupils' knowledge and understanding of lesson content. In these circumstances, therefore, the learning that had taken place was linked to events in which the pupils had participated in some way, such as in a physical or imaginative sense.

Even older pupils seem to appreciate what might seem to be quite minor ways of participating actively rather than simply being asked to understand and remember what teachers teach them:

> When we do the 'Show Me' board things, they're quite good because they make people think about what they've been taught. They're the little pieces of laminated paper that you write the answer on. But when we just sit there and listen to stuff from a textbook that tends to go straight over your head. And maybe something more interactive would help.
>
> (LP1, Year 11 pupil)

> What helps is if you make a story yourself – if you go through it and almost . . . not act it out, but go through it like different characters. I think that's better than a video because people relate to it more. Getting involved.
>
> (LP1, Year 11 pupil)

> Recently we had to do this thing where we had to find out about Hitler's childhood and we all got different things off the Internet from different places and then at the beginning of the lesson we all said one of the facts we found out and if you didn't have that fact you'd just write it down and it was quite good doing stuff like that.
>
> (LP1, Year 9 pupil)

Relating abstract ideas to concrete experience

Often combined with active pupil participation is another favourite pupil idea for facilitating meaningful learning, that of studying or representing the ideas to be learned at a more practical or concrete level. This can take the form of gathering evidence, conducting practical experiments, engaging in role play, making visual representations or constructing diagrams, posters or spidergrams. All of these methods combine pupil agency with the study or representation of ideas at a more concrete level in ways that, by pupils' accounts, help them to make the ideas their own. Pupils are also, however, quite ready to admit that another part of the attraction of such activities is that they are simply more enjoyable than some other possible learning tasks:

> So it's like if I don't understand maths, if you draw pictures and everything to help you get it, then it can help you to understand it

more. So . . . if you're enjoying something you're doing, then maybe you'll be more eager to do it more.

(Pedder and McIntyre, 2004: 13, Year 8 pupil)

[Role plays] help you build up your confidence for doing things in front of the class and help you understand characters in books more, it makes it more fun and, I don't know, you might be more willing to learn if you do more like that kind of thing.

(Morgan, 2000: 39, Year 8 pupil)

[W]hen you went there (to First World War battlefields) you actually saw everything so it wasn't just someone telling you loads of people died because you already assume that with a war but you actually saw it so it's beginning to relate to something.

(LP1, Year 9 pupil)

A couple of months ago we did a lesson about the slave ships from Africa and we did this thing where sir turned out the lights and we had fourteen people under the table and he was trying to show us what it was like and that was pretty cool. And then we watched a video and it was actually like that and then we studied some stuff out of the textbook – that was quite good that lesson.

(LP1, Year 9 pupil)

When pupils claim that teaching approaches involving storytelling, visual stimuli, their own active participation or concrete experience help to make learning meaningful, it is important to recognise that they frequently assert, and almost always imply, that such activities are also enjoyable and avoid the constant danger of tedium. Whereas some teachers may be inclined to suggest that 'having fun' is what *really* motivates pupils to ask for such approaches, pupils themselves seem to find nothing inappropriate about suggesting a multiple rationale for such preferred classroom activities. Similarly, there are several other kinds of classroom activity that pupils frequently claim to find helpful in making learning meaningful, but which they also find attractive for other reasons. We now go on to consider two other such criteria that pupils tend to use in judging good lessons, criteria that are frequently asserted alongside a concern for meaningful learning.

The need for togetherness

Young people like being together much of the time. They take pleasure, confidence and security from being a member of a peer group and from interacting with one another. In classrooms, therefore, they value collaboration, in whole-class discussion, in groups or in pairs. Although, in the studies we have reviewed, pupils rarely seek to justify such collaboration simply on the grounds that they enjoy it or that they feel a need for it, the pleasure that they manifest in such collaboration is abundantly clear. Rudduck and Flutter (2004: 80) quote several expressions of such pupil enthusiasm:

> I like it when everyone joins in and it's not just the teacher talking and pupils listening, like when the whole class gets involved and everyone's like giving their point of view.

> Sharing ideas amongst the class helps you to feel more involved in the subject.

> The thing that I liked was that the whole class got up and participated in the activity.

> I like working in groups. It gives me confidence.

Pupils also offer convincing rationales for collaboration in terms of its contribution to their meaningful learning. Cooper and McIntyre (1996: 107, 109), for example, found that

> from the pupil standpoint, the most valuable shared aspects of these approaches [discussion, question–answer and pupil collaboration in group or pair work] were the opportunities they created for pupils to generate and be exposed to new representations of knowledge and ideas, as well as providing possible confirmation or denial of their own ideas . . .
>
> [P]upils were virtually unanimous in describing the major value of group-work as being . . . that it widened the pool of available ideas, and through this, enabled pupils to advance their thinking in ways which they could not achieve alone.

Pedder and McIntyre (2004: 18) similarly found that

> Effective social contexts for learning were those that allowed pupils to collaborate with their peers . . . Foremost among the benefits

that pupils identified was the scope provided by such arrangements to express themselves, to negotiate meanings and to develop understandings interactively through the medium of classroom talk.

Pupils also repeatedly claim that class or group discussions can be very helpful in mediating ideas that have come from the teacher, through representing these ideas in more accessible language.

The same kind of dual rationale of the pleasure and comfort of doing things with friends and the contribution such collaboration makes to meaningful learning is apparent whenever pupils are consulted, as in these examples from the East Sussex study:

> You don't want the teacher to talk the whole time. When your friends are talking you tend to listen more. You can just relate to them more.
>
> (LP1, Year 9 pupil)

> With more discussion, you'd have people to question what you say and you'd think more about it.
>
> (LP1, Year 9 pupil)

> If you work in groups and you don't understand, there's always people to talk to. Of course your teachers will help you, but with your friends it's a bit more comfortable.
>
> (LP1, Year 9 pupil)

> I think it's really helpful the way we get to talk to our friends about our work and we get to look at it, like, ourselves, and then we've also got the teacher telling us. We've got loads of different points of view and you can incorporate them into your work and it helps in the long term.
>
> (LP1, Year 10 pupil)

The aspiration for autonomy

A dominant theme in research findings on secondary school pupils' perspectives on life in schools (e.g., Rudduck et al., 1996; Rudduck and Flutter, 2004), and, as we have seen, on pupils' views on good teachers, is the need for teachers to show respect for pupils and not to treat them like children. One important aspect of this is pupils' felt need for space to act with some measure of independence and autonomy. Pedder and McIntyre (2004: 15, Year 8 pupil) record that

> pupils spoke about agency and ownership in terms of opportunities for developing greater independence and autonomy in their classroom learning. They wanted to be trusted to learn: 'It's nice to have a teacher who trusts you to do something on your own.'

Again, Rudduck and Flutter (2004: 83–4) quote several examples of pupils' desire for such freedom in their classroom work:

> I like lessons . . . when I am given freedom in my work.

> I enjoyed this lesson as we worked in partners and didn't have to have any help from the teacher.

> I like to be set tasks with some variation or element that I control.

Not 'being trusted' and the lack of autonomy and of independence in action and thought are frequent sources of considerable frustration to secondary school pupils, as exemplified by these comments by Year 9 pupils from Nick Brown's East Sussex reports (LP1):

> I can't remember the last time we had a choice about what we did or any independence.

> I don't think students are trusted enough. I know it's a big school and there are people who are untrustworthy, but they're always checking up on you and always trying to, like . . . trick you. Catch you out. I don't think we're trusted enough. It causes a lot of confrontation.

> Most teachers won't accept that someone doesn't agree with them. That's why people argue with teachers, because they won't accept that you have another opinion . . . Some teachers are just stuck on 'I'm right, you're wrong' and whatever you say is not going to change it.

Here again, however, pupils do not just ask for more independence simply because they want it, but offer convincing rationales for some degree of independence in terms of its contribution to their meaningful learning:

> We should have written the conclusion ourself I think cos then we can think of what we'd actually learned instead of him telling us what we were meant to learn from it . . . so it makes us realise basically what the lesson was all about. If we had to do it ourself I think it sticks more in your mind because it's like your experience instead of someone else just doing it for you.
>
> (Pedder and McIntyre, 2004: 17, Year 8 pupil)

> I think if you've done it yourself it just helps you learn . . . It means you've had to think through what you're doing and do stuff yourself like go and get equipment out, and think for yourself about the safety issues and make sure that you're doing all right, instead of if someone else is doing it, it's them that's having to think about how to do it, what to do, and so you don't get that experience.
>
> (CPTL1, Year 8 pupil)

Pedder and McIntyre (2004: 16, Year 8 pupil) also note that some pupils were keen to take a pragmatic view of the need to balance independent learning opportunities with more controlled opportunities:

> It's just sometimes you need the teacher and sometimes you don't really. It was just good to be like working with your friends, doing your own work . . . Like at the beginning of the lesson . . . she's got to tell you stuff and [you] use her to help you through it if you're stuck on something. But if you're doing an experiment that you've made up by yourself, you don't need a teacher at all because you've made it up yourself and it's your work.

Conclusion

In this chapter we have suggested some quite strong generalisations about the teaching and learning preferences of secondary school pupils. Studies in recent years have consistently shown a strong preference among pupils for *meaningful* learning. We identified three broad ways in which such meaningful learning is facilitated. One of these is through clear and coherent explanations by teachers, with a particular emphasis on making connections between what is being explained and pupils' personal experience and also, especially with older pupils, connections with other aspects of the subject, including criteria for success. Second, pupils emphasise their own active participation, including collecting evidence, personal projects and class discussion, as a crucial element in meaningful learning. And third, pupils see meaningful learning as depending on the representation of abstract ideas in terms of their engagement in practical activities.

However, the strong consensus among pupils about preferred classroom activities seems to stem not only from a desire for meaningful learning, but from other shared concerns that point in the same direction. Priority concerns that influence most pupils' preferences include a strongly felt wish to avoid the tedium that seems to be characteristic of much schooling, a pleasure in doing things collaboratively and a felt need for more autonomy than they are often allowed in schools. From pupils' perspectives, these things are both desirable in themselves and contribute to meaningful learning.

But pupils do, of course, vary widely in their experiences and concerns. Partly that is because they have different teachers, each with their own distinctive ways of teaching. Partly it is because pupils have different identities and social positions and so have different experiences, even within the same classroom. In the next two chapters, therefore, we shall be concerned with the implications of these differences for pupils.

Summary

We learned, in line with the findings of earlier studies, that there is a high degree of consistency in the views of secondary school pupils about what makes for good lessons. This may not only be because of a large measure of consensus among pupils as to the criteria to be used in judging lessons, but because the use of these criteria in combination with one another leads to highly reliable preferences for some approaches to teaching and learning over others.

The preference for certain approaches derives in large measure from a widespread concern among pupils that learning should be meaningful. 'Meaningful' learning is our term and it is useful in that it enables us to bring together some interesting things that pupils value in their teachers' approaches that help to make learning meaningful. The most commonly cited features are these:

- clear and thoughtful explanation of what pupils are supposed to be doing in a particular lesson or task, and the kind of feedback that helps them to understand how they can improve their work. Pupils want to recognise the connections between earlier knowledge and their present work and/or between present work and its relevance outside school;
- opportunities for active participation and engagement. This can take many forms but appears essentially to be about pupils being able to make a contribution to the learning process.

Pupils' preference for approaches which ensure that learning is meaningful is generally sharpened by the simultaneous application of three other important criteria: avoiding tedium; experiencing a sense of togetherness in the classroom; and having opportunities for autonomy.

Chapter 5

What pupils say about their own teachers' teaching

This chapter is about the comments pupils make about the teaching of the particular teacher consulting them and the suggestions they make about how that teacher might develop his or her teaching. How positive or negative are they? How much do they focus on the particular characteristics of individual teachers? How well do they concentrate on the task of helping their teacher to help them learn? How much, in contrast, do they engage in gratuitous personal commentary? How much are their suggestions grounded in their experience or, in contrast, how much do they rely on creative imagination? How radical are their suggestions? How much thought do they seem to have given to how realistic their suggestions are?

What pupils say about the teaching they have experienced depends on the opportunities they are given and most specifically on what they are asked. We shall concentrate here on what pupils say when they have the most open opportunities, drawing especially on interview data from Enquiry 1 of our TLRP Project (CPTL1), which involved semi-structured interviews with Year 8 pupils conducted by researchers on behalf of their teachers. It is, we believe, when pupils have such open opportunities that we get the best indication of what they are generally inclined to say about their teachers' teaching.

There are seven points we want to make about pupils talking about their own teachers' teaching.

A distinctive perspective

It is important to remember that when pupils speak about the teaching they have experienced, they do so in terms of their own experiences, including their own learning. Like any participants or observers in classrooms, pupils observe teaching selectively from a particular perspective, and in their case it is the perspective of those who are taught. The insights that we can therefore expect from them are about the learning opportunities available to them in the classroom situations that they experience, about how helpful they judge these opportunities to be, and about how their opportunities for learning in these classrooms might be improved. We cannot expect pupils to talk about teaching as a professional craft to be understood in all its complexity, nor have we found them doing so. Sometimes, however, they do try to take the teacher's perspective, thinking about what it is possible for teachers to do and what is not. Similarly, they sometimes recognise that other pupils have points of view that are different from their own.

Taking consultation seriously

One important conclusion that we can report is that pupils hardly ever – *never*, in our experience – take advantage of the opportunity of being consulted to make unpleasant personal remarks about the personality, appearance or foibles of their teacher in ways that are unrelated to their learning. In our experience they show great seriousness and self-discipline in talking about their teachers' teaching only as it influences their classroom lives and especially their learning and that of their peers.

Accentuating the positive

A second important conclusion is that pupils are generally very ready to recognise and to comment on attractive features of their teachers' teaching. That certainly does not mean that they are uncritical; but a normal major outcome of pupil consultation, in our experience, is for teachers to be reassured that in many respects their teaching is admired and appreciated. Pupils recognise the helpfulness to their learning of things that teachers do and say as part of their routine classroom practice, including, for example, their careful planning, the carefully judged language they use, the quality of their explanations and demonstrations, the support and guidance that they provide, both publicly and privately, the quality of notes that they provide, their responsiveness to pupil needs, their patience and sense of humour, and their thoughtfulness, for example in the timeliness of the support that they provide. Other examples of things that pupils appreciate are teachers' readiness to recognise and amplify pupils' good ideas, their approachability, the varied nature of the tasks they set (especially writing tasks), the imaginative projects they devise, the helpful revision strategies they teach, and the connections they make with 'real life' in the learning tasks they set. They especially appreciate teachers' trust in giving them opportunities for independence in their learning and also the opportunities they give them to learn collaboratively with their friends or other peers. Pupils' alertness to what their teachers do for them and the warmth of their appreciation cannot but be very heartening for their teachers. Just a few examples of pupils' positive comments about individual teachers from our Enquiry 1 data will have to suffice:

> I like the way she does it, like tells everyone in lots of different ways instead of just one . . . She like tries to explain as best she can in as many different ways as she can.

> Well, she's like nurturing everybody . . . She's like saying to the people who don't really understand, 'This is how you do it.' We will do easy exercises to start with . . . She'll give you time. She'll draw pictures if you want about how to do it and she'll give you examples.

> She explains it loads of times and you understand it . . . She was explaining it in a form which you can understand . . . She explains it and you just like understand it in that instance . . . She explains it in detail.

> She helps you understand your ideas in full . . . She helps you make your ideas matter.

> He makes sure that people aren't stuck and they know what they are doing . . . He'll come round you all the time and just ask if you are all right.

He does quite a lot of practical things which is an advantage in science . . . We hardly ever get the textbooks out, except for revision and things like that because he tends to teach from the board . . . I think mixing it with a bit of practical and teaching from the board, that's an advantage to my learning.

Pupils often seem to find it easiest to explain what their teachers do that they find valuable by starting from particular incidents, and such accounts certainly provide the most vivid pictures of what helps them. Sometimes pupils explicitly use these incidents to exemplify general features of the teacher's teaching. Sometimes the task of determining the general implications of the particular incident is left more open:

I think she talks through what we have to do quite well . . . It was the mystery of a disappearing girl and we had to develop stories against that. And she like did press conferences so it really got us into character so we could like really get the story going because we knew what our characters were.

We had about six or seven people and we had to make an ear out of it. Someone was the sound wave and the pinna and the things in the ear . . . and then we had to act it out. So the ear, the sound wave went into the pinna, through the ear canal and made the bones vibrate . . . You knew exactly what actually happened in your ear.

When we first started doing drama, she helped us understand different acting techniques that we could use . . . She told us about it, she helped us to understand it, she helped us to use it . . . Remember to keep still when you freeze, for example, not let your eyes move about . . . She explained it, but not as going on and on and on about it . . . It was brief but full if that makes any sense . . . so even though she sort of told us at the beginning of the year I can still remember different techniques that we have used.

I said to her I found the question really hard. I don't know how she explained it . . . I don't think she explained about the mathematics. I think she explained about how to go about the problem. Mm. I don't know what she said though, I can't remember. But what she said helped me because I clicked on then. I knew what I was doing.

Sometimes pupils give the explicit message that they would like more of something that they have found helpful:

> If you write a large piece of work that's quite significant you'll quite often get an individual session with your teacher [where] you can just talk to them about [it] in the lesson and that usually is very helpful and . . . it would be good if you had that more often, for smaller pieces of work even.
>
> (LP1, Year 10 pupil)

Identifying unhelpful practices

Pupils are, however, perfectly willing and able to talk about what their teachers do that they do not find helpful. So far as we can judge, such negative comments tend to cover the same range of concerns as positive comments do, addressed to different teachers or sometimes to the same teachers on different occasions:

> She talks too much. It's like she explains what we have to do but then she just says it again and you know what you have to do but she's just saying it again and it's annoying.

> Sometimes we do book work a lot where you just answer a question, so we just look at the text and find the answer. It just gets a bit boring and you just know that you're going to do the answers and it's very boring . . . I don't think that [you learn anything from the book work] because [you are] just answering a question and then moving on to the next question so you don't really have to think about it much.

> We were putting the cubes into two rows of three or whatever, and we had to say how many faces of it you could see, and what faces were hidden that you couldn't see . . . I don't see why we should learn that because I don't see how I can use that information when I'm older . . . I found it really boring and not much use, so I just talked with my friends.

> She got like this long stick out and we had to count upwards and downwards [with] the stick, which was really babyish I thought . . . something like you do in primary school.

You've done an activity . . . and I like doing the activities and everything but it's only when we have to sit in the front and explain it to everybody. It's like if you say something wrong everyone will laugh at you and everything.

Well, usually, I'm put in groups with difficult people . . . I feel that I'm definitely being asked to sort of get these people to work and stuff but not necessarily just to be a teacher. It's more that she [the teacher] feels like I'm responsible and I'm able to get them to work and stuff . . . I feel it's holding me back.

It's always the same thing – we never do anything else apart from write up . . . you never really *talk* about it . . . they tell you what to do and you have to do it . . . it's nothing about us, always about the teacher.

(Morgan, 2000: 56, Year 8 pupil)

As many of the above examples indicate, pupils usually make themselves very clear both about *what* they do not like and about *why* they do not like it. Furthermore, in our experience pupils are generally inclined, if given the opportunity, not simply to say what they do not like but to go on to explain what they would prefer. They have several ways of doing this.

Modifications

One way in which pupils can be helpful in the way they talk about teaching approaches that they do not like is that they frequently indicate how a modified version of the approach would be more helpful for their learning and more attractive to them:

We don't actually get to think for ourselves all the time when we're doing science . . . And it's like when we're shown experiments as well, he shows us what happens instead of what we would like to find out for ourselves . . . But I thought that we could have done it ourselves if he'd just given us a little bit of help.

When you're reading something, you often can have your mind on something else, so not actually take it in. So you don't have to even concentrate when you're revising that way. Whereas if you have questions then it means you would have to think, to try to think about the answer.

And it was a bit hard because there were some people that wouldn't co-operate, and I think . . . we could've chosen more people that we wanted to be with because there are some people that don't really pay attention as much as others and they mess about and you can't get anything done.

And then, they always put the video on towards the end. If they put it on at the beginning and we all talked about it, that would be better.

(LP1, Year 11 pupil)

I think some people get a bit dependent on the teacher. They'll be doing a sheet and then it's 'Oh, Sir, what's the answer to this?' and they write it down and it's just like 'Oh, we've done the sheet.' So the teacher's got to say, 'No, I'm not going to tell you. Get on and do it yourself.'

(LP1, Year 9 pupil)

In this lesson, she asked me to read which I didn't want to do cos I don't like reading like that . . . but the fact that she tries to get people involved without asking . . . if you get them to do it for some reason they don't mind so much. And that helps a lot.

(Morgan, 2000: 39, Year 8 pupil)

The use of contrasts

Another way in which pupils can sometimes be critical in a constructive way is by presenting their criticisms in terms of contrasts between the less helpful things that teachers sometimes do and more helpful things that they do on other occasions:

So it's best when he writes on the board and explains it well and everyone listens more than when he just talks.

I think if you've got that in a block of writing it doesn't really show you anything. It's just like there and you're not going to understand it. But I think when it's done in a role play . . . it's not just kind of explained, it's kind of shown as well. So it's like every time someone says something, it's actually happening so it kind of goes together and makes a lot more sense that way.

We did the poster of the sound thing . . . It was all right. It was more fun. It was a more fun way to learn because we normally do spider diagrams and all that . . . I think it helped me to learn a bit more as well. Just like I'd got it exactly right, like all the facts and stuff. But with the spider diagram it's just writing loads and it's really boring.

I much prefer to do experiments myself than to watch our teacher doing them. I think when you're watching you kind of don't pay as much attention as you do when you're doing it, when you're actually doing it yourself. Because if you're doing it yourself when you're not paying attention then something's going to go wrong.

Well, it helped us remember more cos like you don't often go outside in the field and stuff in science lessons . . . So it was actually fun to take part in it . . . It was just kind of a change from copying off the board.

Sometimes what the teacher says you don't exactly get so if you get pupils [to] explain it to you then you could get some more ideas . . . It's actually easier because they could explain it more so you actually understood . . . The teacher will sometimes explain it like at a higher level.

But what we've done in some lessons is we've all sat in a circle and we've all gone through as individuals about certain things and you get everyone involved rather than one person reading from a book and then everyone going 'OK.'

(LP1, Year 11 pupil)

Other comments offer teachers morale-boosting contrasts between their own practices and those of other teachers:

I think she explained it very well. It was very easy . . . She talks different from other teachers because she's like younger and she sounds more like us.

Usually some teachers really do not trust us to go outside on our own without a teacher. Our teacher let us go outside on our own in pairs.

> It would help if other subjects were as clear [after a detailed account of the teacher's good practices].
>
> (LP1, Year 10 pupil)

Contrasts with other teachers (and other classes) can also highlight preferred practices of the other teachers:

> We had a teacher called Miss Smith and the first lesson we had with her she asked you to write down some things that you enjoy and things that you like about the subject . . . whereas he just like came in one day and just started off with the lessons so he doesn't really know anything about anyone at all, so.
>
> (Morgan, 2000: 56, Year 8 pupil)

> My friend's class . . . do more interesting things. Like in 'Burning Issues', they did about bombs and how they work and stuff, which I thought would be quite interesting, but we didn't do anything about that in our lesson.

Whatever the nature of the contrasts, however, pupils' articulation of contrasts between preferred and relatively disliked practices is surely helpful in making their meanings clear to their teachers.

Constructive alternatives

One of the striking things about pupils' comments and their suggestions is that they are generally very firmly grounded in their own experience of classrooms. They are not lacking, however, in creativity, and another way in which they often make their criticism constructive is through developing alternative ideas:

> Well, it would be helpful to watch certain bits of film or something, or tapes of a musical . . . Like, if we are doing a play that is really sad, you just run a sad bit of film and see how the people act it and how they stand and . . . their body language and stuff . . . I think we ought to go and see a play . . . Yes, a school trip to go and see a play because then we would get to see how other people do it.

> I'd like her to use the computer with us because we haven't ever used the computer in maths yet . . . It's more fun . . . It don't just ask you the question it just leads up to it. It's like a game . . . if you

like, see how many you get right in a certain time and try to beat this person or that . . . It's more fun and everyone you know is wondering about their maths, they just look forward to going to maths.

I think he has to change the order of the lesson around. So it's like have the practical trying to work it out yourself first and then writing down what actually happens and what you found out about cos it's worth it. And bring all the things you've done in the lesson together to like help you, to give you a conclusion and to help you like that.

Then we had to write it down, which kind of took up loads of time when we could've just remembered it. But I suppose she has to mark it and stuff so that's understandable, but it took up some time and I'd rather just sort of acted it out or something . . . She could just pull people out of the group in turn and say, 'Well, what are we doing at the moment then? What are you doing now? What character are you playing? Do you understand the story OK? What's the story about?' So then she understands directly with the pupil rather than just what they've written.

I'd like to be given more practical things like the graphical calculators and stuff. And if we're measuring things to go outside and do stuff that is more practical instead of just sitting and writing loads of stuff down.

Conclusion

When pupils are asked to give their views on their own teachers' teaching, they generally take advantage of this opportunity by offering serious and constructive comments. Teachers generally find these comments quite reassuring, because pupils' comments are usually rather positive, both praising their teachers for what they normally do and formulating many of their suggestions as requests that their teachers should more frequently do things that they currently do sometimes. But pupils also seem to be very honest (but still polite) in telling their teachers what they find unhelpful in their classroom practices. They make practical suggestions about how their teachers could modify their practices. They contrast what teachers do on different occasions, or what other teachers do. They also often offer their own constructive ideas about what teachers might helpfully do. Overall, pupils offer their own distinctive perspectives in very thoughtful and sensible ways.

Summary

When pupils speak about teaching they do so in terms of their own experiences, including their learning. The kinds of insight that they offer are to do with the learning opportunities available in the classroom, about how positive they are about these opportunities and how they might be improved.

In commenting on teaching and learning pupils sometimes try to see things from the teacher's perspective and also to recognise that other pupils may have points of view that are different from their own. The research suggests that pupils are invariably serious and disciplined in talking about how their teachers teach and avoid making gratuitous personal comments. They seem very ready to identify what they consider to be good features of their teachers' teaching and their comments are often communicated in accounts of particular episodes that are easy to interpret. Pupils are also ready, however, to comment on things that their teachers do that they do not find helpful for their learning. In these situations they will sometimes suggest directly how a modified approach might be more helpful and engaging, or they might make their point by contrasting the more and less helpful things that teachers do. Pupils may also offer their own suggestions for different teaching strategies.

We learned then that pupils are eager to make constructive suggestions for their own teachers' consideration. The energy and thought and, overall, the tendency towards positive and constructive suggestions that is apparent in their comments are most impressive. Yet, this is not so surprising when one considers how much of their lives are spent in classrooms and how much the quality of their classroom lives depends on what their teachers do and decide. What remains surprising is how little these thoughtful voices have been listened to until now.

Chapter 6

What pupils say about conditions for their learning

In previous chapters we have focused on what pupils have to say about teachers' approaches to classroom teaching and learning, both in general and in terms of what their own teachers do and could do. In this chapter the focus will move on to what pupils have to say about what facilitates or constrains their own individual learning. This means attending to pupils' experiences of the social realities of classrooms, since schools still depend on classroom teaching, providing for the learning of twenty to thirty pupils simultaneously. We therefore need to think about what such classroom provision means for the learning of all the very different pupils in each class, and we need especially to learn what these different pupils have to say about the conditions that classroom teaching provides for their individual learning.

We shall rely in large measure in this chapter on the work of Enquiry 5 of the TLRP Project (CPTL5), on how the conditions of learning in school and classroom affect the identity and participation of different groups of pupils. Arnot and Reay conducted in-depth studies of one Year 8 tutor group in each of two schools: one (Mandela) a largely working-class London inner-city school with a very mixed ethnic pupil population and a tradition of mixed-ability teaching; the other (Greenfield) a community college in a regional city with a predominantly white but socioeconomically very mixed pupil population and an established policy of teaching pupils for the most part in classes set according to 'ability'.

Up to this point, the evidence we have reviewed has allowed and even obliged us to talk in surprisingly undifferentiated and unqualified terms about 'what pupils say'. Apart from some differences between younger and older pupils, we have reported strong and sustained consensus among secondary school pupils about the kinds of teacher–pupil relationship, the kinds of teacher and the kinds of teaching that they find attractive and helpful. We have also reported common patterns in the comments and suggestions that pupils make for the attention of their own teachers. It is true that, as Pedder and McIntyre (2004: 9) report, 'some were more articulate than others', but, as they go on to say, 'the substance of their concerns was remarkably consistent'. Now, however, when the focus shifts on to the conditions for classroom learning that different pupils experience, the story could hardly be more different. On that subject, as Reay and Arnot (2003: 171) report, 'a . . . challenge for effective student consultation clearly indicated by our data is that there is no homogeneous student voice, but rather a cacophony of competing voices'.

'A cacophony of competing voices'

That lack of homogeneity should come as no surprise. Countless studies of English secondary school pupils' perspectives on their schooling have emphasised the contrasting experiences and perspectives of different pupils. Some of these studies (e.g., Hargreaves, 1967; Lacey, 1970; Willis, 1977; Ball, 1981; Dubberley, 1988; Troman, 1988; Abraham, 1989) have emphasised the sharply contrasting pro-school and anti-school subcultures of different groups of pupils, closely related both to differences among them in their social class and, in the more immediate context of the school, to the ability streams or sets to which they have been allocated. Much of the evidence from these and other studies has supported Lacey's (1970) theory that these subcultures develop as a result of the schools' differentiation among pupils in the ways they are organised and taught, and the resulting polarisation of pupil perspectives as reflected in their friendship choices and attitudes to school.

Other researchers (e.g., Furlong, 1976; Turner, 1983; Measor and Woods, 1984; Davies, 1984), taking an 'interactionist' rather than a subcultural approach, have emphasised that the diversity among pupils is generally much more complex than accounts in terms of such pro- and anti-school subcultures may suggest, and have put more emphasis on the ways in which individual pupils define their situations and decide for themselves, sometimes in quite complex ways, how they will act. Furlong (1976), for example, emphasised the several 'interaction sets' into and out of which pupils move as they agree in particular situations on how to see things and how to act; and Measor and Woods (1984) described the subtle 'knife-edging' behaviour in which pupils frequently engage in order to maintain their preferred identities, for example as neither 'clever' nor 'thick', as being good at practical but not academic subjects, and as being perfectly capable but not prepared to work hard. Woods (1990: 137) comments that 'these "knife-edgers" might appear as totally different people to different teachers on different occasions, but all these appearances were essential parts of the composite identity'. And he goes on to quote Davies's conclusion that:

> The subculture may be less a place to celebrate similarities than to demonstrate differences. The task for pupils in an anonymizing institution is to remember and prove that they are *unique* (although not too unique); the subculture provides a safe foil for this display, especially in the face of the inevitable depersonalisation of the large classroom. Subcultures are not a kind of superglue where pupils must instantly 'adhere' to the rules of the group, but at most a cavity foam filling with plenty of air space to manoeuvre.
>
> (Davies, 1984: 57)

Woods (1990: 121–2) summarises the findings from many of these studies of pupils' experience of secondary schools as follows:

> Major influences bearing on pupil school experience are social class, gender and 'race'. The relationship between these is intricate and diverse . . . Having said that, there is considerable contrast in the institutional climates presented among some of the studies discussed here . . . significant factors like school ethos, school resources, school organization and structure, staff culture and ideology, neighbourhood factors like mix and stability of ethnic groups in the community, relationships in the community, and the local labour market. Variation among these yields a variety of patterns which attach variable importance to class, race and gender in different places at different times to different people.

He notes too (*ibid*.: 139) that interactionist studies

> emphasize individual interests and choices, and situational influences upon them . . . there is too a different set of concerns

among these interactionist studies arising from their different starting point of the pupils' own construction of meaning . . . The research studies are not all concerned with the same thing, or pitched at the same level. The individual, the group and the sub-group, the institution and society are all represented. Though we may analyze at one level, we need to take others into account for a full understanding.

While this literature extends back over the last forty years, and while the complex differences in pupils' experiences have no doubt changed over that period, there is no reason to believe that the differences have decreased. On the contrary, reviews of differences among social class, gender and ethnic groups in their educational attainment tend to indicate that, if anything, differences have increased. Among the conclusions of Gillborn and Mirza (2000: 18, 22, 23, 27), for example, were that:

> According to DfEE figures, in 1997 children from the most advan-taged [social class] backgrounds . . . were more than three times as likely to attain five or more higher grade GCSEs than their peers at the other end of the class spectrum . . . Since the late 1980s the attainment gap between the highest and lowest social classes has widened . . .
>
> Data supplied by the DfEE confirms that the [gender] gap is increasing . . .
>
> The gender gap is considerably smaller than the inequalities of attainment associated with ethnic origin and social class background . . .
>
> Ethnic inequalities of attainment vary from one area to another but, despite this variability, distinct patterns of inequality are consistently visible . . . evidence shows that in some cases the inequalities have increased in recent years. African-Caribbean and Pakistani pupils, for example, have not shared equally in the rising levels of GCSE attainment.

Considerable and complex differences in pupils' experiences can therefore be expected to emerge when pupils are consulted about the conditions that classroom teaching provides for their individual learning. In planning Enquiry 5 to explore such differences, Arnot and Reay therefore deliberately set out to explore the perspectives of pupils who differed in class, gender and ethnicity, and did so in two schools ('Mandela' and 'Greenfield') with contrasting contexts and pedagogical traditions. However, given that their concern was specifically with consulting pupils about *conditions for learning*, they approached the study using the distinctive theoretical lens of Bernstein's (1990, 1996) sociology of pedagogy. Thus, as well as being alert to the impact of class, gender and ethnicity, and to the influence of community and peer cultures, they recognised that pupils' accounts of classroom life and learning would be most directly influenced by the ways in which their teachers had taught them to think. Most significantly, pupils' classroom identities were likely to be directly shaped by their self-perceptions in terms of classroom behaviour in relation to school norms (the 'regulative regime') and 'ability' at schoolwork (the 'instructional regime').

Arnot and Reay's (2004a) report of their findings shows that in schools, pupils' most salient perceptions of themselves and of each other did indeed tend to be in terms of 'ability' and classroom behaviour as well as gender, and much of their commentary was about how their conditions of learning differed according to these perceived characteristics. (The part of their study on which we draw here was about what pupils had to say when consulted by researchers, without any suggestion that their views would be passed on to teachers. It does not therefore confront the issue of how willing the pupils would have been to share these thoughts with their teachers.)

Constructions and consequences of 'ability' differences

As Cooper and McIntyre (1996: ch. 7) show, teachers in English secondary schools tend very quickly and confidently to attribute high or low levels of 'ability' to pupils. Arnot and Reay (2004a: 46–7) demonstrate that pupils themselves are quick to get the message:

> Working-class boys, in particular, articulated a painful awareness of the readiness of schools to attribute successful learning to 'ability' . . . These working-class boys were the only ones to describe invidious evaluations of their own intelligence – 'Other people saying you are thick' . . . These boys vividly described how they were made to feel stupid and childlike in classroom encounters with teachers.

In Mandela's 'mixed-ability' classes, teachers' classroom comments are highlighted:

> Kenny: Some teachers are a bit snobby, sort of. And some teachers act as if the child is stupid. Because they've got a posh accent. Like they talk without 'innits' and 'mans', like they talk proper English. And they say 'That isn't the way you talk' – like putting you down. Like I think telling you a different way is sort of good, but I think the way they do it isn't good because they correct you and make you look stupid.
>
> (*Ibid.*: 47)

In Greenfield's system of setting, the trivial nature of the work in the lowest sets tells working-class boys how stupid they are seen to be:

> Neil: It's too easy, it's like they think you're stupid or something . . . things like that make you feel stupid and it's not that much of a challenge.
>
> (*Ibid.*)

As these comments suggest, in 'mixed-ability' classes it is primarily through the insensitivity of individual teachers that pupils may be made to feel stupid, whereas with setting it is the system itself which gives lower-achieving pupils that message. Therefore, as Ball (1981) and others have found, anti-school cultures are less likely to develop where 'mixed-ability' teaching is used. When pupils in an East Sussex school who had experience of both systems were consulted, they were in no doubt as to which was better:

> I think mixed ability's better because if you're lower down in the set or whatever then you get to hear what other people think and if you're higher up you get to hear what other people think and you just have completely different opinions on stuff. That's quite cool.
>
> (LP1, Year 9 pupil)

> If you're mixed, you don't feel, 'I'm in the bottom set, I can't do anything about it.' If you're mixed, you think, 'Well, I've got as much a chance as anyone else.' And it's different characters that make a class.
>
> (LP1, Year 9 pupil)

Arnot and Reay (2004a: 48) found that lower-achieving pupils had learned to be heavily dependent on others in relation to schoolwork, both in their motivation to learn and in their judgement of how well they were learning:

> Rather than using their own assessment of their learning [something which higher-achieving groups were confident to do], the lower-achieving groups sought reassurance for the quality of their work from their teachers, other pupils and their parents. Working-class boys indicated their reliance on others to motivate them and assess whether they were doing well at school. They reported feeling most successful at learning when the teacher or their parents said 'Well done'.

The issue of whether to rely on the judgement and support of teachers or of parents was important. Carlene and Candice, two black working-class girls at Mandela, reported that they were reluctant to seek the teacher's help and so relied on their parents:

> Candice: I'm not really comfortable asking for help from the teacher. I don't know why. But it's because they don't listen to you. I just prefer to talk to my mum and dad and my brother.
>
> Carlene: With your parents . . . you've got a special bond. You can tell them stuff. With the teacher you don't have anything. You can't exactly tell them how you feel, that you're stuck on something; you can't actually speak to them.
>
> (Ibid.: 70)

Reliance on parents can lead to problems, however. Lower-achieving working-class boys at Greenfield claimed that their parents too had been accused by teachers of stupidity because of their inability to help adequately with homework: 'Well, then, they must have been stupid or something like that.' As Arnot and Reay comment, 'Their trust in school is breached by such moments' (ibid.: 48). The cultural gaps between schools and working-class homes that lead to such attributions are also evident to and confusing for these working-class pupils:

> Sean: My mum tells me something and teacher tells me different.
>
> Craig: Like your parents give you like different methods of learning and then when you come to school, they say something different

and you get confused and then you mix it like together and then you get it like wrong because you get confused.

(Ibid.: 49)

Teachers' responses to perceived differences in 'ability' are frequently a source of feelings of injustice in classrooms. At Mandela, for example, lower-achieving working-class girls expressed a deep sense of unfairness:

Jodie: Yeah, our English teacher. He likes the three clever girls a lot because they are always answering questions. He never gives other people a chance to say . . .

Carlene: If we put our hands up and we want to answer the question, the cleverest person, he will ask them, and we all know it's the right answer. And then he starts shouting at us saying that we are not answering.

Jodie: . . . and I'm like 'what's going on here?' And there's no point me taking part if he's not going to hear me out.

Candice: I think Tim and Hasmi are seen as more important cos they're the goody-goodies . . .

Alexa: And it's the clever girls as well. They get treated better than us.

Candice: There are things I don't like about teachers and the main one is they have favourites and they let the clever girls do whatever they want.

(Ibid.: 53, 54)

And from the lower-achieving boys:

Matthew: The new [subject] teacher, she doesn't respect the way we learn cos some of us learn at a slower pace than others and she has no respect for the slower ones.

Kenny: And she just treated us like a load of shit, man.

(Ibid.: 56)

These concerns that teachers unfairly give more attention to the 'clever' pupils are echoed in other studies:

I would like her not to always take more notice of the more able people in the group like when we have our hands up she goes to them first.

(Morgan, 2000, Year 8 pupil)

When he does ask questions . . . he tends to favour just the cleverer people cos there's some really, really clever people in our class . . . and he doesn't really give anyone else a chance . . . it sort of makes you feel like he thinks you're not really good enough and you just like may be wasting time saying the wrong answer . . . Lots of people don't actually put their hands up really cos they think he's not going to ask them.

(CPTL1, Year 8 pupil)

Arnot and Reay (2004a: 53) point out, however, that

This sense of unfairness in relation to teacher attention was found amongst most Mandela pupils who thought that groups other than themselves received disproportionate time and attention from the teacher. Besides 'the cleverest', those pupils who received most attention were thought to be the low-achieving children, and specifically the boys who received extra support from the Learning Support Centre.

As we have noted, these pupil reports of the multiple ramifications of being labelled as more or less able were not communicated to their teachers. We therefore do not know how surprised the teachers might have been, although we suspect that some might have been quite shocked. Since it seems important to us that teachers should know that pupils experience life in their classrooms in these diverse ways, we are left with two questions. First, what kinds of consultation procedures would be necessary to inform teachers of such pupil experiences in their classrooms? And second, how might teachers be able to respond to such information?

Perceptions of gender differences

The resentment felt by lower-achieving pupils at teachers' favouritism of the 'clever' pupils is matched only, in Arnot and Reay's (2004a) account, by the resentment of working-class boys at both schools of teachers' favouritism towards girls. The boys felt that the girls were trusted by teachers, and that they themselves were not trusted:

As a result of such trust, girls were seen as getting away with all sorts of breaches in the code of conduct . . . If boys like Dane are late (because he has to get his brothers ready for school in the morning) then they could be in quite a lot of trouble: 'If you're late, they think you've been walking and mucking around.' But one girl in the class was always late and always left her bag on the table: 'If a boy did that he gets in trouble straight way.'

(*Ibid.*: 50)

Moreover, when boys do make an effort, teachers can be critical and/or punitive and the pupils are reluctant thereafter to maintain their effort:

Nick: It's like when they give you detention and think that you aren't trying hard enough and you're trying your hardest.

(*Ibid.*: 50)

The teachers' lack of trust meant that the boys felt that they were under constant surveillance:

Kenny: The teacher doesn't ever give me any attention except when I chat.

Jason: Teachers notice me too much, but you don't want them to notice you for bad work, only good work.

(*Ibid.*: 54)

In contrast, the girls not only 'got away with more than boys' but received what Martin called 'nice attention' from teachers. Teachers' favouritism for girls is seen as extending even to where boys and girls sit in the classroom. The boys were agreed that sitting in the middle of the class was best for learning because of the disadvantages of both back and front, as described by Carl:

The teacher will get suspicious if you are up to something at the back and they can't see you that well, but if you are at the front, you won't muck about so much because you are right in front of them and they think you wouldn't dare talk cos you are right in front of them . . . say you are at the back, you are working and the teacher keeps looking at you and you get a bit nervous . . . I hate it when they like breathe on you.

(*Ibid.*: 60)

However, teachers allowed the girls to go into the classroom first:

> Carl: They let the girls go and sit in all the good spaces in the middle so we have to sit in the front or the back.
>
> *(Ibid.:* 61)

Overall, it was clear to the boys that the girls were treated better, being trusted more and being much less likely to be punished for bad behaviour:

> Neil: You hardly hear about a girl getting detention.
>
> Sean: No, if you go in detention there're all boys.
>
> Neil: Well some of the teachers they all treat like the girls and boys the same but if there are boys talking they will be more likely to get split up but if it's a group of girls, they will have five warnings before they get split up.
>
> Craig: And when they do, they only split up a couple of people, not the whole lot.
>
> *(Ibid.:* 61)

The girls, however, were equally resentful because their own learning and their reputation were undermined in several ways by the boys' bad behaviour:

> Carlene: It's unfair because the naughty boys stop us from learning because the teacher can't teach us.
>
> Lisa: And then the teacher will put 'class very noisy' on the class sheet and it's not the whole class.
>
> Carlene: And then they'll say, 'I can't come and help you. I have to stand here and watch who is being naughty.' So they can't come round and help us. So the boys stop us learning better.
>
> *(Ibid.:* 54)

The boys' perceived laziness and extreme dependence on the teachers also slowed down the work of the whole class. Boys would, for example, ask for more 'grammar, verbs and stuff' that had already been covered:

Candice: That's what you are meant to learn in the first year. I can understand them teaching us in the first year, Year 7, but going on to Year 8 we are still learning it.

Carlene: [All boys have to do is] just sit back in their chairs and the teachers will write it down for them – so they don't ever make any effort.

(Ibid.: 70)

Again, we are left with questions about how aware teachers are of these experiences of gender differentiation in their classrooms, about what consultation procedures would enable them to find out, and about how they could fruitfully use such information.

Peer-group relations and conditions for learning

Relations with peers emerge from Arnot and Reay's (2004a) account as being of central importance both positively and negatively for pupils' classroom learning conditions in both schools. Positively, it is the support of friends that emerges as being crucial, especially for lower-achieving pupils:

[L]ower-achieving working-class boys . . . frequently . . . described the role of friends in helping them cope with what, for some boys, was not a developed or comfortable relationship with the teacher. By consulting these boys, it is possible to get a sense of just how often they see relationships with teachers as tense and fraught with difficulty and the supportive role which their peer group and friends play in mediating this relationship and encouraging their learning.

(Ibid.: 49–50)

In pupils' minds, teachers do not realise that it is possible to work and talk and still be a reasonable sort of learner. Carl summarised the feelings of others in his group with this comment: 'Talking helps me cos it makes me feel comfortable . . . And when the teacher is walking around you, you think they're kinda thinking you've done it wrong or something' (*ibid.*: 51). Arnot and Reay expand on this:

Friends play many roles. They can cover up the effects of poor performance – by mediating the evaluation of learning; they can tell

you when you have done well and give you a reference point and
they protect you from individual humiliation . . . This reliance on
friends is not just about friendship or social chat.

(*Ibid.*)

While pupils themselves see their friends as playing these many
roles, and see talking with friends as a necessary condition for working
and learning, they see their teachers as having no understanding of
this positive role of friends and as being very ready to undermine this
crucial source of support for their learning. Other studies have
frequently found that pupils tend to believe that working with friends
is an important source of support for their learning, whereas teachers
are more inclined to see friendships as a potential source of distraction
from learning. Sometimes, however, it seems that this general
conclusion needs to be qualified. In Enquiry 1, for example, it was found
that pupils saw the formation of groups that were helpful to their
learning as being of particular importance. While they emphasised most
the benefits stemming from friends' knowledge of each other's language
and understanding, some of them were ready to recognise advantages
of non-friendship groups:

[W]e adapt to different groups and come together with different
groups and people, and the fact that she puts us with people that
we don't usually work with is quite good . . . I think sometimes
people work with their friends and it doesn't work out so well . . .
but today it was people we don't usually work with. It was a
different scene, different people and everybody had different ideas
and putting all the ideas together came together really well.

(Pedder and McIntyre, 2004: 18, Year 8 pupil)

It is also necessary to remember the intensity of emotions and the
instability of friendships that children and teenagers can experience, as
reflected in this plaintive comment:

I've had to sit next to people I've fallen out with and sit at the same
table with them. It's just not nice. At the end of the lesson, I've
gone to the teacher and said, 'Look , Miss, next lesson would it be
possible for me to sit somewhere else?' and the teacher has said,
'No, that is where you sit.' And I just think they may think it's silly
but at the same time it feels really serious and I don't think teachers

realise how horrible it feels to be sat at a table with people taking the mick out of you.

(LP1, Year 9 pupil)

Rudduck and Flutter (2004: 94) concluded that

pupils are in fact very discerning when it comes to choosing their preferred working partners: they are able to judge which friends they work well with and which they don't work well with and under what circumstances. We concluded that it is often better to consult pupils about who they work well with rather than to impose seating patterns that they may find arbitrary and unproductive.

Against this wider background, the significance of the Enquiry 5 findings about the unqualified importance for lower-achieving working-class pupils, especially boys, of being with friends in the classroom would seem to be that this is a distinctive need for these pupils. Their relationships with teachers are 'tense and fraught with difficulty', contributions from their parents are discounted and, as Arnot and Reay (2004a: 52) report, 'the vulnerability of working-class boys in particular, who appeared to have little to feel really confident about, [is] striking'. In such circumstances, it is not surprising that friendships are seen as of crucial value for their learning as well as for much else.

While pupils see friendship groups as a key positive resource for their learning, in other respects relationships with peers are experienced as generally having a negative impact on learning conditions. Arnot and Reay (*ibid*.: 57) report

a continuous and engrossing interplay of resentment and challenge [between small friendship groups] . . . Such fractiousness expresses itself in terms of the differences among pupils in relation to learning requirements, competing needs and yardsticks by which to compare favourable or not favourable attention by teachers. Moreover the social hierarchies of the classroom exacerbate the divisions.

There seem to be two quite different but interacting sources of these 'fights all the time' (*ibid*., Jake). On one hand, there are the frustrations felt by most pupils about their difficulties with learning due to their failure to get enough positive attention from teachers, combined with the boys' resentment at the undue amount of negative attention they receive. While teachers are blamed for such unfairness, there is also strong resentment against those other groups of pupils who are treated as 'more important'. On the other hand, tensions also emerge from peer-group culture and from differences in popularity among pupils. Peer-group culture, while not itself a focus of study in Enquiry 5, clearly interacted with other classroom concerns, for example in the way in which the two most studious boys were marginalised (Lisa: 'No one likes the geeks'; *ibid.*: 58) and more generally in diverting attention away from the schools' agendas. Arnot and Reay (*ibid.*: 64) point out that 'it is difficult to disentangle [boys'] genuine feeling of estrangement from much of the knowledge on offer from the pressures of the peer group to appear "cool" in front of one another'. Some of the different strands in these inter-group tensions are apparent in this commentary from higher-achieving, middle-class pupils at Mandela:

> Katherine: Some people are definitely seen as more important in our class.
>
> Megan: But it depends on what they are seen as more important for. Some people seem more important because they have to be helped a lot with their learning. So they get helped a lot more and shown what to do better.
>
> Laura: But also just in terms of class relationships people think they're more important if they're more popular.
>
> Jasmine: Not the girls so much. It affects the boys more.
>
> Laura: Yeah, definitely.
>
> (*Ibid.*: 57–8)

Again, are teachers aware of these positive and negative peer-group relationships, which are of such great importance in pupils' eyes? How difficult would it be to develop consultation procedures so that they could find out? And would they be able to use the information constructively?

Feeling in control

Do pupils, especially perhaps lower-achieving, working-class or male pupils, feel that they are helpless victims of the school system, as some of the above accounts seem to imply? Enquiry 5 explicitly sought to find out how much control pupils felt they had over their own learning activity.

Some of the pupils were aware, Arnot and Reay (2004a) report, that even their teachers had very little control over the school curriculum. In any case, some of the lower-achieving, working-class boys were ready to assert that, even if they had a choice, there was 'nothing' that they would want to learn at school. However, further exploration made it clear that, like their higher-achieving peers and the pupils in other studies we have reviewed, they could find subjects interesting and enjoyable if these involved sufficient activity, variety or games, and they were ready with suggestions about how subjects could be made more interesting through practicality, relevance or 'fun'. In practice, however, they seemed to be dependent on teachers' varying commitment, imagination and skill in making the learning of their subjects interesting and attractive; and, since they were not consulted, they appeared to have no influence upon the learning activities in which they were asked to engage.

What about control over the pace of learning? Arnot and Reay (*ibid.*: 67) report that they 'appear to have little if any':

> Dean: Some teachers, they write it on the board and then they say it really fast. Teachers, like, they should explain it more clearly, more slowly.
>
> Paul: When you're just on the last line he rubs it off quick.
>
> Dean: Before you've managed to write it all down!
>
> Paul: Teacher should wait. Or write it down for you.

Arnot and Reay (*ibid.*) explain how these boys

> use as many opportunities as possible to keep the teacher's attention whilst clearly worrying about the disciplining elements and surveillance that they receive by way of return . . . getting stuck, particularly in Mathematics or English, and being unable to get sufficient support brought learning to a halt. Central to these boys' assumptions was that their learning required additional teacher support.

Lower-achieving boys and girls in both schools seemed to get frustrated by work that was too slow or too easy because it was boring and implied that they were 'dumb', but they had difficulty in telling the teachers this, and also feared the greater danger that the work would subsequently become too fast or too difficult. It was socially difficult, too, to admit that work was too hard because you could be laughed at or shouted at; and, at Greenfield, there was the additional danger of being relegated to a lower set. They found little opportunity for effective communication with the teachers because teachers 'didn't listen', and it was easiest to keep the lesson slow, to present a front of not being bothered, or simply to maintain a resistance to teachers' efforts to get them to work.

Arnot and Reay (*ibid.*: 72) conclude that

> Those who arguably most need to control learning appeared to experience the least control over their learning. The only methods of seizing control of their learning for lower-achieving working-class boys appeared to be manipulation of the teacher's attention through disruptive behaviour – and this could have negative effects on their learning.

The difficult conditions that these pupils, and therefore their teachers, experienced were such that even the researchers themselves seem ambivalent in their attitudes. While asserting optimistically that 'it is important to recognise that, despite such difficult conditions for learning, even the least successful learners expressed a rather cautious yet, on the whole, a positive approach to learning – they wanted to learn and they wanted to do well' (*ibid.*: 52), they also sound a pessimistic note in suggesting that 'the culture of resistance was so ingrained that it could not easily be broken' (*ibid.*: 69).

Conclusion

The findings of Enquiry 5, as we have outlined them in this chapter, exemplify very well the diversity of pupil experiences of schooling in English secondary schools, even within the same schools, and therefore the different pupil voices that are there to be listened to, should we choose to do so. This diversity clearly indicates some of the basic challenges that face secondary schooling, challenges that have remained unresolved in a system in which pupils are not consulted. We cannot be certain that consulting pupils will enable schools and teachers to resolve these challenges within a classroom teaching system. We can, however, be certain that these challenges will not be resolved unless teachers consult their pupils effectively, and thus lay the foundations for the deliberate teacher–pupil collaboration that will be necessary for their resolution.

We need to recognise that teachers' systematic consultation of their pupils, directly or indirectly, about those pupils' diverse experiences in their own classrooms is something about which very little is known. It is something about which more research is urgently needed. How can such consultation be effectively conducted? And would teachers be able, in the light of such consultation, to take constructive action to meet the diverse felt needs of pupils that are exposed? The importance of this issue is matched by the great care that will be needed in pursuing it further.

Summary

In sharp contrast to pupils' consensual views about the kinds of teaching that they find helpful, this chapter has shown that when pupils are consulted about the social realities of their learning in classrooms, even those in the same class can report very different kinds of experiences. The findings of Enquiry 5 of our project are consistent with findings from earlier studies in exemplifying how pupils of different social class, different gender and different attributed levels of ability tend to see themselves as having very different classroom learning opportunities. Low-achieving, working-class pupils could not only see themselves but their parents as being treated as 'stupid' by their teachers; and they saw themselves as not being given the help with learning by teachers that they therefore believed they needed. In addition, they seemed to feel themselves to have very little control over their classroom learning. Both more and less academically successful pupils, and boys and girls, tended to see themselves as being discriminated against by their teachers in favour of other groups of pupils.

Given this 'cacophony of competing voices', we have raised questions about how aware teachers are of these widespread but diverse pupil frustrations, about the kinds of consultation through which teachers could become better informed about such pupil experiences and about whether teachers might be able to develop classroom strategies through which they might better meet such diverse pupil needs.

Chapter 7

What pupils say about being consulted

What intrigued us about our overall data was pupils' apparent acceptance, before they had experience of being consulted, of the principle of consultation. This became clear in interviews and discussions with our research teams who had asked pupils what might make school itself and learning in school better for them.

Their support for the idea of being consulted came in part, we think, from an awareness of the national debates about young people's right to be heard but it also reflected their frustration with the institutional habit of treating them as children rather than as the young adults they were in their out-of-school lives. Pupils want to be treated as people and to feel trusted. They want to be able to talk about their experiences as learners and to know that what they say will be taken seriously – and they express dissatisfaction at the gap between their aspirations and the daily realities of school.

This chapter is about what pupils say about the principle and practice of being consulted. We draw on data gathered by Bethan Morgan in a linked study (LP2) in which teachers from the same school were consulting their pupils for the first time and giving them an opportunity to share their concerns and insights.

Consultation is an opportunity to change some of the daily situations and strategies that get in the way of pupils' learning and their commitment to learning. A teacher comments on their 'generous' attitude to improving what happens in the classroom:

> There was one student making a point about teaching and learning who just said, when asked about her involvement, 'It's something we think needs improving, and it interests us. It's something we already know a lot about. Some people aren't learning and we can help.' They feel they have something to contribute, they feel they can actually make a difference, and they want to make a difference.
>
> (Mulliss, 2002: 3)

Pupils are able to pinpoint situations and strategies that do not work and that, if teachers were made aware of how pupils experienced them, could easily be changed. They are, on the whole, insightful, reasonable and constructive – but sharp and sure in their identification of weaknesses in the system, whether at the level of the school or the classroom. And yet their observations, in the absence of a structure which enables teachers to see things from their pupils' perspective, are likely to remain unspoken and unshared.

What pupils say about being consulted

A study, designed and carried out by Bethan Morgan, focused specifically on what pupils thought about consultation. Here, we draw on data from three Year 8 classes in the same secondary school. The school was one where the senior management team had a strong public commitment to pupil voice and encouraged pupils to comment on school-wide issues; there was, however, a more varied pattern of commitment at classroom level. The pupils involved had had no previous experience in the school of being consulted about teaching and learning in particular subject lessons.

Their teachers (Miss A, Science; Miss B, Science; Miss C, English) agreed to take part. They were not the only teachers involved but we had fuller data on their consultations and therefore decided to narrow the analysis of pupil responses to these three data sets. At various points in the year, each of the three teachers gave their class a questionnaire that asked for opinions about teaching and learning approaches. (Miss A's class completed a second questionnaire – after she had responded to many of the suggestions they had made in the first;

we have distinguished between the interviews that followed the completion of the two questionnaires, referring to them as 'Miss A1' and 'Miss A2'.) Morgan talked to pupils in the three target classes individually or in very small, self-chosen groups shortly after they had completed the first questionnaire and again during the summer term. This chapter is based on the transcripts of those interviews (each interview lasted about thirty minutes). The pupils' names have been changed – Morgan invited them to choose their own pseudonyms. (Some names may appear in two of the groups. This is because six pupils in Miss B's Science class were also in Miss C's English class. Furthermore, two pupils, from Miss A's and Miss C's groups, chose the same pseudonym, Marshall, so the latter is referred to as Marshall II.)

The overall picture that emerged was broadly consistent across the three groups. Pupils responded positively to the idea of being consulted but thought that its potential depended on how committed teachers were to taking seriously what they had said and to making explicit use of it; they also expressed some concerns and anxieties. Their responses are discussed under these headings:

- the potential of consultation as pupils saw it;
- pupils' perceptions of the authenticity of teachers' responses;
- pupils' perceptions of questionnaire-based consultation;
- whether being consulted helps you learn.

The potential of consultation as pupils saw it

Pupils were positive about the idea of teachers asking them for their opinions and were in agreement that it's 'good that . . . a teacher wants to like know your points of view' (Ellie, Miss C). As in other schools, they were aware of the absence of opportunities for talking about learning; they also anticipated, given some of their experiences of teacher–pupil relationships, that it would be difficult with some teachers to effect any fundamental change: 'Some teachers you just can't talk to cos they just bite your head off! Eat you for lunch!' (Jason, Miss C). Another boy commented, rather cynically: 'Like they got all their like boffy degrees, they got to like think they're God Almighty and they don't even bother listening to pupils' (Ben, Miss B). In a sudden flash of irritation, another pupil said that if you wanted to get any attention in lessons you had to do something wrong because then teachers *did* listen (Jemma, Miss C). Consultation, they thought, might be a better and fairer way of capturing a teacher's attention.

Indeed, pupils had high hopes of consultation, for their teachers and for themselves, but their aspirations for their teachers were perhaps easier to articulate:

> It's quite a useful thing to do cos if you like just carried on teaching without knowing what the pupils think, you're going to end up teaching them things that they don't find enjoyable or what they don't really want to pay attention to.
>
> (Marshall, Miss A1)

> [It's about] trying to find out what you think of the way she's teaching you, if there's anything that like could be done different.
>
> (Richard, Miss C)

> I think it's a really good idea because then they can see . . . if they're a good enough teacher for the pupils . . . if they're making any sense to them.
>
> (Sandy, Miss C)

Usually, they said, teachers did not ask pupils to talk about teaching and learning, so they did not know what pupils felt – nor what they had to offer. Indeed, several suggested that they knew better than their teachers what helped pupils learn and what could make things better:

> It's been ages since [they] went to school . . . yep? And [they] might not remember basic things . . . But . . . we're learning 24/7 . . . so . . . we know, we should know more than them.
>
> (Zoe, Miss B)

> They can't see theirself when they're teaching, can they? But we can.
>
> (Marshall II, Miss C)

> I think it's about the teacher feeding off our minds, instead of us learning off them, sort of like switching the process around.
>
> (Stan, Miss A)

Pupils were very appreciative of their teachers' efforts in introducing opportunities for consultation:

We're telling them stuff that we want and they're trying their hardest to do it, so they're caring for us. They're not just teachers that like teach. They're like trying to understand, trying to help you with your education.

(Brenda, Miss C)

Pupils' perceptions of the authenticity of teachers' responses

I think it's good . . . but only if the teachers refer back to it.

(Ellie, Miss C)

Although pupils could see the potential of consultation as a strategy, they learned that in practice what mattered was the authenticity of teachers' responses to what they had said – in their case, in the questionnaire. This is what *should* happen:

If she like read all of them then she might like put them together and say . . . 'I'm going to try my hardest to attempt all the reasons you've put down [about] how I could improve' . . . So then everyone's got a chance to know that she's read it and she's taken it to action.

(Brenda, Miss C)

The pupils had a great deal to say about what happened to their comments. First, it is important to point out that the teachers involved were well regarded by their classes; however, this did not stop pupils in two of the classes from feeling disappointed that more had not happened in response to their comments in the questionnaire:

Cos she doesn't do anything about it. It's like they never referred to it, they never change anything according to it.

(Michaela, Miss B)

Well, if they're going to do it they should . . . seem to pay any attention to it. Cos if they're going to consult us about something . . . then make a change about what we've asked them to do.

(Dawn, Miss C)

Pupils became suspicious: perhaps their teachers were not reading the questionnaires carefully enough, or perhaps not at all:

> [Y]ou don't get the teacher saying back about what they did and then it really makes you wonder if they actually read them. Or they've just thrown them in the bin!
>
> (Mary-Kate, Miss C)

> [T]hey just flick through and that . . . teachers don't refer again to them. They don't ever bring them back up again.
>
> (Ellie, Miss B)

> [They should] just speak to you for a little while [about it] . . . so you'd know that she's read it, thought about it and, like, decided.
>
> (Dorothy, Miss C)

There is a great deal at stake here. The lack of response can be experienced by pupils as discourteous; further, to have no clear evidence of a response could make the pupils lose faith in the principle of consultation. It was interesting how quickly, in reflecting on why the teacher had not followed their advice, the pupils reverted to the traditional authority image of the teacher:

> [Perhaps] she just looks at it and thinks, 'Oh, they've got different opinions to me but I'm the teacher – so they have to do what I say.'
>
> (Michaela, Miss B)

For pupils, the potential of consultation to transform the teacher–pupil relationship can easily unravel.

However, a few pupils from each group thought they *could* identify some small signs of responsiveness. What was missing in two of the groups, it seems, was the teacher's readiness to talk through her responses with the pupils, making clear which recommendations she had chosen to act on and why there were some suggestions she would not be able to implement. But explaining yourself to pupils was not part of the teachers' repertoire; they were still operating within the framework of traditional teacher–pupil relationships. However, although disappointed, some pupils were sympathetic to the pressures on their teachers that might account for their minimal response:

> She can help us only as much as she can help us, like . . . She's not someone who can do everything in the whole world, like Mary Poppins or something.
>
> (Roger, Miss C)

Feedback and follow-up were different with the third teacher, Miss A. She had recently qualified and with fewer administrative demands on her time was able to give considerable attention to developing consultation; her pupils were quick to recognise and approve of her responsiveness. Pupil satisfaction with being consulted was high – if, occasionally, somewhat dramatically expressed:

> Makes us feel happier – makes us feel better. Feels like you're actually . . . part of . . . [the lessons]. Like some days I think . . . 'What's the point in me living? What's the point in me getting out of bed? I've got nothing to do at school. It's just . . . boring.' Some days you don't seem to learn anything.
>
> (Damien, Miss A2)

Other comments emphasised pupils' sense that they were now getting more out of the lesson:

> It's good because you know then it wasn't like a wasted half hour or something and that it's actually working. And we're like kind of making more use of the time. And doing something that actually is good for our learning, [not] doing something that won't work.
>
> (Meg, Miss A2)

> [L]ike when she's saying, 'Oh, all the majority of you thought this, so in future we're going [to] try and do this' . . . it's nice cos she's like trying to help us learn more better.
>
> (Melissa, Miss A2)

Through Miss A's care with the procedures, including following up on what had been suggested, pupils were beginning to trust her: she referred back to the questionnaires and discussed the responses with her class without disclosing who had said what, and they liked that. One boy offered useful advice to teachers who are new to consultation:

> [A]lways tell the pupils [the] results – so they know what's happening, cos otherwise they feel a bit lost and then confused and that doesn't help.
>
> (Peter, Miss A2)

Pupils could point to changes that Miss A had made as a result of the consultation – and, importantly, as we saw above, they thought the changes were enhancing their learning:

[S]he's kind of . . . changed a lot the way she teaches . . . because
. . . she used to just set us work and . . . that was it. And now we
have a lot more freedom and independence on how we can do
things.

(Meg, Miss A2)

[O]ur lessons have changed so much. More practicals . . . more
project work. She doesn't speak for as long.

(Jonathon, Miss A2)

They felt flattered that Miss A was prepared to change her approach
'just for us to like it more', whereas most teachers were not seen as
either responsive or flexible enough to do this: 'they are just like, "this
is the method – you're going to learn from it"' (Marshall, Miss A2). We
can see that a different kind of teacher–pupil partnership could develop,
one that is based on mutual trust and a joint commitment to learning.

Pupils' perceptions of questionnaire-based consultation

Most, but not all, pupils thought that communicating your ideas through
a questionnaire was better than having to 'tell the teacher face to face'
– although, one pupil commented, unprompted, that she didn't mind
talking to the microphone (and by extension, the researcher). There
was a lot of discussion in the interview groups about procedural
issues and consideration of confidentiality and anonymity featured
prominently in pupils' explanations of why written evaluations were
better. This was evidence of the insecurities that they felt in these early
stages of consultation about the boundaries of trust. They wanted
neither the teacher nor their peers to know who had said what.

Commenting in front of your peers could be embarrassing and peer
pressure could make you echo what your friends thought rather than
your own opinions. Commenting directly to the teacher was problem-
atic for different reasons: if you were harsh in your criticism then
the teacher might take it out on you or become stricter and abandon
opportunities for dialogue. One pupil was pragmatic – 'There's no
point being scared because . . . if the teacher didn't want comments
or anything then she wouldn't give out a questionnaire' (Frederick,
Miss C) – but his logic was not reassuring to others.

If some pupils were scared about what would happen to them as a
result of their comments, others were concerned about the effect on the

teacher. They acknowledged that their honesty in writing what they really thought was sometimes compromised because of this:

> I'd, like, sort of feel sorry cos then . . . they would go [mournful tone], 'Oh God, why'd you say that about me? Why'd you say that about me?' And I'd get a bit worried and feel sorry that I said it.
>
> (Marshall II, Miss C)

> [Y]ou get asked a question but you don't really want to hurt the teacher's feelings or you'll think, 'Oh, I can't say that cos then they won't like me.' If they say a question like, 'Do you think I teach very well?' and [pupils] say, 'No', then you'll think, 'Oh, should I have said that?'
>
> (Frederick, Miss B)

Some had clearly softened their views in the questionnaire:

> You automatically put some stuff that . . . you know she'll like.
>
> (Michaela, Miss B)

> You feel a bit awkward so you have to say something nice about her.
>
> (Judy, Miss C)

These pupils were demonstrating a capacity to look at things from the perspective of others. Some said that if the questionnaire had more open questions as opposed to boxes to tick – most of them wanted this because then they would have more opportunity to express their views – then that would be hard on those pupils who found writing a struggle and 'can't spell or anything'. Some also saw that an advantage of the questionnaire for the teacher was that it was a permanent record that would enable her, they hoped, to keep looking back at what they had written and discuss and try out different suggestions. This readiness of pupils to see situations from different angles indicated that there was a potential for them to move beyond their traditional view of the teacher and to conceive of a different kind of teacher–pupil relationship. Indeed, a few pupils were concerned about the one-sidedness of the approach and felt that the pupils should be designing a questionnaire for the teacher to complete so that they would know what her preferred ways of teaching were.

Asked whether they could think of any alternatives to the questionnaire for gathering their views, pupils came up with a number of suggestions. One pupil who resented the time taken up by the questionnaire – 'You go there to learn Science and we're doing questionnaires about it' – thought a better way 'would be to just at the end go up to her and if you have any suggestions to tell her, like that' (Michaela, Miss B). However, taking into account the demands on the teacher as well as the pupils' own preferences, pupils thought the questionnaire was a good compromise: 'She's not going to ask all twenty-eight people about each of them things [in the questionnaire] cos it would take too long' (Luke, Miss A). But if the teacher chose to talk to pupils, their advice was to do so on a one-to-one basis, because if they had to comment in front of their mates some pupils would try to be funny or outrageous.

A few pupils who clearly felt somewhat impatient with the detail of the questionnaire suggested that there should be an occasional on-the-spot class discussion:

> I reckon the easiest was for 'em to do it in one lesson . . . then go, 'Right everyone' – just take it in the gut and say, like, 'Everyone just tell me what you think about the lesson,' instead of all the questions that [were] on the questionnaire.
>
> (Marshall II, Miss C)

A variant of this idea was for the teacher to stop the lesson at a particular point and invite comments on the strategy she was using (somewhat like the 'spot check' approach described by MacBeath *et al.*, 2003). Some pupils thought that a computerised questionnaire might be interesting because 'people generally like computers' (Honey, Miss B). Zoe (Miss B) favoured writing individual comments and putting them in her teacher's pigeon-hole. Derek (also in Miss B's class) liked the idea of a large sheet of paper on which pupils could write short comments when they had something to say – or in response to specific questions about some aspect of the lessons to which the teacher wanted their reaction. One pupil suggested that each member of the class keep a diary of things they liked or did not like in the teacher's lessons, and another thought that a group exercise might be useful: a small number of pupils would sit at each table and the table leader would invite responses and record agreed key comments. One group thought that five pupils should act as 'key informants' (our term) at the end of each lesson and give the teacher an immediate view of what worked well in the lesson. With more time, the pupils would have been able to identify and discuss the different issues that their suggestions raised – such as whether all pupils would have a chance to express a view in the whole-class setting, or how the five pupils would be chosen and whether they would be seen as 'representative', or how the various suggestions related to the issue of confidentiality and anonymity that seemed so vexing for them. But, as one pupil said pragmatically of the alternative strategies mentioned in her interview group: 'It's always worth a try, isn't it? Anything to help the children learn better' (Sandy, Miss C).

Whether being consulted helps you learn

> It probably contributes to our learning quite a bit.
>
> (Philip, Miss A2)

Pupils claimed that consultation *does* help them learn. Moreover, they were able to explain why. First, they argued that they knew better than their teachers what strategies helped them learn and prevented them learning, so if the teacher included more of the former and avoided the latter, they would learn more – the teacher would 'let us out into better learning' (Peter, Miss A1). A good example was 'research': teachers assumed that pupils liked research-based tasks but they were wrong because what it usually entailed was little more than 'copying and pasting' and 'we don't learn from it'; they wanted to 'make the most of our learning time' instead of wasting time on things that do not help them learn (Meg, Miss A2). As a result of the consultation, although other teachers continued setting 'research' tasks, Miss A knew that they did not work, and why, and changed her approach. Simply, as one pupil maintained, as a result of seeing some suggestions taken up, 'In the end we learn more because we're finding it better to . . . be in the lesson' (Dawn, Miss C). Their teachers, particularly Miss A, were creating more opportunities for approaches that pupils enjoy and believe support their learning: less copying, less teacher talk, more active and interactive work – and the occasional game, which pupils justify in terms of learning:

> [W]hen the teacher mentions a game . . . it's still about the subject but you're enjoying it ten times better than writing out stuff off the board. You're not thinking about learning neither but it's still going in.
>
> (Hazel, Miss C)

Second, and related to the first explanation, is the simple logic that if you enjoy a particular way of working then you are likely to learn more:

> If you improve the lesson to make them like it they won't just switch their brains off and they'll listen more . . . And then they'll enjoy it when they come, and learn . . . a lot more.
>
> (Philip, Miss A2)

> I think it's good because [teachers] get a view of how the pupils basically want the lessons to be run cos if it's run how they don't want it they're just going to switch off basically.
>
> (Ralph, Miss A2)

The 'fun' word appears in several responses but, as pupils explain, 'fun' can mean having a laugh, doing things you are really interested in, or doing things that are novel and challenging. Consultation is 'fun' too – a good way of making pupils feel alert, attentive and involved:

> [T]he questionnaires really make a difference because . . . we used to be like [bored tone], 'Oh, Science' . . . and it's like now [brighter tone], 'Science!' – like more perky sort of thing.
>
> (Melissa, Miss A2)

The pupils' comments are not, as might be thought, statements about the dominance of their wishes over their teacher's, and the need for entertainment at all costs; the group seemed genuinely concerned about their learning. Indeed, one group of interviewees explored the possibility that the pupils might be mistaken about what helped them to learn – and if the teacher took up their suggestions and then discovered that they were wrong, she had to tell them:

> If she says, 'You said you learn well [by doing this] but you're not actually learning well' then it actually makes us stop and think . . . rather than just letting us assume.
>
> (Philip, Miss A2)

Another pupil said that it might not be right to have only the things that the pupils said they liked but a balance of 'the stuff we like . . . and the stuff that we don't like' (Jason, Miss C).

The third part of the argument was this: if a teacher bothers enough about you to ask your opinion and then takes time to think about and

respond to what you have said, you will respect and like that teacher –
and 'you tend to work better if you like the teacher' (Melissa, Miss A2).
Another pupil sums it up:

> I know it's a bit weird but it'll actually get the kids to like the teacher
> more because they're actually asking them what they think about
> . . . the lesson. The kids will just like the teachers for asking them
> about it – for letting them have a say in what goes on.
>
> (Christine, Miss A2)

Miss A had been exemplary in these respects. And the response of the
class was positive:

> It's definitely changed the lesson and stuff . . . so a lot of us are
> listening and more attentive . . . We're doing a lot more fun things
> so we're all kind of trying to get a bit more involved and stuff.
>
> (Meg, Miss A2)

> I think she feels better about it as well because we're listening to
> her more.
>
> (Melissa, Miss A2)

Consultation, pupils suggested, can improve the classroom climate and
relationships:

> Definitely ask your pupils because you'd kind of get close to them
> [and] you'd get better work out of them and you wouldn't waste
> proper learning time with stupid . . . exercises. You'd make their
> learning worthwhile.
>
> (Meg, Miss A2)

This pupil goes on to explain that with consultation you get 'more of a
bond' and adds that it is especially helpful for the quiet and enigmatic
pupils:

> Like some kids – they're a bit hard to figure out – and they just kind
> of sit there and the teacher's thinking, 'How can I make them learn?'
> but they don't think of asking them. [Now] they know what would
> make them learn more. [Consultation will] definitely, definitely
> bring . . . exam results up higher.
>
> (Meg, Miss A2)

Conclusion

The feelings and thoughts of the pupils discussed in the last section were consistent with those of other secondary school pupils who were interviewed about being consulted. Pupils from Morgan's project explained how consultation influenced learning through ensuring that teachers understood – and where possible acted on – pupils' advice about strategies that helped them enjoy lessons and consequently learn more. Pupils from other schools provided insights into the broader impact of consultation. They talked about becoming more confident about expressing an opinion and about their pride in seeing their ideas translated into action. Some pupils – as did the pupils quoted in the last section – clearly felt good about recognising the power of their own insights: they knew things about their own learning and about learning in their class that were useful to teachers; this was a different kind of knowledge from the knowledge of curriculum content that was normally valued in school.

But these positive responses are dependent on the process of consultation being carefully introduced and sustained long enough for pupils to feel that teachers' interest in what they have to say is genuine and will be thought about and followed up, and for both teachers and pupils to feel that mutual trust is opening up the possibility of a more partnership-oriented way of working together.

Summary

Teachers who engage in pupil consultation and researchers who explore it generally find that pupils appear very positive about consultation and pleased to be involved in it. That strong general impression is confirmed in this chapter, where we have summarised findings from research that explicitly asked pupils about their thoughts on consultation shortly after their teachers had consulted them. These pupils welcomed the idea of consultation in principle, because it implied that these teachers wanted to hear their views, in sharp contrast to other teachers who did not want to listen to them. They were confident that teachers could usefully learn from them and they appreciated teachers making an effort to do so. In practice, their appreciation depended on the authenticity of teachers' concern to listen to them and to take their views into account; and they gauged such authenticity from evidence – through explicit feedback and through evident changes in teachers' practices – that teachers had read and thought seriously about what they had said. The pupils also commented on methods of consultation. The majority favoured the questionnaires that their own teachers had used, because of the confidentiality and anonymity that they allowed. They were, however, very ready to suggest other possible consultation procedures, a prominent concern being that the chosen procedure should genuinely allow them to communicate their ideas about what helped their learning. Finally, pupils who had experienced what they were sure was authentic consultation were in no doubt that it had helped their learning, for three clear reasons: their teacher was now concentrating on teaching approaches that really helped their learning; they were enjoying the classes more and were therefore learning better; and the relationship between teacher and pupils had improved because of the former's readiness to 'let them have a say in what goes on'.

Chapter 8

Teachers' responses
to what pupils say

The literature on pupil consultation, although quite strongly research based, has tended to be a literature of *advocacy*, promoting the case for consulting pupils. In particular, it has strongly emphasised the rich, perceptive and thoughtful things that pupils undoubtedly have to say about classroom teaching and learning. Many of the previous chapters of this book have followed this common pattern. This has been an entirely proper tendency since it has been necessary to show the merits of an innovative idea. However, a balanced consideration of the idea of pupil consultation needs to be equally concerned with the implications for teachers. Even from an advocacy perspective, the main value of consultation must depend upon the use that teachers make of what they learn from pupils. This chapter is therefore concerned with teachers' responses to pupil consultation. What do they learn from it? Can they use what they learn from it? How helpful from their perspective is what pupils have to say?

Is pupil consultation helpful to teachers?

To understand what may be involved from the teacher's perspective, we need to ask why, after some two hundred years of classroom teaching, teachers have not generally engaged in pupil consultation before now. There would seem to be a number of contributory factors. One, certainly, is the 'ideology of immaturity' (Grace, 1995) that we mentioned in our opening chapter, according to which children and adolescents have not developed sufficient wisdom to be able to contribute to responsible decision-making about their own lives. Another important factor has surely been the ideology of professionalism, according to which teachers, especially in the UK, have persuaded themselves – and for many years succeeded in persuading others – that by virtue of their professional positions and expertise, 'teachers know best' in relation to all school and educational matters. Both of these seem indeed to be 'ideologies' in that they are claims that are much too sweeping to be rationally justifiable and also in that they have seemed to serve the interests of teachers by legitimating their unilateral exercise of power over their pupils.

A more sympathetic view of the teaching profession might, however, emphasise other more practical and less self-serving factors underlying the lack of pupil consultation. Such a view could be rooted in an understanding of the extraordinary complexity of classroom life (e.g., Doyle, 1986) and the vast amount of potentially relevant information with which classroom teachers are confronted. From this perspective, expert teaching is critically dependent on simplification of this vast amount of information and on the careful prioritisation of information that is needed for classroom decision-making (e.g., Berliner, 1987). Given the availability of so much other information, much of it about pupils, consulting pupils may seem an unnecessary and unhelpful extra task for teachers to undertake.

Teachers do tend to have a great deal of information about their pupils, and have many ways in which they can learn about them, including observing them, assessing their work, and listening to their contributions to classroom discussions, all of which they do on a daily basis. It is clear too that it is to information about their pupils that teachers give most attention in their classroom teaching (e.g., Brown and McIntyre, 1993). Furthermore, responsiveness to their pupils seems to be a fundamental aspect of many teachers' views of successful teaching (see Cooper and McIntyre, 1996). So not explicitly consulting pupils about teaching and learning does not indicate any lack of concern about pupils or even a lack of attention to pupils' concerns. It may simply mean that teachers have felt they knew enough about their pupils' concerns and perspectives without consulting them. (But, as we have seen in the previous chapter, this is certainly not a view shared by pupils themselves.)

Although apparently not an attractive idea in the past, pupil consultation seems to have become increasingly popular in recent years, so it may be that teachers are spontaneously recognising the benefits that it can offer them. Enquiry 6 of the TLRP Project offered support to selected schools wishing to explore the benefits of pupil consultation, and it is interesting to consider what excited the enthusiasm of teachers who took up this offer. In some cases, schools wanted to explore the benefits of school councils or other whole-school initiatives proposed by senior management teams, but there were others in which the enthusiasts were classroom teachers. For example, Paul Freestone, Head of Science at Exmouth Community College, was concerned that pupils in the school were not achieving as well in Science as in other subjects but he did not know why. So he consulted a representative sample of Year 11 pupils and on the basis of what he learned from them he experimented with new approaches to teaching the subject (Flutter and Rudduck, 2004: 34–7). Ingrid Cox, of Rivington and Blackrod High School near Bolton, was uncertain about the benefits of target-setting as a way of supporting Key Stage 4 pupils, and was keen to explore what kinds of support pupils found helpful in raising their standards of achievement. As a result of the consultation that she and her colleagues conducted, it was possible to develop a whole-school target-setting policy that involved the pupils more actively and was much more sensitive to their needs (*ibid.*: 41–4; see also Project Newsletter, No. 11, November 2003). In such cases, the motivation seems both rational and clear: teachers recognise both that they have problems to resolve and that their pupils may be able to provide the information necessary for the solution of these problems.

In some cases, teachers' initial thinking about consultation changes as a result of the experience. Gill Mullis, teacher-researcher at Hastingsbury Upper School, for example, described teachers' experience there as follows:

> We began with the aim of developing students' involvement in decision making within the school by working with Student Council members. In doing so, we slowly redefined the 'we', began to challenge discourse and practice which excluded pupils from decision making, and transformed the 'that' – no longer a discussion about paint pots and social areas, but a dialogue about relationships and teaching and learning.
>
> (Flutter and Rudduck, 2004: 66; see also Project Newsletter, No. 6, September 2002)

More generally, it seems that although teachers may be positively disposed towards pupil consultation, they often – and not surprisingly – develop clear views of its benefits only as a result of engaging in it. Sometimes, therefore, teachers develop an enthusiasm for pupil consultation after participating in initiatives from outside, often from researchers. Sarah Bennett of Worthing High School, for example, describes the West Sussex Learning and Improvement Project as 'an exciting project which aimed to encourage schools to learn from each other, and from pupil voice'. And, while noting that 'the whole process would have been meaningless without support from the staff', she explains the valuable insights that the teachers learned from the project, concluding that 'above all, what we've learned is that we all still need to keep listening' (Project Newsletter, No. 8, February 2003).

Similarly, MacBeath *et al.* (2003: 6, Enquiry 2) quote secondary school teachers who have learned the benefits of pupil consultation from experience. Some of these benefits are for themselves:

> We've had some very clear pointers from students about how they like to learn and I think it's given quite an encouragement to different ways of teaching. We've modified things or developed things further – and had the courage of our convictions.
>
> Staff that you thought wouldn't ever listen, who'd seen this going on and who'd said, 'Fine, yes, but that's not for me' – once they've seen the students reacting and hear what they're saying . . . they're suddenly thinking, 'Well, maybe they *do* know what they're talking about.' And that brings more staff in.

Other benefits noted by these teachers are for the pupils:

> We've learned a lot . . . about how students rapidly improve in their learning and their self-esteem and their motivation through dialogue with staff, through feeling important, feeling cared for, feeling their views matter. I think it's had a really significant effect.
>
> I think it's essential to consult pupils about their learning . . . it's educational in its own sense, it develops their ability to take responsibility for their learning.

Similarly, Fielding and Bragg (2003: 19, Enquiry 4) quote secondary school teachers who have learned from their experiences of working with pupils as researchers the multiple benefits that this can bring:

> We hope that the findings can be used by both students and staff to improve learning and teaching across the school. This is what I find so exciting, this research can make a positive difference to everyone. It's not about students picking holes in teachers, it's about achieving together.

> Kids amaze me. They astonish me. They just knock me out. Working with these students in a completely different way has been fascinating. My relationship with them is different.

While some teachers, then, are spontaneous enthusiasts for pupil consultation about teaching and learning, many, sensibly enough, need to be persuaded of its advantages; and they are most readily persuaded of these advantages through having some practical experience of them. This being so, it makes sense that our richest evidence about teachers' responses to pupil consultation comes from situations in which teachers have agreed that researchers should consult their pupils on their behalf, should feed the evidence of what the pupils say back to them, and should then explore with them their responses to what the pupils have said. That was the approach adopted in Enquiry 1 of the TLRP Project (Pedder and McIntyre, 2004, 2006; McIntyre *et al.*, 2005) and also in a small parallel project by Morgan (2000). The following sections are based mainly on the findings of these projects.

How do teachers respond to the different things pupils have to say about their lessons?

From the four schools that were keen to be involved, one volunteer department from each school and two volunteer teachers from each of these departments were chosen to participate. One Science, one Mathematics and one English department were involved in the main project (Pedder and McIntyre, 2004) and a second English department was involved in Morgan's broadly similar but smaller study. For each of the teachers, the research focused on one Year 8 class; and each teacher worked with the whole class to identify six fairly articulate representative pupils, three boys and three girls, three of whom were doing well in the subject and three who seemed neither to enjoy the subject nor to be doing well in it. These six pupils were invited to take part in individual post-lesson interviews. During the first phase of the enquiry, which consisted of five researcher visits to each class over a three-month period, the focus was on eliciting from the pupils their ideas about teaching and learning in the relevant subject teacher's class, taking a lesson observed by the researcher as a starting point; and then, after giving the teachers time to read the transcripts of their pupils' interviews, eliciting from the teachers their responses to the pupils' ideas.

Throughout this first stage, teachers were increasingly asked to focus on planned changes that they might make in their practice in response to the pupils' ideas. In the second stage, over the next two months, the teachers tried to implement such selected changes in their practice, and after each of three lessons the same six pupils and the teacher were again interviewed about the impact of the pupils' ideas on the teacher's practice. A third phase of the main study involved follow-up interviews with the teachers about six months later, to explore the longer-term impact of the initiative. Except when otherwise stated, quoted teacher responses in this section and the next are from this enquiry.

As is reflected in the design of this study, at least three levels of teacher response to pupil consultation can be differentiated: the fairly immediate impact on teachers' pedagogical thinking; the short-term impact on their practice; and the longer-term impact on their practice. We shall consider each of these in turn, starting with teachers' responses as they reflect upon what their pupils have to say. A primary determinant of such responses is, of course, what the pupils say. So a very important and consistent finding, both of these particular studies and much more generally, is that teachers tend to be reassured by the politeness, the forbearance and the constructiveness of pupils' comments on their teaching. The most negative response from any of the teachers in Enquiry 1 was that the pupils were telling them nothing that they did not know already. But most of the teachers found some surprising and pleasing things, such as the quality of the pupils' understanding of what teachers did, the positive feelings expressed by them about the subject, the consistency across the six pupils in their perceptions, and the pupils' capacity to think not only about their individual needs but about those of their classmates. On the whole, the teachers agreed that, as one put it, the pupils 'were generally, in a very polite, nice way, good at criticising the lessons' (Pedder and McIntyre, 2004: 21).

The teachers, however, were equally critical in their consideration of pupils' comments and suggestions. None of them was ready to accept pupils' ideas without very careful reflection on their implications. For example,

> I mean I'm quite flexible but . . . I'm not going to have the curriculum dictated by a class . . . 'Well, we want to do this and we don't want to do what you tell us to do' . . . cos I'm there to guide their learning and what's in the curriculum cos they don't actually know.
>
> (Morgan, 2000: 58)

But this did not mean that the teachers rejected all of their pupils' ideas. For example, the teacher quoted above demonstrated that he was indeed flexible by thinking hard about what the pupils were saying:

> One of them said, 'Well why can't we do things based on ourselves rather than it's always dictated to us?'. . . . That made me smile . . . but it did make me think quite carefully about how do we make something like Shakespeare relevant to a Year 8 or any year group for that matter without it being boring?
>
> (*Ibid.*)

Pupil ideas had to meet several demanding criteria before teachers would consider acting on them. The criteria used most by the teachers are addressed below.

Educational effectiveness

Teachers would generally accept only those pupil ideas that they considered to be both educationally desirable in principle and effective for achieving their educational purposes:

> [T]he *huge* thing that they kept saying was how they loved drama . . . I think there is room for drama, but it can't be every single lesson because it's an English lesson. And if you do drama things every lesson you're neglecting the English skills that they need.

In response to a pupil comment that it would be useful to learn from their mistakes in planning and conducting experiments:

> That's one comment I do disagree with really . . . I can't see the point in having them plan an experiment if it's not really up to standard or if it's basically wrong.

Validity

Suggestions would be considered only if teachers accepted that they were based on valid accounts of what actually happened in classrooms:

I disagreed with what she said. She said that there were about four titles [to choose from]. There were loads, about fifteen. I think she had enough choice there, I really do.

They say they don't want so much homework. They give the impression, one or two of them, that they do homework every night, but we only have it once a week.

Practicality

Teachers commonly saw their pupils' ideas as being very sensible in principle but not necessarily feasible in practice. There were various considerations that might lead to pupil ideas being viewed as unrealistic, including compatibility with the National Curriculum and constraints of time, equipment and space:

Some of them said they'd like to do computers more often . . . but there's actually not any availability on the timetable for that Year 8 group to get into an IT room, which is why I'm using the calculators more.

In response to a suggestion of open-ended group projects:

I'm always thinking I've only got three weeks to get through the content before they're assessed. It's a different type of learning and they will remember an awful lot more from what they've presented and because they're proud to achieve, but again it's weighing up whether the time spent on that is going to be useful when they've got all these hurdles to jump over.

Representativeness

When similar suggestions came from several pupils, teachers were usually much more interested. In their consideration of pupil ideas, phrases such as 'A lot of them said . . .' and 'Quite a few suggested . . .' kept recurring. Teachers were also very interested in identifying the pupils from whom comments came, as a way of helping them to judge how helpful a suggestion would be for the whole class. (This was possible because, although the interviews were anonymous, pupils made no attempt to disguise their identities and so teachers found it easy to locate them.) Ideas were accepted only if teachers judged that they would enhance the learning experiences of all their pupils or at least that none would be disadvantaged by them:

> I think that the pupils who are making the suggestions are ones that see themselves as good at drama, who perhaps assume that they will get a big role.

> You see, I know who that is . . . it wouldn't work well with the class as a whole, I'd lose too many of the class.

From the ideas suggested by their pupils, the teachers were invited to select some that they would incorporate into their practice. What that meant depended on the nature of the pupils' ideas. Most of the teachers seemed to be faced with five different scenarios.

Affirmation of teacher practices

The easiest suggestions for teachers to accept were those which encouraged them to do more of the good things they already did, and there were plenty of such suggestions:

> They did enjoy the things that I went to the trouble to do so that they would enjoy them.

> I think the strongest point that came out was the idea of trust . . . the fact that I'd allowed them to go off around the school in pairs or threes to collect their own leaves in the sites they chose . . . and they all seemed happy and very pleased with the idea they've been trusted to do that . . . and that's quite interesting to reflect on about how that might get used in other lessons.

> A lot of them were saying how they like the fact that I don't make them work in silence all the time and they like to chat a little bit with their friends . . . I think partly because they can help each other with their work but also . . . it's a happier working environment.

> Here they are actually saying, 'Oh, I thought being told to be in a certain group was a good thing' . . . a couple of them actually acknowledged that they worked better when they weren't with their friends because there was less possibility of getting side-tracked . . . I think I will probably do it more now.

The tricks I tried with the counting sticks to help with axes is something that was new this year . . . and because of the feedback from the interviews I shall definitely go on to do that again, because they've actually helped me identify ways they've understood it.

Weaknesses identified in teachers' practices

The pupils were also ready to identify weaknesses of specific lessons or of the individual teachers, and the teachers were often ready to accept these judgements:

> On a couple of the interviews I got the impression that the pupils wanted more ownership really of their planning practical work and actually writing up conclusions of their practical work. They wanted more involvement in that. I think what I do is perhaps I'm the central pivot . . . but possibly we could develop that a bit more and once I've perhaps told them a little bit about the experiment . . . let them think a little bit more about the safety precautions . . . about planning a fair test . . . and then, you know, they own the experiment.

> I think one of my main observations from reading the transcripts was that I talked too much and I think I do. I agree with them. More than one of them said I talk too much.

> One of the things that struck me was that the aim and purpose of the lesson wasn't actually that clear to a couple of the pupils . . . I think partly that was my fault . . . the golden rule is ensuring that they understand the aim and purpose of a lesson. I think I've got to work at that a little bit.

> What was mentioned by some pupils was that they couldn't bear the noise . . . they couldn't hear what each other were saying and I thought . . . I could actually find, say, a room for one group and a room for another group and actually try and siphon them off really . . . I'll just try and find out which rooms are free.

Good pupil ideas accepted by teachers

Pupils did not limit themselves to judging the merits of the teaching they had already experienced: they also offered their own ideas. In many cases teachers welcomed these ideas as good, sensible and practical, and were ready to incorporate them into their practice:

> One of the things that somebody brought up was that another teacher . . . picked on people without them having their hands up and it keeps them on their toes, and I know I don't do that much. And I don't know why I don't do it and I've never really thought of it much . . . but, as a way of classroom management, I think that's quite a good idea, really . . . I tried it a bit today.

> That was one of the ideas I thought I could use – to have individual extension exercises available for one or two . . . it's something I used to do when we had a more individualised scheme really. It's bringing back the old ideas.

> Other suggestions included 'cut the story and use more of an outline' and that definitely was a good idea; and I think personally, as a teacher, I should have thought more to make that introduction punchier, livelier, more dramatic.

> I think one thing that came out was that they would like to discuss wrong results more, which I think is fair comment really . . . Perhaps I'll try to make an effort to at least do one piece of investigational work where we spend a lot of time evaluating it and so forth.

Pupil ideas developed by teachers

Frequently, however, teachers were not content simply to accept or reject pupil ideas but instead took them as a starting point for new thinking of their own. For example, they would adapt the idea to produce one that better fitted their own purposes, or develop a specific idea from a pupil into a more general idea:

> They were referring to enjoying doing the poster work and presenting information in poster pictorial form. They found that easy to remember . . . so I suppose the key issue from a teaching point of view is how much quality information they're getting down . . . It's set me thinking . . . possibly I could give them a spider diagram – they've got the information in a spider diagram – and get them to translate that into a poster, something that they seem to get a lot of enjoyment out of and would be keen to refer back to.

I think this one particular student had some lovely ideas about merging different ways, like having a story and having props from another story and merging these ideas . . . It would be quite nice to use that, or perhaps get her on her own, or with a couple of other people, and get their suggestions . . . Rather than me being the focus, I could actually get other students to introduce a scenario or their ideas and develop it further.

Ideas about which teachers were uncertain

Teachers were not always ready to commit themselves one way or another about the merits of pupil ideas. Quite often they reported instead that what pupils had said merited serious reflection:

[O]ne or two commenting on the fact they don't feel that we did enough practical work. I found that interesting because I think in my planning one of the things I know that I do try and do is wherever possible to fit practical-type work into whatever we're doing . . . so that's there for me to reflect on whether that's actually happening.

In other cases, teachers decided that the best way to decide on the merits of a pupil idea was to try it out in practice:

She's obviously very keen on this whole-class drama . . . whereas, my reality, I'm seeing that I'll have three or four groups that I'm trying to direct and [some] people who don't have a concrete task to do . . . so I can see it falling apart really . . . I'll see how it works . . . It's a learning experience, for them and for me.

How do teachers differ in their responses to pupil ideas?

Attitudinal differences

As is apparent from the evidence given above, while most of the teachers examined pupil suggestions critically, they were also impressed by the quality of much of what their pupils had to say and seemed ready to respond in practice to many of their ideas. As they moved into the second phase of the project, however, differences in teachers' attitudes became more apparent. While three of the teachers wholeheartedly followed up their initial responses by planning and implementing units of work that took extensive account of pupil ideas, the other three teachers had distinctive attitudes which significantly influenced their responses.

Lack of belief in pupils

In retrospect, it was clear that one of the teachers, Lorna, held an ideology of professionalism which led her to be very doubtful about the possibility of her learning anything useful from her pupils. Teaching, she believed, was a complex business; and while she accepted most things the pupils said as having some merit, she also viewed them as telling only half the story. Everything, she emphasised, was a matter of judgement, with a balance having to be achieved among the various needs of the pupils, various teaching purposes and practical concerns, so whatever the pupils said had to be balanced against other considerations. None the less, Lorna did commit herself to making changes in her practice and, according to at least some of the pupils, she successfully fulfilled her intentions of talking less and having more open problem-solving tasks, more discussion and more use of peer explanation. She herself, however, was not happy: 'On the whole it did work,' she said of one lesson, but then went on to express multiple disappointments. She concluded, 'I feel that the contributions the pupil ideas have made to my teaching have been limited and I've been disappointed that I haven't been able to do more.' It seems that for teachers to benefit from pupil consultation, they probably need a basic confidence that pupils do potentially have something to offer them. Lorna did not have such confidence.

Expecting too much of pupils

At the opposite extreme, Jane was perhaps the teacher who was most impressed by the pupils' comments and most responsive to them. She was so excited by the maturity, perceptiveness and imagination of many of the pupils' comments that she seemed to assume that they would also share aspects of her own expertise as a teacher that she probably took for granted. Having identified a number of suggestions from the class representatives that she wanted to follow up, she saw it as important to integrate the pursuit of these ideas with substantial delegation of decision-making to the class, starting with whole-class consultation.

She therefore delegated most of the planning and conduct of this whole-class consultation exercise to the class representatives. She had not anticipated, however, the fragile status of this small, elite group, the contentiousness of some of their suggestions, and especially the enormous difficulty for them of managing the social processes involved in the planned small-group and whole-class discussions. What should have been the triumphant culmination of a highly successful consultation process instead ended in conflict, incoherence and distress. Jane had clearly underestimated the expertise that pupils would need for the planning and management tasks that she had delegated to them, expertise that they had never had any opportunity to develop.

There are important wider lessons to be learned from Jane's experience. While it is clearly evident that young people do have the opportunity as pupils to develop helpful ideas about how to enrich teaching and learning in their classrooms, it would be unwise to assume that they can undertake new classroom roles without having support in learning how to do so.

Scepticism

One of the six teachers whose initial responses did not give grounds for confidence about his readiness to use pupil ideas was Matthew, the head of a Science department who was working with one of the lower Year 8 sets. His responses to pupil ideas were characterised by sympathy with the pupils' general perspectives but a sustained scepticism about their specific suggestions. He was highly sceptical, for example, about such common pupil claims as that they did not do enough practical work, that they had to do too much writing, and that peer explanations helped their scientific understanding. He was ready, however, to try out and evaluate many pupil suggestions; and, as the project developed through the first two stages, his enthusiasm seemed to grow. At the end of the second stage, Matthew commented:

> The opportunity to get some insights into pupils' thoughts about teachers has been fascinating . . . you become aware that some of them have more positive attitudes towards their learning than is necessarily apparent in the classroom . . . it's made me . . . aware that I've got into a routine way of working and it isn't necessarily the routine they would want. And then to be able to change that routine and see if it had an effect – and that they do recognise that a change has taken place. Quite how that would have improved

the quality of their learning is hard to evaluate . . . certainly it's had an impact on their motivation.

When Matthew was visited six months later, this enthusiasm was equally apparent. He was confident that his teaching had been significantly changed by the previous year's consultation, and he had actively developed formal consultation procedures with his new Year 8 class, through questionnaires followed up by whole-class discussion. Furthermore, 'I'd like to think I could keep this going and perhaps extend it beyond this Year 8 group. I might look at disseminating it to the Science department through talking about it at a departmental meeting.'

Matthew's enthusiastic long-term espousal of pupil consultation, as a consequence of his readiness to examine ideas critically and to try them out in his own practice, showed the healthiness of his sceptical attitude. There will be many teachers who are equally sceptical about the fruitfulness of pupil consultation, but who, if they try it out for themselves, as he did, are likely to be persuaded of its value.

Practical constraints

It will be remembered that one of the main criteria teachers used in assessing pupil ideas was their 'practicality'. Differences among teachers in their responses to this aspect of pupils' ideas depended partly on the contexts in which they were working, but also partly on them as individuals. Constraints such as those of time, equipment and space did, of course, vary across contexts; but it was also the case that, while one teacher might quickly dismiss a suggestion as impractical because of such constraints, another in similar circumstances might make more vigorous or imaginative efforts to turn the idea into a practical possibility. Our most striking example of practical constraints making it difficult to implement pupil suggestions was with Laura, the head of a Mathematics department who was keen to respond to pupil suggestions that, among other things, she should use computer facilities more. Initially the facilities were not available, then there were technical problems, and finally things didn't work very well because Laura had not had previous opportunities to find out that the pupils' ICT knowledge wasn't as good as expected. None the less, Laura persisted, had some limited success in using pupil ideas and was able to distinguish what she saw as the inherent merits of pupil ideas from the temporary practical problems. In particular, 'the fun thing was what came out the most': Laura's pupils convinced her that the extra efforts she sometimes made to make the lessons more practical, more game-like and more fun really did help their mathematical learning, and that she should therefore continue to make these extra efforts, despite all the constraints. She was so impressed that her thoughts moved on to how she could effectively engage in pupil consultation without the support of a researcher:

> I mean, there's a lot that they're saying here . . . Are there ways that I can get this kind of feedback from my students . . . so that I can use it? They can use it to help me give the right approach to that class . . . an approach that works for them.

Like Matthew, Laura was still enthusiastic about pupil consultation when she was interviewed six months later, and committed to developing it further. But her case exemplifies the potential significance of practical constraints on teachers' responsiveness to pupil ideas.

Expertise and confidence in teaching

We had wondered whether teachers would vary in their ability and in their confidence to change their practices effectively in response to pupil ideas. In terms of teachers' short-term responses, however, we had no indication that this was the case. On the contrary, all our evidence indicated that where teachers were persuaded of the desirability of changing their teaching in response to pupil ideas, they were capable of doing so very effectively. The clearest examples of this were from two young teachers, Catharine and Richard, teachers of English and Science, respectively. Each had generated, in the first phase of Enquiry 1, substantial lists of pupil ideas that they thought might usefully be incorporated into their teaching, although neither was entirely confident of the practicality of all the ideas on their lists. During the second phase, they each planned with great care and commitment a unit of work that incorporated some of these ideas. (As Richard had discovered, such care and commitment were necessary, his first attempt having lacked both qualities and having been spectacularly unsuccessful.) In both cases, the units involved imaginative projects, in which there was relatively little teacher talk and various kinds of practical and collaborative work for which pupils were given considerable space and responsibility. In both cases, the teachers clearly showed excellent judgement in their planning and management, the pupils were highly motivated and seriously engaged, and the units were judged by both teachers and pupils to have been highly successful. Although the teachers were both teaching in ways that were very different from their normal practice, it was clear that they were entirely capable of teaching very effectively in ways that were highly responsive to their pupils' ideas. (For fuller accounts, see Pedder and McIntyre, 2004: 28–32.)

However, even immediately after these highly successful units, neither Catharine nor Richard saw them as having major significance for their future practice, either in relation to the teaching approaches preferred by their pupils or in relation to their use of pupil consultation. Both were very conscious of their obligations in terms of coverage of the National Curriculum and related assessments; and both saw these obligations as preventing them from being very responsive to their pupils. It was towards the end of the summer term that they had planned and taught units in response to their pupils' ideas and they both saw this as an exceptional time of year:

> Richard: [T]his is just a relaxed time of year and . . . I'm probably a little less concerned . . . I'm probably allowing myself the luxury of experimenting a little bit more with these kinds of ideas.

> Catharine: Of course, it's getting towards the end of the year so it doesn't bother me as much now, but if this was earlier in the year I would be worried that I would be neglecting basic literacy skills by doing all these things. At other times, I couldn't be quite so responsive; we need to balance it with learning all the specified skills, writing and comprehension.

Six months later, their views were much the same. They thought that the consultation of pupils had been enlightening, but that there were severe tensions between most of the pupils' ideas and their own 'really serious' curriculum obligations as teachers. They had both concluded that occasional informal 'chatting' with individual pupils or classes was a fruitful and feasible form of consultation in which they could engage, but it was only around the margins of the curriculum, such as 'just before Christmas', that they could be responsive to what their pupils wanted.

Richard and Catharine, it seemed, were both willing and able to be very effectively responsive to their pupils' ideas, but not while fulfilling their obligations to deliver the National Curriculum; and they were in no doubt that, whatever their personal views, it was to that latter task that they had to give priority. In this respect, they contrasted sharply with Matthew and Laura, who, as more senior and experienced teachers, did not appear to feel any such tension. We may tentatively conclude that many teachers would be capable of responding effectively in their practice to their pupils' ideas, but that a large proportion of them might need opportunities to develop more confidence and to learn new skills before they could combine such responsiveness with fulfilment of nationally imposed obligations.

Comment

Our study was designed to maximise the quantity and quality of the ideas about learning and teaching that pupils, when consulted, could offer their teachers. And certainly, although the six teachers examined the pupils' ideas critically, they found plenty of thoughtful and sensible pupil suggestions that they seemed willing to assimilate into their practice. Even among this very small sample of teachers, however, we found considerable variation in their readiness and ability to make their actual practice responsive to pupils' ideas. Three main factors seemed to be important.

Attitudes

While a thoughtful scepticism about the merits of pupils' ideas does not prevent teachers realising that they have much of value to learn from their pupils, a firm preconception that 'teachers know best' is likely to be a formidable barrier against such learning. Teachers need to be sceptical, furthermore, to prevent them being so impressed by pupil ideas that they assume the pupils are capable of playing new classroom roles without first having the opportunity to develop the expertise that these roles require.

Practicality

Many pupil suggestions are likely to depend on the use of different kinds of equipment, space or time, or simply on more of these resources than many teachers have immediately at their disposal. Teachers' responsiveness to pupil ideas will therefore depend on a combination of a school's capacity to provide such practical conditions and on the teachers' own perseverance in trying to make such conditions available.

Expertise and confidence in teaching

We have no evidence of qualified teachers lacking the ability to plan and manage successful classroom teaching that is responsive to their pupils' ideas. Teachers do vary, however, in their confidence, and probably also in their expertise, in combining responsiveness to their pupils' ideas effectively with conscientious implementation of demanding government requirements, such as those currently in place in England.

Given the evident importance of these factors, we need to recognise that teachers may not feel able to take advantage of the opportunities that pupil consultation offers them unless they work in contexts where they are strongly supported in doing so. In secondary schools, that probably means that intelligent and thoughtful leadership at both whole-school and subject-department levels is needed to facilitate the use of pupil consultation.

Conclusion

As we suggested at the beginning of this chapter, classroom teachers generally know a great deal about their pupils and make intensive use of that knowledge in their everyday teaching. Furthermore, given the vast amount of arguably relevant information available to teachers, about their pupils and other things, an important aspect of their professional expertise is giving priority attention only to information that really helps them to teach as effectively as possible. So it is important to ask whether consulting pupils gives teachers information that in practice enables them to teach more effectively. Even accepting that pupils have a right to be consulted, we would probably find it hard to persuade individual teachers to consult their pupils if we could not argue persuasively that their teaching could be improved by doing so.

So what have we learned from the research reviewed in this chapter? First, we can say with some confidence that most teachers, when they are able to gain access to the range and depth of ideas and suggestions that their pupils can offer them about teaching and learning in their classrooms, are likely to find these ideas impressively sensible, thoughtful and potentially helpful. Second, it seems that, provided that they are not debilitated by their own ideologies or constrained by too severe practical problems of time, space and other resources, many teachers are likely to be able to use their pupils' ideas to develop their teaching successfully, both in their pupils' eyes and in their own. Third, however, rather fewer teachers are likely to have the confidence and expertise to be able, without help, to combine such responsiveness to pupil ideas with meeting the demanding obligations imposed on them by centralised systems, such as the National Curriculum in England.

A further reservation has to be that all our evidence is about teacher responsiveness to pupil ideas that are consensual or that the teachers judge to be beneficial for their whole classes. Fortunately, as the evidence we reviewed in Chapters 2, 3 and 4 indicated, pupils' ideas about classroom teaching and learning tend to be consensual. On the other hand, the evidence we reviewed in Chapter 5 suggested that the social conditions of learning experienced by different pupils in the same classrooms tend to be highly diverse. It seems likely, therefore, that teachers might find it much more challenging to be responsive to consultation concerned with the conditions of learning experienced by pupils. As yet, however, we do not have any evidence about teachers, without the support of a linked researcher, gaining access to pupils' reports of their learning conditions, far less about their responses to such reports. Further research about such consultation and about teachers' responses to it should be given high priority.

Our evidence, then, strongly suggests that, under certain conditions, teachers can be enabled to teach more effectively through pupil consultation, which can bring real benefits to them. But we also need to ask about the costs that pupil consultation involves for teachers. Such costs, it seems clear, would be associated with the *processes* of consultation and with the *conditions* necessary for fruitful consultation processes. We have not, in this chapter, attempted to look at the implications for teachers of the different kinds of consultation process they might use, as this was previously considered in Chapter 2.

In Chapter 9, we shall attempt to summarise the case for consulting pupils about teaching and learning in terms of the potential beneficial impact that it can have, not only for teachers but for the pupils themselves.

Summary

Irrespective of the rights of pupils, of their keenness to be consulted, or even of the quality of the ideas that they can offer, teachers are likely to consult their pupils seriously and on an ongoing basis only if they find that what they learn from their pupils is helpful. In this chapter, therefore, we have focused attention on teachers' responses to pupils' ideas. In particular, we have concentrated on the findings of Enquiry 1 of our TLRP Project, in which teachers were helped by researchers to consult their pupils in some depth and were then asked to try to respond in their practice to the pupils' ideas. The teachers were generally very impressed by the constructiveness and thoughtfulness of these ideas, but examined them critically in terms of such criteria as their practicality, how far they reflected the whole class's needs, the validity of the perceptions of classroom reality on which they were based, and their educational soundness. Each of the teachers then developed and taught a unit of work that was responsive to those of their pupils' ideas that they found helpful, and these attempts to be responsive were evaluated by both the teachers and the pupils.

Our evidence strongly suggests that, under certain conditions, teachers can be helped to teach more effectively by pupil consultation. The teachers varied considerably, however, in their responsiveness in practice to their pupils' ideas, both immediately and in the longer term. Among the most important factors underlying this variation were teachers' different attitudes to pupil ideas, the multiple practical constraints that limit teachers' freedom and, perhaps most fundamentally, the different levels of confidence and expertise with which teachers felt able to respond to their pupils' suggestions while also meeting their nationally imposed obligations.

Chapter 9

The impact of pupil consultation on pupils and teachers

In previous chapters we have reported what we have learned from research about what pupils have to say when they are consulted about teaching and learning, and about how teachers respond to what pupils have to say. In this chapter, before moving on to discuss conditions for effective pupil consultation, we aim to summarise the research-based claims that can justifiably be made about the impact that pupil consultation about learning and teaching can have on pupils and teachers.

The claims that we can make about the impact of consultation reflect the nature of the research undertaken within this TLRP Project. One of our research strategies was to bring together schools already active in pupil consultation, to study the diverse initiatives in which they were engaged, and to try to develop shared understandings of the various possibilities open to schools for successfully fostering pupil consultation. One strand of this work focused on the different methods of consultation used, and led to the generation of *A Toolkit for Teachers* (MacBeath *et al.*, 2003). Other strategies involved initiatives by members of the research team to explore the impact of consultation through, for example, acting as intermediaries in the consultation process or helping schools to develop 'students as researchers' projects. On the basis of these various strategies, we have been able to report what happened in different schools, and to develop evidence-based understandings of consultation processes and their impacts.

We are unable to make strong evidence-based generalisations about the impact that pupil consultation about classroom teaching and learning has on pupils, teachers and schools. Such claims would, minimally, have had to be based on surveys of samples of schools engaged in such consultation, samples that were representative of specified populations of schools. Such surveys can reasonably be undertaken in relation to initiatives that impinge on virtually every school in the country, such as the National Literacy Strategy. In 2000 (and even today), however, schools engaged in pupil consultation into teaching and learning were relatively rare; and both what they were consulting about and how they were doing it were very diverse. In such circumstances, therefore, it would not have been productive to engage in a major survey investigation. (We did, though, conduct a fruitful, small, end-of-project survey of teachers who had been involved in the project.)

In the absence of evidence from a representative survey, the kind of evidence-based claims about impact that we can make with confidence relate to the *potential* impact of pupil consultation. Although we cannot make justifiable assertions about the *normal*, far less the *inevitable*, impact of pupil consultation, we have abundant evidence about the many benefits that pupil consultation about teaching and learning *might* bring.

Pupils: defining the potential impact

The evidence from our various projects, including that reported in earlier chapters, shows that pupils can benefit in several ways from being consulted.

Pupils' changed attitudes to school and to learning

When pupils are consulted about teaching and learning, and especially when they see evidence that their teachers have listened to their ideas and responded positively to some of them, in our experience this has a significant impact on their motivation. In an end-of-project survey of the views of teachers who had been involved, 80 per cent of the 96 respondents thought that consultation had helped pupils to 'feel more positive about school' and 76 per cent that it had helped them to 'develop more positive attitudes to learning'. Teachers also commented that among the impacts of consultation on their pupils were:

- greater willingness to learn;
- improved attendance;

- more positive attitudes and improved attainment;
- improved motivation and less willingness to be intimidated by demotivated peers;
- increased talk and interest in lessons;
- greater ability to understand and control their own learning.

Pupils' changed perceptions of teachers

When teachers start consulting pupils and taking account of what they say, they themselves tend to be seen in a new light, as more human and in the same social world as the pupils. For example, when asked if they had noticed any changes after their teacher had started consulting them, two pupils commented that:

> She like reacts with us like you would with your friends – like if you said something and your friend would find it funny, Miss [name] would find it funny.

> She does ask for our opinions a lot more like I said . . . and so it's almost as if we're one big group and we're all friends because we all learn from each other and that does help a lot.
>
> (Morgan, 2000: 46)

Similarly, student researchers came to perceive teachers differently:

> When you're working very closely with teachers, you can't be scared of them.

> Teachers' honesty in explaining that they didn't have a structured idea of what the project was about and where we were going was strangely liberating.
>
> (Fielding and Bragg, 2003: 17, Years 9 and 12 researchers)

In the end-of-project survey, 75 per cent of the teacher respondents thought it had helped pupils develop 'more positive perceptions of teachers'.

A stronger sense of membership among pupils

When pupils are consulted seriously, it can make them feel, often for the first time, that their school and their class are to some extent *their* school and *their* class. This is important to them. When Birkett (2001) analysed 15,000 responses from pupils aged five to sixteen who had been asked to describe 'The School I'd Like', she identified nine main themes. One of these was 'A listening school'; another was 'A respectful school – where children and adults can talk freely and student opinion matters'. As we saw in Chapter 7, it is important to pupils that their views should be listened to, and equally important that their views should be acted on (or that it should be explained to them why this cannot be done). When that happens, pupils can see teachers starting to treat them as partners:

> It changed how some staff at the school considered their students, encouraging them to think of students more as equals and a source of help in making the most of their teaching.
>
> (Fielding and Bragg, 2003: 20, Year 12 researcher)

And when pupils find themselves treated as partners in the educational enterprise, not merely as its objects, they can come to see themselves as members with a stake in the enterprise.

Pupils' developing capacity to reflect on learning and to talk about learning and teaching

Gill Mulliss, after two years of consulting her pupils, from Year 9 to Year 11, comments:

> When you work with the students in this way you can see they're learning about all sorts of things – about themselves, about the subject and how they learn, and about other students. What we're enabling them to do, I think, is to be more critical of their own education, and I mean that in the positive sense in which they're beginning to understand, and to be able to articulate more about what's going well, what's going badly, why it's going badly, and actually what their rights are. You know, they have a right to a decent learning experience and they're not always getting it.
>
> (Mulliss, 2002: 3)

A recurring observation from researchers from our different projects concerns the wide differences among pupils in their developed capacity or readiness to talk about learning and teaching, differences that are very closely related to the success that pupils have previously achieved in their school work. The easy way for schools to react to this is to listen to those pupils who are keen and demonstrably able to articulate their views. A more fruitful reaction, however, is to develop strategies for encouraging and supporting the lower-attaining pupils in developing their readiness, their confidence and their ability to articulate their views. This is not only more likely to give teachers new insights into pupils' experiences in their classrooms, but can have important benefits in developing pupils' capacity to reflect on what facilitates, and what constrains, their learning. There is no doubt that even simple practice in articulating their views, with reinforcing evidence that teachers are taking these views seriously, can have a big impact on pupils' capacity to reflect on their learning. Here, for example, a Students as Researchers co-ordinator comments on the impact of such work on students' thinking:

> Our students tell us that things have changed for them in their ability to see themselves as learners, that their ability to understand the process of learning has been affected by becoming able to conduct research themselves, and that they've been able to use those skills specifically in their own research for subjects. But I think it's more than that. They can see themselves as people who can control their own learning and can direct it because they can understand it.
>
> (Fielding and Bragg, 2003: 18)

Pupils' new skills and capacities to take on new roles and responsibilities

It is especially in the context of Students as Researchers initiatives that pupils and their teachers observed other new skills and capacities that pupils had developed through these initiatives. The following two quotations are from two Year 10 pupils.

> We learned communication skills that helped us in the way we carried out the interviews, we also learned about creating a key question and developing our understanding around it. This skill has recently helped us with our History and English coursework.
>
> During our research we were independent researchers . . . it was up to us as a group to get everything completed. We set targets, tasks

and deadlines so everything was done. Our independence has helped us in lessons as well as in our research.

(CPTL3)

However, it is also clear that all pupils who are consulted, faced as they are with new tasks, begin to develop new skills. They report on how they don't want to upset teachers, but at the same time they want to use these new opportunities to get messages through to teachers about what they do too much, or not enough, or not very well. They listen too for feedback from the teachers which shows that they have thought about what the pupils have said; and they monitor what teachers do to see whether their practice has been influenced. While we certainly would not claim that pupil consultation leads to democratic classrooms, it does encourage pupils to develop skills of diplomacy and of exercising political influence.

A positive impact on pupils' sense of self

In their responses to the end-of-project survey, 84 per cent of teachers thought that consultation had helped pupils feel more positive about themselves. As this statistic suggests, it may be in this respect that pupil consultation has its most immediate impact on pupils. And that should not surprise us, because pupil consultation suggests to pupils, perhaps for the first time, that 'teachers actually care what you think':

> I think it's just what teachers should do. I think that all teachers should do it because it's just so helpful cos you know your teachers actually care what you think and they're not just there to teach you and get money for it.
>
> (Morgan, 2000: 47, Year 8 girl)

In some cases the impact can be more dramatic:

> I had found the extra niche that I needed in order to keep me interested in my studies and motivate me to come to school. From some work that I had done I influenced the school's feelings about profiling so much that they had changed it. That gave me a great sense of achievement.
>
> (CPTL3, Year 10 student researcher)

Overall, members of the project team, reflecting on what pupils and teachers had said about the benefits of consultation for pupils, suggested that being consulted can help pupils develop:

- a stronger sense of membership, feeling more positive about school and more included in its purposes – *the organisational dimension*;
- a stronger sense of respect and self-worth so that they feel positive about themselves – *the personal dimension*;
- a stronger sense of self-as-learner so that they are better able to manage their own learning – *the pedagogic dimension*;
- a stronger sense of agency so that they see it as worthwhile to contribute to improvement in teaching and learning and wider school matters – *the political dimension*.

But these impacts start to become apparent only when the process of consultation has been carefully introduced and sustained, when pupils feel that teachers' interest in what they have to say is genuine and will be thought about and followed up, and when both teachers and pupils feel that mutual trust is opening up the possibility of a more partnership-oriented way of working together.

Teachers: defining the potential impact

For teachers, too, there are several benefits that can come from pupil consultation.

A more open perception of young people's capabilities and attitudes

As we reported in Chapter 8, teachers are frequently impressed and surprised by the insightfulness revealed by their pupils' comments on teaching and learning in their classrooms. They learn that pupils are thoughtful about teaching and learning in ways that they had not suspected. Two of the Enquiry 1 teachers, for example, commented:

> You become aware that some of them have more positive attitudes towards their learning than is necessarily apparent in the classroom.

> They were . . . generally very perceptive on how they were learning and they weren't dishonest at all – they were quite critical when

they thought something wasn't right for them. It made me wonder if they always reflected like this without me knowing.

Teachers are also frequently relieved to discover how maturely pupils take advantage of being consulted, being very polite and constructive in their comments and frequently showing sensitivity to the constraints upon teachers and to the different needs of other pupils. Such experiences encourage teachers to develop more trust in their pupils, more respect for them, and above all a readiness to be more open to new possibilities for what their pupils are able and willing to do.

The capacity to see the familiar from a different angle

Whatever comments pupils make about life in a particular teacher's classroom, these comments are based on different perspectives from that of the teacher. Most teachers recognise the value of such different perspectives, whatever they offer. They can reassuringly confirm the teacher's own understandings and judgements. They can offer new information or insights about what life is like for pupils in that classroom, thus giving the teacher valuable food for thought. For the receptive teacher, these different perspectives are perhaps most useful when they challenge the teacher's limited view: 'it's made me kind of . . . aware that I've got into a routine way of working and it isn't necessarily the routine they would want'.

A readiness to change thinking in the light of these perceptions

Many teachers show themselves ready to change their own thinking in the light of new insights and suggestions offered by their pupils. This can be at a very simple level: 'More than one of them said I talk too much. I think I do.' But, equally, it can be at a much more profound level, like the teacher above reflecting on the limitations of 'the routine way of working' he had established; or another teacher, already quoted in Chapter 8 but worth repeating here, who was ready to think again about the degree of teacher-centredness of his lessons:

> On a couple of the interviews I got the impression that the pupils wanted more ownership really of their planning practical work and actually writing up conclusions of their practical work. They wanted

more involvement in that. I think what I do is perhaps I'm the central pivot . . . but possibly we could develop that a bit more and once I've perhaps told them a little bit about the experiment . . . let them think a little bit more about the safety precautions . . . about planning a fair test . . . and then, you know, they own the experiment.

A renewed sense of excitement in teaching

Teachers have commented on the ways in which pupil consultation has given them new confidence and enthusiasm for their teaching, and a new sense of inspiration. Increasingly encouraged as they are to rely on standardised approaches to teaching propagated by central government, teachers find from pupil consultation both a freshness in the ideas of their pupils and renewed confidence in their own professional judgement. Lynne Webb, one of the Enquiry 1 teachers, wrote of her experiences in the Project Newsletter No. 2:

> The fun thing is what came out the most. I do try to make my lessons fun, and sometimes I think, 'Am I just doing it to make it fun? Or is there some true learning happening behind that?' . . . But sometimes in Maths when you do something that is practical, physical and fun, it gives them the slow-down thinking time that they need to work things out as well as the enjoyment and enthusiasm to carry on. So I learned from them that they thought it important to be given time to think more . . . You get so that schemes of work are getting in the way if you're not careful.

Another of the Enquiry 1 teachers was excited by how her professional thinking and practice could be enriched by working collaboratively with her pupils and drawing on their creative ideas:

> You know, that's what made me enthusiastic because I suddenly saw all that untapped creativity really . . . You can use pupils' ideas in a very valid, interesting way and it can make the pupil excited, the teacher excited and you know obviously the lesson will take off from there . . . It's like going on a teachers' conference and sort of thinking, 'Oh, that's a good idea,' and planning a series of lessons together. You know . . . although you do a bit of collaborating with other teachers, there's not that much time any more so, you know,

if you can actually collaborate with pupils it's equally – I didn't realise it – it's equally exciting, isn't it?

(Enquiry 1, English teacher)

And a teacher working with Students as Researchers summed up the excitement felt by many teachers:

It constantly reminds me of what teaching should be about, puts me in touch with the inspirational side of it, because their insights into their lives in school always exceed my expectations.

(Fielding and Bragg, 2003: 19)

A practical agenda for improvement

Whatever feel-good factors pupil consultation generates, it would not be of much value to teachers in practice if it did not offer them practical agendas leading in their own eyes to improvements in their teaching and in their pupils' learning. Fortunately, as Enquiry 1 has demonstrated, it can offer teachers agendas of just that sort. Each of the six teachers involved had little difficulty in generating a substantial agenda for developing their teaching, based on their pupils' ideas. It is true that one of the teachers lacked enthusiasm, another had an agenda that turned out to be unrealistically ambitious, and the other four varied in their confidence about the long-term implementation of their agendas; but each had a substantial agenda of ways of improving their teaching, and four of them were able to implement these agendas successfully, at least in the shorter term. If there were constraints, these were not in the lack of richness, consensual nature, value or practicality of the pupils' ideas as judged by the teachers. In other projects, too, there has been no lack of pupil ideas judged by teachers to be both valuable and practical. For example,

I particularly notice that some of the teachers now try to set homework earlier and they say, 'Oh, we're doing this now because this is what you like us to do.' They try to promote a better teaching and learning environment in our school so that the voice of our students is valued.

(CPTL3, student researcher)

Pupil consultation does, then, 'deliver' for teachers at the most practical of levels. Among all its other benefits, it can help teachers to improve their teaching.

Teacher–pupil relationships: defining the potential impact

In Chapter 3, we reported the priority importance that pupils attach to teacher–pupil relationships being of a human and personal nature, with an emphasis on mutual respect and trust. Significantly, therefore, it is perhaps in relation to just these aspects of teacher–pupil relationships that pupil consultation has its most striking impact. As teachers see pupils differently so they are more likely to respect and trust them and to offer more opportunities for them to take responsibility for their learning. And this is what students say they want. Both teachers and pupils testify to such changed relationships and ways of working as a result of consultation:

> I know from working with students that the more you talk with them and involve them, the more it changes the learning relationship . . . When you work with students in that way, you can see they're learning about all sorts of things – about themselves, about the subject and how they learn, about other students. And I've found that has impacted on the way I operate in the classroom . . . I've actually handed far more over to them in lessons than I would have done a year ago.
>
> (Fielding and Bragg, 2003: 20, secondary teacher)

> It's given us more freedom but yet more fun . . . and we get to do it on our own, we can go off and do it at our own time and take our time and understand how we got our results rather than just copying it off the board.
>
> (Enquiry 1, Year 8 pupil)

> She's kind of changed a lot the way she teaches . . . now we have a lot more freedom and independence on how we can do things. And . . . [it's] kind of like she knows what we want and she knows what we don't want . . . and she's a lot more kind of relaxed and laid back . . . if we don't like it.
>
> (LP2, Year 8 pupil)

> Well, . . . she's like always got time for everyone now and she never leaves anyone out – she's always with everyone, helping them out and stuff.
>
> (LP2, Year 8 pupil)

Mutual respect and trust between pupils and teachers can grow from teachers' consultation of pupils and from their responsiveness to what they say; but the connection is not an entirely simple one, since effective pupil consultation also *depends* on mutual trust and respect. Pupils have to show a measure of trust in their teachers to reveal to them their views of what happens in their classrooms; and teachers have to have some trust and respect for their pupils in order to attend seriously to what they say. Pedder and McIntyre (2006) used the idea of social capital, and especially Portes's (1998) analysis, to examine ways in which pupil consultation relates to trust and respect between teachers and pupils. They concluded that the idea of 'norms of reciprocity' seems crucial in understanding pupils' and teachers' instrumental motivation to engage in pupil consultation, with a recognition on each side that they might have something to gain from it. If, for example, teachers fail to act on what they have learned from pupils, or fail to explain why they are doing so, or respond to pupil consultation only on a short-term basis, they may be seen to breach the norms of reciprocity with the consequence that pupils' trust in them may diminish. But in some classrooms they found a sustained growth in teachers' and pupils' confidence and trust in each other, and these were classrooms where teachers persisted despite difficulties in conscientiously trying to use their pupils' ideas. In doing so, these teachers were demonstrating a strength of commitment to 'norms of reciprocity' that was possibly lacking in some other teachers, and also perhaps a sense of obligation to a 'solidarity' with their pupils and to classroom life as a collaborative enterprise. Pupil consultation can certainly lead to enhanced mutual respect and trust between pupils and teachers, but probably only where teachers find themselves able to commit themselves wholeheartedly to it.

Conclusion

We therefore have strong evidence that, under suitable conditions, and if it is pursued wholeheartedly, pupil consultation can have a very powerful beneficial impact on life and learning in classrooms. Pupils tend to be very enthusiastic about being consulted and respond very positively if it is clear that the consultation is being undertaken seriously. The potential effects on their learning are both direct and indirect. Directly, being consulted tends to have a beneficial impact on pupils' self-esteem, on their attitudes to school and to learning, on their sense of membership of their class and their school as communities, on their view of teachers, on their capacity to reflect on their learning, and on other valuable cognitive and social skills. The indirect effects, through the impact of consultation on teachers, may be equally or even more important. We have seen that consultation can lead to significant changes in teachers' perceptions of their pupils, to them being able to see their teaching from a different perspective and to a consequent readiness to be open to change, to a renewed sense of excitement about their teaching, and to rich and realistic practical agendas for improving their teaching. Such changes in teachers and in teaching could be very important for their pupils' learning. It is true that we do not yet have evidence that this combination of direct and indirect effects of consultation leads to improved attainments, but their potential beneficial impact on the quality of classroom learning is very evident. Perhaps the biggest impact – certainly from the perspective of pupils – is likely to be one that is inherent in the very *process* of consultation: the change that it both signals and fosters in the relationship between teachers and pupils.

These various ways in which consulting pupils can have an impact on classroom life, and therefore on classroom learning, are summarised in the model on page 152.

Summary

In this chapter, we have sought to summarise what we have learned from our research about the impact of pupil consultation on teachers and pupils. We noted that, since pupil consultation has so far been pursued only in a limited number of schools, it is possible at this stage only to talk of its *potential* impact; and we concluded that much depends on supportive conditions and on teachers engaging *wholeheartedly* in it. Given such engagement, however, the impact is likely to be considerable. We have summarised the evidence about the impact on pupils, in strengthening their self-esteem, enhancing their attitudes to school, to their teachers and to learning, helping them to feel a stronger sense of membership of their school and their class, and enabling them to develop new skills for learning and for democratic citizenship. Evidence about the potential impact on teachers is equally strong, in that consultation tends to lead to a greater awareness of pupil capacities, to new perspectives on their

continued

PUPIL CONSULTATION

tends to

ENHANCE PUPIL COMMITMENT AND CAPACITY FOR LEARNING

through

strengthening self-esteem

+

enhancing attitudes to school and learning

+

developing stronger sense of membership

+

developing new skills for learning

IMPROVE TEACHERS' TEACHING

through

teachers' greater awareness of pupils' capacity

+

gaining new perspectives on their teaching

+

renewed excitement about teaching

+

transformed pedagogic practices

and to

TRANSFORM TEACHER–PUPIL RELATIONSHIPS from passive and oppositional to more active and collaborative

and so is very likely to

IMPROVE PUPILS' LEARNING

own teaching, often to a rekindled enthusiasm about teaching, and to realistic practical agendas for improving their teaching. Most fundamentally, perhaps, consultation contributes substantially to the development of more collaborative relationships between teachers and pupils. All of these impacts are likely, in turn, to lead to improvements in the quality of both learning and education.

Chapter 10

Reservations, anxieties and constraints

> There will often be problems for teachers in building a new teaching and learning culture in schools but we have to be aware that pupils are also likely to experience anxieties – even if, as is the case with consultation, they tend to be supportive of what it is seeking to achieve. In this chapter, we discuss first the things that make it difficult for *teachers* to develop consultation and then those things that get in the way of *pupils* trusting in consultation as something that can make a positive difference to their experiences of learning in school.

The experiences of the pupils, teachers and schools with which we worked suggested that consultation can have a 'transformative potential' but we are cautious about making great claims because we are keenly aware of the difficulties, in the system and in schools, of realising that potential. We are also aware of David Hargreaves's reservations about a casual use of the term 'transformation':

> Transformation has recently become the language of educational policy makers . . . They seem very comfortable with the term, though I am not at all sure they know what they are talking about. When virtually every new development is allegedly transformative, it is vital to ask what the term really means.
>
> (Hargreaves, 2003: 1)

In relation to pupil voice, transformation is about seeing pupils differently; it is about recognising a wider range of capabilities in young

people, and responding to their insights about teaching and learning in
school; it is about changing the power relationship between teachers
and pupils so that learning becomes more of a shared responsibility;
it is about reviewing the status of the pupil group in schools so that it
can have greater influence on ways of improving learning and the
conditions of learning.

If the term 'transformation' has worn thin through overuse we can
instead use Maxine Greene's (1985) words: she talks about 'creating a
new order of experience' for young people in schools – one which goes
beyond the incremental, and somewhat conservative, model of change
and instead aims for something more *radical*, something, as Robin
Tanner (1987) says, that can 'transcend the cramped conditions of the
time'. But in the present climate of constant policy-led change that is
rarely radical in conceptualisation and rarely sustained long enough for
its impact to be recognised, radical innovation can seem daunting.
Teachers may well be drawn to the values that pupil voice represents,
but it is not easy for them to take radical change on board in a thorough
and coherent way in this climate of perpetual motion. Its appeal to
pupils – the chance to make their views known and to feel that what they
say might make a difference – is strong, and has been for some years.
For example, the young people who sent their ideas on 'the school
I'd like' to Edward Blishen in the late 1960s were impressive, but the
ideas were probably not deemed significant enough to be seriously
translated into policy and the listening was not sustained. What a loss!
In his introduction, Blishen (1969: 9, 10, 13) comments on the pupils'
contributions:

> an enormous, remarkably good-humoured, earnest, frequently
> passionate and, at best, highly intelligent plea for a new order in
> our schools . . . The radical note that was so pervasive was aston-
> ishingly steady, reasonable, and supported by instances . . . From
> all quarters of the education scene it comes, this expression of
> children's longing to take upon themselves some of the burden
> of deciding what should be learned, how it should be learned . . .
> Standing out above everything else . . . is a great restlessness about
> classrooms, timetables, the immemorial and so often inert routine
> of schools.

The young people who took part in our project also wanted to have a
more active, responsible and trusted role in their learning in school.
Consultation offered a way forward, but one that was often difficult to

initiate and sustain: adults had reservations, pupils were wary and the demands of the performance agenda created some sharp tensions.

From the teacher perspective

There were three main areas of reservation, anxiety or constraint that emerged from the data and needed to be worked through if teachers were to make a wholehearted and sustained commitment to consulting their pupils about teaching and learning:

- Constraints coming from the system or the school:
  - pressures of time and curriculum coverage;
  - lack of institutional support;

- Reservations reflecting personal doubts and concerns:
  - teachers' feelings about the pupils they teach;
  - concerns about possible criticism;

- Anxieties rooted in the procedures:
  - balancing the individual and the group perspective.

Pressures of time and curriculum coverage

As teachers see it, the main constraints on their developing consultation with pupils are the result of pressures from outside rather than inside the school. The urgency of the performance agenda raises issues of coverage and time that can make it difficult for teachers to develop a coherent practice of talking with pupils about their work. Moreover, the boundaries of what counts as learning are now tightly drawn and pegged to curriculum content and short-term success in tests and examinations: while consultation can bolster achievement, there are other outcomes that go well beyond the narrow definitions of achievement that currently prevail. However, support for school self-review – now a high-profile initiative – can legitimise time spent working with pupils on the analysis of teaching and learning, although the tension between reflection/reviewing and 'getting on with the work' doesn't necessarily go away, as one teacher in our project explains: 'We are very often pushed for time because there's very often a lot of content to get into, even in a double lesson' (CPTL1).

Compare this, a typical and understandable response, with the approach of a teacher who has developed a habit of consultative partnership with one of her classes. She talks *with* them about the time pressures: 'This is what we need to learn in the next nine weeks . . . What do you think we need to do first?' – and the pupils respond. They understand the challenge and the pressure that it brings but they commit themselves to making the strategy work because it is 'theirs' (Mulliss, 2002: 3).

One outcome of the tensions about time and coverage is that teachers may opt not for dialogue but for written reviews of teaching and learning which tend to take less time to complete and analyse. Teachers may try to conserve time by asking pupils to complete their written commentaries in the last few minutes of the lesson – and some pupils can find this dispiriting because they have no time to respond thoughtfully. However, written evaluations have other advantages in pupils' eyes (see Chapters 7 and 11): for instance, in offering anonymity. But if a new spirit of partnership is to develop then the writing about learning needs to be balanced by discussion of learning in which pupils *and* their teacher take part.

Lack of institutional support

In the project we saw teachers as the 'professional creators' of a new culture of learning and we saw the process of 'building capacity among teachers and focusing that capacity on students and their learning' as the 'crucial factor' (Sergiovanni, 2000: 140). But there were problems in building the new culture of learning. The government's commitment to 'innovation, innovation, innovation' made it difficult for schools to practise the discipline and economy of sustaining a core of coherent values which all new initiatives had to work to (other, of course, than the values that are reflected in the performance agenda). This meant that there might, at any one time, be a diversity of initiatives in a school, each reflecting rather different concerns and values. In these circumstances it is difficult for the senior management team to offer adequate encouragement to every initiative.

Some innovations are more at risk than others. Teachers considering getting involved in a new approach that requires a redrawing of conventional power relations and/or some fundamental changes to their present practice need to feel that the risks are worth taking and that there are colleagues who will be interested in the outcomes and prepared to offer support. Sometimes, of course, that interest and support can come from teachers in other schools who have already embarked on the innovation and who have put an account of their experiences on an accessible website. It can also come from a linked researcher who is part of the team responsible for developing or disseminating the innovation. But teachers who are new to pupil voice may need to feel that there is some degree of understanding of – and commitment to – what they are contemplating doing in their own school. The burden of carrying a demanding innovation alone can be daunting and, as we found in the project, the compromise may be not to see consultation as part of their regular practice but to keep it in their repertoire and use it as an 'end-of-term treat' once the pressure of the tests/exams has subsided. Such teachers might be ready to incorporate consultation in their practice in a sustained way if they knew that there was a secure backdrop of interest and support in their school.

However, as we saw in a few schools, while there may be a rhetoric of encouragement for pupil voice from the senior management team, the level of practical commitment in terms of resources for effective implementation may remain low; in the absence of active and high-profile support, it is easy for teachers to identify other priorities. And even when there *is* a school commitment to pupil voice the focus may not be on the classroom and the improvement of teaching and learning. For example, consultation and participation may have a firm foothold in the school but may be contained in designated spaces, such as citizenship education and personal social and health education (PSHE) or in meetings of the school council; talking about classroom teaching and learning may be a marginal concern. And again, in some settings the aspiration has been more to develop young people's social and communicative skills, so energy is consequently invested in preparing them to present their views to others at local, regional or even national student conferences. Pupils are quick to acknowledge the benefits of such experiences but the danger is that pupil voice can become a vehicle for showcasing pupils in ways that enhance the reputation of the school rather than a way of encouraging reflection on teaching.

In the context of institutional support we have not so far mentioned the role of parents. In some settings, they can be a force to be reckoned with – for or against change. In the project, we had no evidence of parents taking any particular stance on pupil consultation, although some teachers admitted to feeling anxious lest parents might think that time was being allocated to consultation to the detriment of work for tests and examinations. That is certainly one possibility, since parents can be relied upon to want what they see as being in their children's best interests. But for the same reason it is also possible that parents will be active supporters of pupil consultation, knowing as they do the responsibilities their children are given at home, and in many cases remembering their own frustration at being 'treated like children' when they were at school. In seeking to ensure parental support, schools have the advantage that they can be confident of pupils' own support for consultation. So there may be some considerable merit in a strategy of working with pupils to plan how to demonstrate the benefits of consultation to their parents.

Teachers' feelings about the pupils they teach

So far we have discussed constraints on the development of classroom consultation that are rooted in the system; these are mainly to do with the performance agenda and time, but also the inherent complexity of involving pupils in reflective reviews of teaching and learning when there are other priorities. Consultation can be a Pandora's box: opening it reveals issues that teachers may not have the time to, or be ready to, address. One of them is recognising possible prejudices in their feelings about some of the pupils they teach.

Amis (1971: 172) was profoundly sceptical about the impulse behind pupil participation, revealing, in his comments, a distrust of young people's commitment to learning: 'Demands for student participation conceal, or do not conceal, a simple desire to have less studying to do.' If this *is* true for some pupils, then instead of seeing the problem as lying within them we need to ask what it is in schooling that is turning them away from learning: disengagement, as David Hargreaves has said, is 'unsolicited feedback'. However, some teachers have also acknowledged that they are sceptical about the motives of some of their pupils, especially the lower achievers: they felt – wrongly, as it usually turned out – that such pupils would not be able to manage opportunities to comment, seriously and sensibly, on teaching and learning and that they would have nothing to say, would ask for more 'just fun' activities, or would criticise their teachers. In thinking about such pupils in the context of consultation it is difficult for teachers – even as it has been difficult for us as researchers – to disentangle the mutually reinforcing tendencies for less successful pupils to have less expected of them by their teachers and therefore to be less motivated to engage with school learning, less enthusiastic about being able to comment on it and less confident that if they do express a view anyone will take any notice of what they have to say. It is therefore unreasonable to claim, simply, that academically less successful pupils will not be sufficiently competent to respond to opportunities for consultation; their reticence or reluctance may be a reaction to their disengagement from teaching and learning and consequently their ambivalence about trying to contribute to its improvement. And yet these are the pupils whom it is important to hear from, and to see whether the respect, recognition and trust that are fundamental to consultation could help restore their belief in schooling.

Indeed, when teachers are able to 'hear' the voices of these pupils through transcripts of interviews conducted by their linked researcher, or even through reading reports of observations made by similar pupils in other schools, they may be forced to admit that they have underestimated their maturity and capability. For example, the following comments were made by several teachers who were all new to the idea of consulting pupils. They were somewhat anxious about it and doubtful of their pupils' capacity to respond but they were able to move beyond their earlier scepticism and recognise how insightful and constructive their pupils could be:

> Pupil voices make us look at things we don't normally think about.

> Their comments have dramatically changed the way I work.

> The most powerful evidence about changing teaching and learning is coming from the students.

> You cannot change the [school] culture by bombarding teachers from outside but more by listening to what pupils have to say.
> (LP1; Rudduck *et al.*, 2006: 36)

Anxieties about the possibility of personalised criticism

Teachers who had not sought pupil opinion on teaching and learning before were understandably edgy about what pupils might say – in particular, about possible criticism of their professional skills and/or personal qualities. But pupils tended on the whole to be rather reassuring and encouraging in their comments, sometimes strategically so. And perhaps it is no bad thing if in the early stages of this kind of dialogue pupils are overly courteous and hesitant, slowly building up trust so that they get a better idea of what they *can* say and about the limits of the teacher's readiness to listen.

If concerns about pupils being sharply critical are generally un-founded, another potentially disturbing experience for teachers is to discover that they are sometimes misreading their pupils' reactions to their teaching. For instance, one teacher (CPTL5) agreed that pupils might complete evaluation sheets once a week for three weeks; the data enabled him to see that different groups of pupils in his mixed-ability class were responding quite differently to the work. Some lower-attaining pupils were expressing satisfaction and he knew that he had been successful in supporting their progress but the higher-attaining pupils expressed dissatisfaction with the pace of the work. The teacher acknowledged that his pupils' comments reflected a reality of which he had been unaware: 'As the kids are making loud and clear, I think you have to accept that sometimes you've misjudged the task and maybe haven't differentiated enough.' He went on, 'A couple of times they *all* said "Boring" – and they were right.' Nevertheless, he was shaken by this response: 'I was a bit disconcerted because any teacher will claim it doesn't matter but of course we are all sensitive to evaluations and when I got the first batch [of evaluation sheets] back I was, "Oh, no!".' However, the presence of the researcher gave him a chance to talk through his feelings. Schools might want to ensure that all teachers embarking on consulting pupils in this way have some such support from colleagues.

Balancing the individual and the group perspective

Teachers standing at the threshold of consultation have expressed concern about how they can respond in practical ways to what their pupils say about teaching and learning, if they say different things. Across groups, across schools and across ages there tends to be a high degree of consensus in what pupils say helps them to learn and what gets in the way of their learning (see Chapters 3 and 4). Indeed, according to data from one of the project's constituent enquiries (CPTL5), the greatest area of difference is not pupils' perspectives on pedagogy – here the consensus tends to hold – but differences in their experiences as learners within sub-groups, the sub-groups reflecting the intersection of gender, social class and individual positions in the popularity hierarchy. These differences exist but are not exposed in more familiar approaches to classroom learning, and the possibility of dealing with them when they become explicit can generate anxiety.

There are also likely to be individual differences that may reflect a pupil's past history as a learner and his or her sense of confidence in relation to particular learning strategies. Teachers who know their pupils well are more familiar with this kind of difference. They also know that part of the process of developing as an individual is to be able to formulate and justify your own view. In consultation, issues of group pressure and authenticity can, however, come into play: teachers are sometimes concerned that pupils may not be offering their own opinion, based on their own experience, but are instead subscribing to a group perspective, either because they do not want to be seen to be stepping out of line or because they think that their own view might be 'wrong'. For instance, one pupil acknowledged in interview that she felt 'insecure' about expressing her views and did not want other people in the class to know what she had written (LP2). Another source of concern is whether pupils' responses merely reflect what they think teachers want to hear (but, as we said earlier, until trust is established in the group such protective strategies are understandable). This may have the effect of deepening the doubts of teachers who are already sceptical about the virtues of consulting pupils.

From the teacher's perspective, encountering and responding to differences of perspective within the working group may underline the complexity of pupil consultation rather than its richness as a source of insight. And if the teacher selects from among the different accounts of experience what he or she might work on, the decision, unless explained and justified, may be interpreted as reinforcing the influence of a particular individual or sub-group. However, one of the strengths of discussing teaching and learning is that it provides the opportunity for pupils to see that different individuals or sub-groups in their class *may* have different experiences of the same situation and different views on how their learning can be improved.

This issue of understanding and responding to diversity of experience is important and worth addressing. Stewart Ranson (2000: 65), writing in the context of citizenship education, argues the need to 'reconstruct a theory of citizenship' which is 'grounded in the experience of heterogeneity' and he elaborates the need for different groups 'to enter a discourse in which they voice claims for their identities to be recognised and accommodated in the public space'. He goes on to argue that 'inclusive citizenship' thus requires recognition of different voices as well as a 'fair distribution of resources which provide the condition for equal participation'. Ranson's argument might prompt us to reflect on – and research further – this issue of difference in consultation. Our data (see Chapter 6) suggest that the sub-group differences that tend to play out their existence below the level of the teacher's gaze could usefully be brought to teachers' attention so that they could review their understanding of the social dynamics of learning in particular classes. This is easier said than done, however, and in the case of our project the mediator was the linked researcher.

From the pupil perspective

Pupils initially find it difficult to believe that:

*   it is acceptable to comment on lessons that they had hitherto seen as the sole responsibility of the teacher;
*   consultation is for *all* pupils.

The acceptability of commenting on lessons

Any sudden change of regime can be unsettling and pupils have said that commenting on teaching and learning is difficult because traditionally it has not been their role to do so. Younger pupils have made it clear that they think it would be 'rude' for them to say anything about what their teacher did, even though they also acknowledged, to the researcher, that there were things they would like to say – including, on one occasion, that the word 'difficulty' had 'two fs'! In many settings, pupils' regular experience has been of the teacher taking charge of communications about learning and making judgements about the quality of their work; any reversal of this process that led to them commenting on what they saw as the teacher's responsibility seemed to them to be bizarre. But once the change was legitimated they learned to make use of it.

Not surprisingly, pupils were sometimes unsure what the boundaries were. How far could they go? Could they be critical? Wasn't it better to play safe and to soften any potentially critical comment? For instance, as one pupil explained, 'It's easier to say, "Oh, it's a pretty good lesson"' and 'If I had to make an evaluation I would, like, put in 3 or above to make [the teacher] feel good' (CPTL5). This tendency was strong in relation to teachers who were popular, and whose feelings pupils didn't want to hurt, even though they could see that teaching and learning strategies might usefully be changed (see Chapter 7). In playing safe, the pupils are prudently avoiding some of the risks of consultation as they see them. But once trust has been established they begin to feel more comfortable with the process, knowing that their teachers genuinely want to hear what they have to say.

While some pupils were concerned in consultation with how their *teachers* would respond, others were uneasy about what their *peers* might think of them if they were actively contributing to a review of teaching and learning – presumably because it was a teacherly initiative, designed, as they saw it, for 'the boffs'. They therefore kept quiet in any class discussions in order to avoid ridicule from their friends. For such pupils, individualised written responses can offer a degree of privacy and personal freedom.

Similar concerns were reported in the survey carried out for the Scottish Parliament by Borland *et al.* (2001). Asked whether they would prefer to comment directly to their teachers or through an intermediary, most pupils opted for the latter approach – but again, we must recognise that it takes time to build up the trust that will make dialogue about teaching and learning seem both legitimate and possible.

Consultation is only for some pupils

In a climate which celebrates high academic achievement, less successful pupils can feel marginalised; they may also believe that they are in low sets where not much is expected of them. These messages are demeaning and leave their mark. It is not surprising, therefore, if pupils who feel that they are second-class citizens in school do not readily believe that opportunities to comment and to make a difference are for them. Some predict, from past responses, that if they do have anything to say it will not be taken seriously. Some believe that teachers are prepared to listen only to 'the good ones' or to 'those who do well'. In some settings the favoured groups may be middle class and/or white (see Mitra, 2001), who are much more articulate in the language of the school – in speaking 'proper'. The key issue is *who* gets heard in the acoustic of the school; and how *what is said* gets *heard* depends not only on who says it but on style and language.

The prospect of being consulted can sharpen existing anxieties among pupils about their competence in expressing their thoughts and lead them to feel that they are not up to it compared with their more articulate peers. And there may be grounds for their feeling less secure, as Shirley Brice Heath (2004: 53) has pointed out: 'For many young people who have not participated extensively at home or at school in open discussions or small group conversation, . . . and as planners and thinking partners, their facility with certain language structures lies dormant.' Indeed, the consultation process can sometimes affirm rather than challenge the existing dividing practices in schools and the regimes which lead to some pupils being valued above others. Another example of quite unwitting language-based divisiveness is when teachers commit themselves to building a new kind of consultative learning community by working in a small-scale and relatively protected way with a few students; this may be the only way that they can bring about change. But the pioneer students are often invited to 'display' their progress to other teachers, to the senior management team and to governors and are given responsibility, and trusted to do well. Such students can quickly develop a command of the situation and learn to meet the different challenges with maturity and confidence. However, these pioneering groups of students can become an elite, creating new hierarchies within the body of students itself – and their status is often rooted in competence in talk which may, in turn, be linked to social class.

Conclusion

Many teachers have acknowledged concerns about being on the receiving end of personal criticism and about what happens if the familiar hierarchical structure of the classroom is challenged by the principle of partnership. Anxiety is, therefore, an understandable response:

> For most individuals in any organisation, the challenge of fear and anxiety is always at least in the back of their minds if not front and centre. People often feel vulnerable, unsafe, and inadequate when trust is not present. Furthermore, all learning involves risks and therefore some fear.
>
> (Mitchell and Sackney, 2000: 107)

Senge *et al.* (1999: 244–50) suggest some strategies that are designed to respond to evidence of unease in the context of trying something different:

- reminding people that fear and anxiety are natural responses;
- starting small and building momentum before confronting difficult issues;
- avoiding full-frontal oppositional assaults;
- ensuring that participation is a matter of choice, not coercion.

This advice is fine as far as it goes, but it does not meet the needs of pupils who also – as we have seen – have concerns about innovations that change the familiar structures of classroom learning and for whom an innovation may not be a matter of choice; they may not be reassured by hearing that anxiety and fear are 'only natural'.

Building trust between teacher and pupils and among pupils is a crucial condition for the open discussion of teaching and learning, and where such trust is fragile it may have to be built up gradually through a series of smaller-scale opportunities that invite comment, offer feedback and reassure students about the security of the procedures. What also seems to be important for pupils and teachers – alongside starting small – is building an understanding of the reason for the innovation and the benefits it could bring.

Summary

In this chapter we have discussed reservations and anxieties that teachers and pupils experience in relation to pupil consultation, as revealed by our research, and some factors that can constrain them from wholehearted engagement with consultation. Both teachers and pupils can feel vulnerable when faced with such a change in their accustomed ways of relating to one another. We identified five kinds of such anxiety or constraint for teachers. The source of two of these is the system in which teachers work, which nationally places them under constant pressure to respond to curriculum requirements that can seem to leave little space for responsiveness to, or even finding out about, pupils' ideas, and at school level may not provide strong enough support for making such space. Two other kinds of reservation can come from teachers' own views of their pupils. If teachers distrust young people's commitment to learning, and especially the commitment of academically less successful pupils, they may well see little point in consulting them; but our own experience suggests that engaging in consultation can be very persuasive for teachers in helping them to move beyond such distrust and scepticism. A related kind of reservation can stem from teachers' anxiety about pupils' evaluative responses to their teaching; and, although we have consistently found that pupils' comments are polite, constructive and only very cautiously critical, it does seem important that teachers should not be asked to undertake such consultation except with strong social support from colleagues. The fifth, and perhaps most fundamental, kind of anxiety that teachers may feel stems from a concern about the complexity of their task of having to respond to the potentially very diverse perspectives of their pupils; and the research findings outlined in Chapter 6 do suggest that, when commenting on the social conditions of their classroom learning, pupils in the same classroom can register very different concerns.

As indicated in Chapter 7, pupils are generally much attracted by the idea of being consulted by their teachers about classroom teaching and learning, and respond equally positively to the practice of consultation when teachers engage in it wholeheartedly. Initially, however, they do tend to display some anxieties. One is about what it will be appropriate to say to teachers who ask for their comments, in relation both to what their teachers and what their peers will find acceptable, and such anxiety can have important implications for the consultation procedures with which pupils feel comfortable. For some groups of pupils, especially those who have experienced relatively little academic success, there can be particular anxieties relating to the appropriateness of their views being sought and given. Given their previous experiences, they can justifiably question whether their views are truly wanted, whether they will be taken seriously, and whether it will be worthwhile for them to invest in such an exercise.

In relation to all these concerns, we must recognise that it takes time to build up the trust that will make dialogue about teaching and learning seem both legitimate and possible.

Chapter 11

Conditions for developing consultation

What conditions does consultation need for its growth and survival? To some extent, but not entirely, they can be deduced from the last chapter on reservations, anxieties and constraints. We look first at conditions in the classroom and in particular at the quality of teacher–pupil relationships. But if consultation is to flourish there it will need a supportive framework at school level – and so, although our main concern is with the classroom, we cannot ignore the characteristics of the school climate.

Classroom teaching has always been a job in which thoughtful teachers can never see the end of the work they could usefully do and therefore in which they have to prioritise some tasks at the expense of others. In recent years, there has been a considerable increase, in the UK and elsewhere, in the number of official external demands to which most teachers feel obliged to respond. In the present climate, it is hard to find the time to try out something as challenging as consulting pupils about teaching and learning – and it can be very challenging if it is new to teachers and to their school.

Sarason (1993: 114) makes the distinction between new ideas that are merely absorbed and adopted without critical reflection and new ideas that are thought about in relation to the context which they might inhabit. This is an important consideration for developing consultation: schools and individual teachers need to be sure why they want to consult pupils – especially if they are to feel that the effort involved is justified. The motivation may be extrinsic and the responses instrumental, such as 'Consultation is popular and will be good for the school's image' or 'Ofsted is monitoring school support for consultation so we'd better be seen to be doing something about it'. More commonly, teachers and schools are attracted by the idea of consulting pupils because they believe it is right to listen to what young people have to say about their schooling. They also recognise that they may be able to learn much of value from their pupils, and they may be interested in building a more partnership-oriented relationship with pupils.

Conditions in the classroom: trust, respect and recognition

Our data from the project, confirmed in various linked projects, suggest that conditions in the classroom that favour the development of constructive consultation are trust, respect and recognition, on the part of teachers towards pupils and on the part of pupils towards teachers.

Trust and respect

These terms are fairly straightforward to interpret. This boy, who had felt that he did not matter in school, started to change in response to teachers who tried to help him by talking to him about his feelings and giving him more attention:

> I'm not really a good lad at school. But if you get to know the teachers like this then you know they're all right and that you can go to them if you need some help.
>
> (CPTL6)

Other interviews with pupils in the project highlighted some specific teacher behaviours that carried a strong positive charge and seemed to be contributing to the building of mutual trust and respect:

- a readiness to engage with pupils in adult ways;
- recognising pupils' desire to take more responsibility for learning as they grow older;
- being available to talk with pupils about their experience of school and about their schoolwork, its strengths and weaknesses, and how they can make improvements (and sometimes, especially for those whose achievement profile in school is poor, about their achievements *outside* school);

- being seen to be fair in dealings with all pupils;
- a readiness not to see some pupils just in terms of 'all the bad stuff' in their past but to believe in the possibility that they can change;
- a commitment to making all pupils feel confident that they can do well and achieve something worthwhile.

However tentatively a teacher and his or her class might start engaging in consultation, if the first steps go well, then trust and mutual respect increase: teachers see that pupils have worthwhile and constructive things to say and pupils see that teachers are taking seriously what they have said and are either taking on board some of the ideas and changing their practices or explaining why they cannot act on some of the suggestions.

We have been talking about building mutual respect and trust in pupils and teachers but for pupils in particular there is also an issue of trust in the consultation procedures themselves. As the discussion of teaching and learning starts to become a reality principles of procedure will need to be put in place. Pupils and teacher together may be able to work these out or the teacher may need to suggest one or two to begin with, such as anonymity in the pupils' review of teaching and learning. It is also important that pupils see consultation as an opportunity for constructive comment rather than as an opportunity for complaining. Pupils may also have things to say about the arrangements for con-sultation – for instance, whether whole-class discussion works, under what circumstances 'representative' voices might be appropriate and how 'representatives' might be identified, and whether they want more opportunity to think about their own learning through individual written evaluations. In short, pupils should come to feel that the mode of consultation is something that they can help shape – so that all pupils feel that they can contribute and feel comfortable about contributing; and so that consultation, because they are its joint owners, does not become a routinely repetitive event that quickly loses its impact.

Good experiences of consultation generate trust and allow confidence to grow: pupils' confidence that they have things to say that will be taken seriously and confidence in talking about teaching as well as about their own learning and teachers' confidence that pupils will talk honestly, constructively and without fear of retaliation.

Recognition

Trust and respect, as we said earlier, are relatively familiar terms, but what do we mean by 'recognition'? What first comes to mind is probably the system of classroom incentives and rewards. They are a way of recognising effort and achievement, and what pupils tend to object to is not the *principle* of recognition that the system embodies but the *nature* of the rewards and their public presentation.

In one school the formal system of incentives and rewards was not greatly valued by the older pupils and was therefore unlikely to be effective:

> The reward system? We're at that age where nothing can really please us that well. It's not material reward we want, there's no point in it. The only thing we really need is confidence and to be told sometimes that we're doing well.
>
> (LP1)

> You get these silly little supersticker things. Last year I got loads. And I think they're quite pointless. The school wastes money on pens and stuff and vouchers and no-one really cares . . . I prefer it when my teachers just pay attention to my work and tell me whether it's good or not.
>
> (Rudduck *et al.*, 2006: 32)

The interviews revealed the disdain that many older pupils felt for extrinsic motivators, such as gold stars. Instead, pupils appreciate it when teachers understand what engages them and is valued by them, and their increasing preference is for recognition that takes the form of supportive comments from teachers. Pupils want teachers to acknowledge the extra effort they are making and, importantly, explain that they feel good about themselves when teachers have recognised their efforts and progress. Pupils say that they want to 'try harder' for such teachers and that they enjoy being a member of their classes. Such a climate favours the development of consultation.

Recognition, here, is about teachers being aware of and responding with authentic pleasure to evidence of pupils' special effort and progress, whether in work or behaviour; recognition is a way teachers have of demonstrating respect and re-enforcing trust. But looked at in terms of *pupils'* agency, recognition is about pupils' capacity to see situations from the teacher's perspective and also to appreciate teachers' efforts and skills. One pupil, talking to a researcher, identified a number of possible ways of improving teaching and learning, and then reflected on the implications of his agenda for his teacher, commenting, with a flash of sympathy, 'I think it's very hard for the teacher [to take on board] all of this. It's almost impossible for them' (LP1). Another pupil, from the same school, talks about the kind of teacher he would like to avoid but is also able to see that he is being unrealistic about the human frailties of teachers:

> [If I could wave a magic wand] I'd choose my own teachers – the ones who enjoy their job and don't seem bitter towards students, the ones that are smiley and positive not the ones who are, like, 'Grrrrrrrrr, who's chewing? Grrrrrrrrr, who's going to get detention today, then, I wonder?' But everyone has off days.
>
> (LP1)

And this pupil realises that in asking for written commentaries on his work he is making a considerable demand on his teacher's time:

> I had my essay marked very nicely. There was a paragraph about how it could be improved. But it did take four or five weeks [to be returned]! It's a bit long to wait, possibly! But if you were always going to get a comment which was going to help you improve, I wouldn't mind waiting the extra week or whatever. It would definitely take teachers longer but it would almost certainly help improve grades if people were pointed in the right way from the start.
>
> (LP1)

Some pupils clearly understand the pressures from outside the school that teachers are under to ensure that their classes secure high grades in tests and exams while at the same time trying to respond to their pupils' agenda, which may pull in a slightly different direction. One pupil commented, sympathetically, 'I don't know, they have to get it just right, don't they!' (LP1).

Mutual trust, respect and recognition are, then, some of the key interpersonal conditions for the development of consultation but it is also helpful if teachers:

- feel obliged to be as responsive to their pupils as they are to top-down requirements;

- see pupils' learning capacities as open to radical development, not more or less predetermined, and that the key to such development is for them to work in collaboration with their pupils.

Time to reflect on learning

In Chapter 10 we looked at shortage of time as one of the main constraints, as teachers see it, on developing consultation. Here we look at time from the pupils' perspective as one of the conditions for consultation. Pupils want something quite specific: if they are to be asked about teaching and learning then they want to be assured that teachers are genuinely interested in what they have to say, which means that the procedures have to be structured in ways that allow them to offer authentic commentaries.

Interestingly, as we saw earlier, many pupils see questionnaires that invite written responses and suggestions as offering greater individual opportunity to make their views known as well as being more protective of anonymity. But they want enough time not only to complete their commentaries but to think about what it is they want to write:

> Pupil 1: Yeah, I would have preferred having time to think about all the classes – how they should be, what we can actually do.
>
> Pupil 2: [W]e had to do it in a minute . . . couldn't concentrate on it.
>
> Pupil 3: He only gives you about thirty seconds.
>
> Pupil 4: If you got five minutes you could really think about 'Am I really good at learning?'
>
> (CPTL5)

Some of Bethan Morgan's pupils (see Chapter 7) also emphasised the importance of time: Danny's (Year 8) advice to his teacher was to 'give them . . . a right amount of time' because without that 'they might just rush it and put any answer'. Another student (also Year 8) commented, 'If you do a questionnaire I think you should give it as homework', because then he would be able to 'give it more time'.

The time issue is important because, as pupils explain, they have few chances to reflect on their learning – and to do this they seem to need the support of teacher encouragement and a formalised occasion. For pupils who know how to handle the opportunity, these moments of reflection can clearly have a positive impact on their learning. Here, the linked researcher, Diane Reay, asks three pupils from the same class whether 'doing these sheets' has been useful:

> Well, yeah, in a way, cos you think, 'Have I really learned anything?' and then you think, 'Well, I'm not sure. Maybe' or 'Yeah, I have.' And then next lesson you come and you think, 'Well, the [last] lesson I learned a lot. I want to learn a lot this lesson.'

> It's given me a lot of time on these three sheets [i.e., given out over three successive lessons] to think about what I've been doing and how it's affected my learning in other classes and in Maths, and how it's affected the teacher thinking about me.

> I managed to come up front with myself – cos I'm often not sure really whether I had or hadn't learned anything and I actually had to sit down and think when I had to write that sheet out.

> (CPTL5)

Perhaps the broader condition to which this time issue relates is 'authenticity': for consultation to be credible, pupils need to feel that teachers will listen and respond to what they have to say about teaching and learning; and, as we have just seen, they feel that if consultation is worth doing, it is worth doing well. That means being given the time to think things through. It is not every day that pupils ask for time to reflect on their learning.

Conditions in schools that support the development of classroom consultation

We have highlighted the roles of trust, respect and recognition in the development of consultation in the classroom and reaffirmed the importance of time – for teachers and for pupils – but there is also the question of ensuring that the values that allow consultation to flourish in the classroom are actively promoted at school level. This tends to mean, as Rachal (1998: 186) has said, that a 'schooling atmosphere' needs to give way to 'a less hierarchical and more collaborative relationship'.

In some settings such transformation would not be easily accomplished. The values expressed through consultation would have difficulty in finding a foothold at school level: for instance, in schools where the majority of pupils are convinced that they do not matter and where only the highest academic outcomes are valued; or where the oppositional stance of large segments of the pupil body is so strong that there can be no suspension of disbelief about the possibility of building alternative teacher–pupil relationships. And where there has been a predominantly authoritarian relationship trust will at best be wary and unsteady and the challenge of change will be considerable – as this deputy head acknowledges:

> We are attempting to change the culture of the school from an 'us and them' hierarchy to a participative learning community. One of the keys to this is creating mechanisms to hear student voice and to increase the level of involvement of students in decisions that affect their school community.
>
> (CPTL6)

In another school the aspiration was also to develop a school-wide culture around the idea of pupil voice:

> We want to nurture the idea of students as commentators and critics and researchers, discussing what helps them to learn and ensuring that they feel that they and their work are recognised and valued.
>
> (LP1)

In these two schools the idea of pupil voice was new and the initiative was being taken by the senior management team. More often the innovation travels in the other direction – from a committed teacher outwards and upwards to the whole school. Gill Mulliss had been working on consultation fairly privately for some time and after two years believed that consultation had something to offer colleagues. She wanted the values embedded in the relationships she had nurtured at classroom level to be adopted more widely:

> I think the students in Year 11 feel very proud and they have been very successful, but the next step for me is a bigger one: it's bringing on board more staff, affecting the whole school policy and practices, and that will be an interesting stage to move on to.
>
> (Mulliss, interviewed 2002)

Mulliss hoped that the school would consider giving a special responsibility to one member of staff for pupil and teacher development.

Meanwhile, she concentrated on persuading colleagues that consulting pupils was worthwhile: she invited some of her pupils to present a summary of their work at a staff meeting – and found that there were 'very few staff who weren't actually interested in what they're saying'. She also invited colleagues to drop in on her lessons and see how the climate and relationship had changed after almost two years of working together on consultation.

Other teachers have also found that pupils themselves are reliable advocates for consultation, and when they are given the task of preparing a report on the process and outcomes of consultation for staff and/or governors their audiences are invariably impressed by their insights, by the quality of their presentation and by their commitment to working with their teachers to 'make a difference'. However, while a presentation by pupils – or even passages from transcripts of their commentaries – may impress other teachers in the school, it is also important that colleagues understand the principles that give structure and security to the work at classroom level – including the fundamental importance of building trust, respect and a capacity for recognition.

Fielding and Bragg (2003) identified five items that appear to be associated with success in building and sustaining a whole-school commitment to pupil voice that would facilitate the work that goes on in classrooms. Together they reflect a coherent set of values that are to do with openness, attentiveness to the views of others and mutual respect and support:

- advocacy by institutional leaders;
- enabling structures and practices;
- a school culture that values and listens to all staff;
- a culture of enquiry and research among teachers;
- a tradition of pupil involvement in decision-making.

'Advocacy' needs to be more than rhetoric and more substantial than persuasive pressure; it should make clear *why* the development of pupil voice is important and how it would fit with the values that underlie other initiatives or aspirations. Senior management teams also need to provide 'enabling structures and practices'. It can be helpful if some senior teachers who are knowledgeable about pupil consultation are given the task of supporting and advising other teachers. Again, teachers in middle-management positions, such as heads of department in secondary schools, could fruitfully be given the remit to help and encourage teachers of the same subject or age phase to collaborate with each other in developing joint approaches to pupil consultation. Indeed, there are many 'enabling structures and practices' that can be provided so that teachers can feel that they have a realistic opportunity to engage effectively in pupil consultation. For instance, teaching assistants can help alleviate the time problem: where there are several teaching assistants in a school who are manifestly good at establishing empathetic relationships with pupils, they could be given some training and become available to interview pupils individually or in small groups on behalf of, but working closely with, class teachers. A session during professional development days could regularly be set aside for reporting on and/or working on consultation; and ICT staff might be asked to help with the analysis of evidence collected from pupils via questionnaires or structured interviews.

The other three items – a school culture that values and listens to all staff; a culture of enquiry and research among teachers; and a tradition of pupil involvement in decision-making – delineate a foundation of existing practice which would provide a positive base for the development of pupil voice.

If there is anything missing or understated in this list, it is the obvious desirability of an explicit policy commitment within the school. In the present climate in particular, teachers – individually and in departmental teams – need formal approval (one might even say 'permission') from senior management to be responsive to their pupils as well as to national directives, and to take the necessary time to do that. Only heads ultimately have the authority to make such an endorsement, to support such a balance. Not all heads may feel brave enough, or feel that the school's reputation is robust enough, to do that, but without firm commitment from the school's leadership it is difficult for individual teachers to take the risks involved. School-wide support for pupil voice can, according to Mitchell and Sackney (2000: 6), mean moving from a technological model that is concerned with targets, efficiency and hierarchical modes of accountability to one that is characterised by 'metaphors of wholeness and connections, diversity and complexity, relationships and meaning, reflection and enquiry, and collaboration and collegiality'. They attribute the style of the former to a 'learning organisation', the style of the latter to 'a learning community'. We would want to emphasise the importance of sensitivity on the part of school leaders to the complex and difficult task of building an authentic learning community in the classroom.

An important part of the process is to build confidence in the potential of pupil voice among significant adults – such as governors, teachers who are likely to be sceptical and parents. Headteachers and senior management teams might find the following check list – devised out of reported practice within the project – a useful guide. The tasks include:

*   reassuring teachers, pupils, parents and governors that consulting pupils is recognised nationally as both legitimate and potentially beneficial – and that it may be worth trying in their school;
*   building support among teachers by presenting evidence of the positive outcomes of consultation – while acknowledging that consultation can initially make for some uncomfortable learnings;
*   being sensitive to the anxiety experienced by teachers who have not before consulted pupils about teaching and learning (see Chapter 10);
*   ensuring that teachers feel confident about strategies for handling consultation – including active listening and providing feedback;
*   ensuring that other policies and initiatives are in harmony with the values that underpin pupil consultation;
*   ensuring that newly qualified teachers and teachers new to the school understand the extent of the school's commitment to pupil voice and feel confident about its principles and practices.

Conclusion

We are in no doubt that the benefits to be gained from pupil consultation are more than adequate to justify the time and work that it involves. It is, however, important to be realistic and to recognise the investment of thought and energy that it requires. The greatest benefits, further-more, are likely to come from those strategies that involve the greatest investment of thought, time and resources. Both individual teachers and school leaders need to recognise that engaging in pupil consultation requires significant commitment.

It is also important that such commitment from school leaders and from individual teachers should be explicitly connected. There are many schools in which valuable pupil consultation initiatives have been taken at the whole-school level, most frequently through the development of school councils. But however imaginative and productive such initiatives may be, they do not necessarily have any impact at the class-room level. School leaders need to recognise that classroom teachers need both encouragement and support in committing themselves to pupil consultation in their own classroom contexts. Indeed, school leaders need to recognise that the challenge of pupil consultation in relation to classroom teaching and learning may be greater than that of whole-school consultation, and certainly involves its own distinctive complexities and risks. So there is a need for whole-school strategies specifically directed towards encouraging and supporting teachers' use of pupil consultation about teaching and learning in their own classrooms.

Summary

This chapter has been about the conditions necessary for the development of classroom pupil consultation. Some of these are conditions in the classrooms themselves, but many teachers will feel the need also for a supportive framework at school level.

At the classroom level, pupil consultation can develop only if there is mutual trust, respect and recognition between teacher and pupils. Teachers can demonstrate trust and respect for pupils in various ways – for example, by demonstrating a belief in all pupils' capacity to do well and a commitment to working with them to develop that capacity – and in doing so they are likely to foster the pupils' trust and recognition of them. Thoughtfully noticing and explicitly recognising pupils' efforts and progress is one important way of doing this. But seriously engaging in consultation and responding to it is itself a way of showing trust and respect for pupils and so of winning their trust. So modest initial consultation efforts can cultivate the ground for more ambitious efforts. Issues of trust arise for pupils in consultation procedures themselves; and consulting about the procedures so that pupils can help to shape them is likely to generate trust and confidence among pupils. Time for pupils to reflect on their learning is another condition that they tend to emphasise as necessary for effective consultation.

While some individual teachers have pioneered classroom consultation on their own, it would be unreasonable to expect most teachers to undertake such a considerable task without the support of their schools. Most generally, classroom consultation will be difficult unless the general climate and culture of the school support the mutual trust and respect on which consultation depends. More

continued

specific support is also needed in the form of active advocacy of classroom consultation by school leaders, explicit school policies that guide and encourage teachers to engage in classroom consultation and practical structures and procedures that support individual teachers in doing so. It is important that school leaders should build a shared confidence in the value of pupil consultation among teachers, parents and other significant adults.

Part III

What are the overall implications?

In previous chapters, we have reported what we learned from the TLRP Project and from related projects. In these final chapters, our aim is to consider more generally what has been learned from research on consulting pupils and where we have got to in the wider political project of using such research to facilitate radical improvement in teaching and learning in schools.

The project has, we believe, made some important and distinctive contributions to our understanding of what is at stake in the pupil voice agenda, and we shall try to indicate what in broad terms we, as an education community, now know and where we think we might go from here.

Chapter 12

Summary

What have we learned?

The data across the different enquiries reported in this book suggest that if consultation is thoughtfully introduced and developed then it has the potential to strengthen pupils' commitment to learning. We can say much about why this might credibly happen – including the importance for pupils' motivation of classroom relationships that are characterised by mutual respect, trust and the sharing of responsibility as well as teaching approaches that allow for active pupil involvement. We also know more about the importance of a coherent relationship between the school culture and the classroom culture.

What we learned about the importance of the personal and interpersonal dimensions of learning

As we saw earlier, for pupils, the personal and interpersonal dimensions of learning are very important but they tend to be ignored either in the face of lingering suspicion of 'child-centred learning' or because they become submerged by the outcomes orientation of the performance agenda. We want to reinstate their significance for pupils' commitment to learning.

In emphasising the *personal dimensions of learning* we do not mean individualised learning nor the spirit of competitive individualism that marked the Thatcher years. And while, as David Hargreaves (1982: 85) has said, 'the shift towards a concern for the individual pupil has been of inestimable benefit', its association with the progressive child-centred movement of the 1970s opened it to criticism for diminishing the importance of the cognitive goals of schooling. Its power was also weakened, according to Hargreaves (1982: 93), by its dissociation from the social dimension of education – hence our highlighting of the *interpersonal* dimensions of learning alongside the *personal*.

When we speak of 'the personal dimension', what we have in mind is captured in the comments of teachers from East Sussex who worked on an exploratory 'personalised learning and pupil voice' project (LP1). The teachers developed their own interpretations of 'personalised learning', which, while differently nuanced, were essentially about changing teacher perceptions of pupils' capabilities and, consequently, about the way they related to pupils:

> Personalised learning for us is about the need to engage, recognise and value students and their achievements – each one – at a personal level.

> Personalised learning in this school is about boosting the esteem of all students so that they can have self-belief.

> It's about adapting what we do in the classroom so that it is relevant to all those we teach – it's about partnership and participation.

Another teacher in the project summed up the range of possibilities when he said that personalising learning was about 'enabling pupils to speak with insight and intelligence about how they learn in school' – and for teachers to understand and respond.

Giving greater attention to the personal and interpersonal dimensions of learning includes recognising and harnessing pupils' strengths in support of their learning. These strengths include:

*   greater maturity and capability than they are sometimes given credit for in school;
*   a capacity – borne of sustained experience in schools – for the insightful analysis of the social situations of classrooms;
*   a disposition – that needs more conscious nurturing – to take into account the perspectives of others, including teachers and fellow pupils.

The data highlighted the importance for pupils of the qualities of trust, respect and recognition, together with a sense of reciprocity, and opportunities to exercise responsibility. Then there are things that young people in school say they want, or want more – and these also tend to reflect the personal and interpersonal dimensions of learning. Pupils want:

- to be respected and trusted, both as individuals and as an institutional group, and to have more autonomy in the pursuit of their learning;
- to feel that they belong in school and to have a sense of membership;
- to feel that they have something to contribute that others will recognise and value.

We have summed these up in terms of the importance for pupils of trust, respect and recognition and also the strong sense of reciprocity that is highlighted in the final bullet point.

Thus, our data lead us to rebalance the traditional primacy of academic aspects of learning by bringing the personal and the interpersonal into the frame, believing, with Berry (2006: 522), in 'the possibility of defining social participation as constitutive of opportunity to learn'. Here we summarise what giving attention to the personal and interpersonal might look like in practice. We would expect to see:

- **A positive sense of learning and of self as learner.** Pupils
  - know that their achievements will be recognised;
  - experience a justifiable sense of pride in their learning;
  - feel confident about how to improve the weaker aspects of their work and know that guidance from teachers will be available in a form that makes sense to them;
  - experience lessons as generally worthwhile and interesting and sometimes exciting but are able to cope with routine tasks and understand why they are sometimes necessary.

- **Relationships with teachers that are based on mutual respect and trust:**
  - where neither party will seek to humiliate, mock, hurt or demean the other;
  - where both teachers and pupils are able to see things from the perspective of others and to be sensitive to differences, of view and need, within the working group;

  - where pupils and teachers feel able to talk about teaching and learning as a shared responsibility.

- **A sense of agency in relation to learning.** Pupils

  - know that they have a contribution to make to the improvement of teaching and learning;
  - know that their ideas and actions can sometimes make a difference to how things are done;
  - know that they will be trusted to organise aspects of their own learning, individually or in groups.

- **Opportunities for unhurried reflection**, so that pupils can think and talk about

  - their own learning and learning within the working group;
  - ways of improving teaching and learning.

Our data suggest that the very process of being consulted strengthens pupils' commitment to learning because being involved and feeling that your views are valued and that you are being treated in more adult and responsible ways make pupils feel good – about themselves as learners, about 'listening teachers', and about the work that these 'listening teachers' organise for them. *Thus, we would claim that a distinctive feature of the project was its identification of the importance of the personal and interpersonal alongside the cognitive dimensions of learning.*

What we learned about the potential of consultation to strengthen teaching

Consultation works to support teaching in two ways, each focusing on the understanding and agency of the teacher.

Consultation offers teachers a practical agenda for the improvement of teaching and learning

As we have seen, there is, in broad terms, remarkable consistency across schools and across ages about what pupils say helps them to learn and what gets in the way of their learning. Pupils have a great deal to say about aspects of teaching that, if changed, might better support their learning as well as about ways of working and tasks that they find engaging and motivating – such as content that connects with their everyday experiences, and interactive learning that includes discussion and group work. They quite consistently call for less teacher talk and less copying on the grounds that these can be tedious, and if they are bored then they will not learn as well or as much. These observations are very familiar and consequently tend to be ignored, but if they were acted on then they could make a significant difference to pupils' learning. And pupils argue, with a simple logic, that they know what strategies engage them and help them to learn, and that if teachers could accommodate more of these strategies then pupils' commitment and achievement would be strengthened.

Commenting on the principle and practice of consultation, one pupil said, 'I think it's been good because you've actually been able to say what should happen but saying it and it actually happening is a different thing' (CPTL6). As we have seen in Chapter 8, the extent to which teachers are likely to act on the suggestions pupils make will reflect their proper professional judgement of their validity and feasibility (such as whether they represent a majority or minority view or whether their implementation would require resources that the teacher does not possess) and how they fit with teachers' other plans or priorities (such as covering topics for exams).

In deciding whether or how to respond teachers are also making judgements about the educational quality of pupils' suggestions and whether the suggestions are likely to deepen their understanding and advance their learning. But, by and large, teachers have found that pupils are serious-minded and insightful when they comment on teaching and learning and tend to recommend modest changes; they are not, in our experience, bent on making outlandish suggestions. And pupils argue (see Chapter 7) that they are prepared to work harder if they respect their teachers and if they think their teachers care about them and are responsive to what they have to say about their learning – even if it means explaining why some ideas cannot be implemented.

Consultation can offer teachers greater insight into the social dynamic of a working group

As we have seen in Chapter 6, a different focus for consultation is the dynamics of the learning group – about which pupils are also very perceptive – and their perceptions are often highly emotionally charged, revealing the complex ways in which sub-group identities and rivalries can affect learning.

The sub-groups may reflect differences in social class, gender and ethnicity, in pupils' perceived acceptance or rejection of the school's learning purposes, or other less predictable and more local dimensions, such as the criteria in a particular school or classroom for determining membership of the 'in-group'. While most pupils tend to agree about the strategies that help them learn, there can be quite marked differences in the ways in which the different sub-groups experience teaching and learning. If teachers can learn more about the 'below stairs' life of their classes it may help them to make differential adjustments to their teaching – such as making sure that the three or four high-attaining boys are stretched throughout the lesson and are not habitually experiencing the last ten minutes as wasted time; or making sure that the working-class girls who want to do well are not bullied by some of their friends into conforming to the 'smart' norm of work avoidance; or making sure that the efforts of those pupils for whom learning is an uphill struggle are recognised even though their levels of achievement may seem unimpressive. Probing the social dynamics of the group can be demanding and we have as yet encountered it only in classrooms where the teacher has the support of a linked researcher who will feed back his or her data, or insights from the data, and aid the teacher in interpreting and acting on the data.

So, on the one hand, consultation can make available an agenda for improvement while, on the other, it may yield information that will help teachers to respond to sub-group differences whose effect on learning is often not apparent.

Comment

Academic achievement is central to the project's concerns and we have come to see it as largely dependent on two things:

* the complex set of personal and interpersonal dimensions that, together, help to build and sustain pupils' trust in school and their commitment to learning;
* guidance from pupils about which classroom strategies and experiences help them to learn and which get in the way of their learning.

However, persuasive as our arguments may be, they do not fit neatly with the government's strategies for improving learning. The dominant 'official' view of learning is heavily outcomes oriented and, despite widespread interest in the principle of consultation, gives insufficient weight, in our opinion, to pupils' views about what helps them to learn and about how learning might be improved. Pupil consultation has been encouraged by government but seemingly more in the context of the children's rights agenda and citizenship education than in support of learning more generally. And in a climate of constant testing, where so much is at stake for the government in terms of its promises of improved national performance and for schools in terms of comparative performance figures as the maker and breaker of reputations, it is tempting to try to work directly on short-term performance goals rather than to take a broader and more generous view of the kinds of learning we value in pupils and the kinds of experience that help build a commitment to learning that will endure beyond school.

Classroom and school

We have deliberately focused on consultation in relation to what happens in classrooms, but it is clear that the values that help build and sustain a commitment to learning there need to be reflected in the school's organisational structures and regimes (see Chapter 11). Indeed, school regimes can exert a strong influence, both positive and negative, on pupils' motivation to learn. By 'regimes' we mean the system of explicit and implicit rules and values that structure pupils' daily experiences in school: for instance, assumptions about what is seen by teachers to matter most in school, which year groups are privileged, how different groups of pupils are perceived and valued. Regimes convey messages that pupils absorb, and to the extent that some feel disenfranchised by these messages they may adjust their attitude and behaviour accordingly.

Particularly damaging to pupils' dignity and self-esteem (see Meadmore, 1993) are some dividing practices, the side-effects of a system that prioritises narrow performance goals. Grouping practices can easily communicate a lack of respect for those who are not high achievers and can be demoralising for those who find themselves in low sets:

> It's better to be in the high sets because you are thought better of by teachers . . . If you are in the bottom set you ain't got no confidence. You think you are just going to fail . . . [P]eople in like the lower group don't learn nowt because of the teacher. He just writes stuff on the board and then gives you the answers straight away so they can't learn nothing.
>
> (Rudduck and Flutter, 2004: 58–9)

Pupils do not want to feel that they are so little valued that they have been relegated and marginalised. Their response may be to seek an alternative source of esteem within the peer group by maintaining a studied disdain for learning.

What pupils want instead are structures that provide a consistent and positive message. They want to feel that the system is reliable; they (mostly) want to feel that every child matters and that all should be treated with respect (although there are occasions when pupils can turn, quite vengefully, on the minority who disrupt the learning of others or on those whose struggles with learning capture too much teacher attention). Pupils want to know that rules and codes of conduct make sense, are transparent and are handled in the same way by all teachers. They want a system that

- will recognise and respect a range of accomplishments;
- is open and fair;
- relies on a minimal set of rules but ones that make sense to pupils, which ideally they have had a part in formulating or reviewing, and which are consistently interpreted by all teachers as well as by the pupils themselves;
- will encourage pupil involvement at a variety of levels and in a variety of ways.

Again, most pupils want to feel that school is for them but they can instead feel that it belongs to the teachers: 'They treat you like it's *their* school and *their* rules but the school policy is for everyone . . . and it seems like it's all them, nothing for you' (LP1). These pupils need to feel that they do belong, that what they say counts, and that they have strengths that will be recognised; then they may find it possible to push back the barriers and recommit themselves to learning. Involving pupils in authentic consultation about issues that matter to them can make a profound difference, as some teachers in the project discovered: 'We've learned a lot about how students rapidly improve in their learning and their self-esteem and their motivation . . . through feeling important, feeling cared for, feeling their views matter' (CPTL1). But in the present climate – and despite evidence of the potential of con-sultation to strengthen pupils' commitment to learning – ensuring that pupils feel 'important', 'cared for' and that 'their views matter' is unlikely to be accepted by government policy-makers as constituting a central plank in their reformist policies. As Rosenbaum and Newell (1991: 10) have said, 'Children may be the subjects of a fair amount of political rhetoric but unfortunately the rhetoric tends to be empty and unconnected to practical policies.'

Indeed, the model of learning embedded in present government thinking relies on the power of rewards, targets and close monitoring – all combining to support the achievement of short-term performance goals. Moreover, government initiatives tend to be presented, whatever the reality, as highly successful, and this strategic display of success is essentially conservative – if everything is successful then there is no need for adjustments, let alone radical change.

Our approach is different: it rests on an appreciation of what pupils can contribute to the improvement of teaching and learning and it requires a fundamental change in the way we see pupils and in the power relations between pupils and teachers.

As Ruth Jonathan (1989: 323) said, school improvement is not just a matter of 'rapid response to consumer demands of the moment' but a question of dealing with the deep structures of school and the habits of thought and values they embody. Our view of students has, for a long time, been held in place by such habits of thought but we are now moving beyond the silenced voices to a re-evaluation of what young people can contribute to the analysis and planning of their experiences as learners. We need to review the goodness of fit between what young people today are capable of and the opportunities actually available in school; and we need to review the 'adultness' of their responsibilities and identities out of school and the 'adultness' of their lives in school. Comber and Kamler (2004) put this well when they reported on research that revealed not students who were 'in deficit' but rather young people whose potential resources remained invisible in the school context.

Chapter 13

The development of consultation and its transformative potential

In previous chapters, we have reported what we learned about pupil voice from the TLRP Project and from related projects – in particular about the importance of the personal and interpersonal dimensions of learning alongside the academic. In this final chapter, we revisit some of the ideas introduced in the first chapter and consider where we have reached in the wider political project of using research on pupil voice to facilitate radical improvement in teaching and learning in schools and radical changes in our perceptions of young people. The main focus is on the potential of pupil voice to transform the structure and experience of classroom learning.

Stages in the development of pupil voice and pupil voice research

> Nowhere have rights to have a say in one's own affairs been won without serious struggle.
>
> (Qvortrup, 1997: 85)

Young people want to have a voice – there is clear evidence of this in our work and in the work of others – but lacking confidence in their power to influence practices in school, it was not pupils but others who struggled for them to win the right to have a say. Support has come from many groups – including researchers who have, for many years, demonstrated in their data that young people have a capacity for insightful analysis and have things to say that are worth hearing.

There are several discernible stages in the development of pupil voice and pupil voice research.

Stage 1

An important first step was when educational researchers started to gather data from young people in order to open up the world of school and classroom. On the basis of observation, interviews or surveys, they offered insights into young people's in-school cultures and new understandings were disseminated to audiences beyond the schools. The audiences might include teachers but not necessarily the teachers whose pupils were involved; indeed, researchers may not have offered any feedback directly to the schools. Pupils, as key informants, may have felt pride in knowing that people from outside the school were interested in what they had to say but their accounts of experience were not leading to a review of practice in their own school that might have made learning better for them. We have already mentioned (in Chapters 1 and 2) the contribution of Laccy, Hargeaves, Meighan, Woods and others who were pioneers in this kind of pupil voice research. Their approach became well established and continues as part of the standard repertoire of educational researchers interested in pupil perspectives.

Stage 2

A boost to the status of pupil voice and pupil voice research was given by the United Nations Convention on the Rights of the Child (1989) and the idea of involving young people in decisions affecting their lives was quickly taken up in the special needs area. The UN Convention led eventually to the passing of the Children Act, and mainstream education started to consider the implications. However, active exploration of the rationale for developing pupil voice and understanding its deeper potential was still limited. Sealander (2003: 216) claimed that even in the 1990s 'few education specialists' were trying to examine students' perspectives critically. Response remained patchy among schools in this country. The situation appeared to be similar in the USA, with real change slow to materialise – as the following comment suggested:

> [Adults] think of [students] as the potential beneficiaries of change [but they] rarely think of [them] as participants in a process of change and organisational life.
>
> (Fullan and Stiegelbauer, 1991: 170)

In England, despite exhortations in government documents to respond to the spirit of the UN Convention, there was still a long way to go.

Additional support came in the 1990s from pioneer researchers intent on building a new sociology of childhood. They were driven by the desire to map the complexities of childhood even as educational researchers wanted to map pupils' experiences of school. These sociological studies highlighted 'the exotic terrains' of children's worlds (Sealander, 2003: 6); they also sought to convince fellow-researchers and policy-makers that children as a social group should be taken seriously. They reminded us (Hendrick, 1997: 43) that in the mid-nineteenth century 'the middle class notion of a properly constituted childhood [was] characterised by a state of dependency'; and of the assumption that had gone unquestioned for a long time that children should be 'harmoniously socialized' to the point of silence and invisibility (Prout and James, 1997: 14). Qvortrup (1997) was concerned to make the children of today visible by establishing reporting systems, including statistical reporting, that made it possible to recognise the contribution they made to the domestic and wider economy (see also Morrow, 1994: 134; James and Prout, 1997: xiv). The legacy of this important body of work – even though it was not necessarily school focused – included seeing young people as actors in their own right.

Both groups of researchers mentioned above helped change our ways of seeing young people. They were in a sense 'consulting' students but not usually in ways that allowed the data to loop back and inform practice in the contexts where the data had been gathered. The improvement of learning and of the conditions for learning was not yet high on the research agenda; indeed, a necessary first step was for research to convince its audience that what young people had to say was worth hearing and that there were many aspects of their learning that were not fully understood, even by their teachers, unless they listened to pupils' own accounts of their experiences in and perceptions of school.

Stage 3

The next stage, which is where we are now, reflects not only the new prominence of pupil voice in educational discourse but wider concerns about the developmental potential of research and how it might benefit the schools that contribute. Stage 3 is a logical outcome of the new interest in the potential of consultation to improve learning: given differences between classrooms, both within and across schools, it is seen as important to follow through the process and impact of consultation in particular contexts. Thus, research into pupil consultation looks not only at what pupils have to say about teaching and learning in different schools but at the responsiveness of teachers and the conditions under which teachers might want, and feel able, to make consultation a regular part of classroom practice.

There are, predictably, calls from policy-makers for evidence of the impact of consultation on pupil achievement but these cannot be responsibly met before we are sure that schools understand the rationale for developing pupil voice and are implementing it in reasonable ways – that is, not just as a reluctant 'quick survey' in the last few seconds of the lesson with no discussion of the outcomes with pupils and no obvious follow-through. There is evidence of the *potential* of consultation to strengthen pupils' commitment to learning but not the kind of proof – that is, a direct cause-and-effect link – that government has wanted: it is clear that successful implementation depends very much on the culture of classroom and school and that the approach to consultation and its impact are, therefore, likely to show considerable variation across schools. Nevertheless, in settings where consultation is thoughtfully developed the signs are encouraging.

Our own findings are echoed in recent comments by some US researchers:

> [When teachers listen] students not only feel more engaged but are also inclined to take more responsibility for their education because it is no longer something being done to them but rather something they do.
>
> (Cook-Sather, 2002, quoted in McQuillan, 2005: 641)

> Where student participation was encouraged and nurtured, classroom and schoolwide changes were more likely to be sustained and to deepen [and] in those schools students often became proponents of change.
>
> (Muncey and McQuillan, 1996: 155)

McQuillan (2005: 664) goes on to summarise the overall pattern of impact in a school he studied:

> Having students exercise a voice in school matters may enhance academic performance, enrich students' understanding of democratic citizenship, and make schools more responsive institutions.

The connections can be systematic – intertwining and building momentum in mutually reinforcing ways.

So, where is consultation at the moment? We hope that the preceding chapters of this book provide some answers. But, to summarise briefly, the status of pupils as an institutional group and also their capacity for constructive and insightful analysis are now more widely recognised among teachers; less well understood, perhaps, is the process whereby consultation can improve pupils' self-esteem and their sense of membership and agency, and how these, in turn, can strengthen their commitment to learning and, ultimately, their achievement.

There is a danger at this stage – and we are already seeing evidence of it – that could minimise the potential of consultation to improve teaching and learning. Because the classroom is the environment that is protected by concerns about academic achievement and therefore the more difficult arena in which to secure fundamental change, efforts are being directed more towards developing consultation *outside the classroom* and also *outside the school*, as we warned in Chapter 1. Indeed, consultation events for pupils that lie outside schools are multiplying – for example, Internet conferences, face-to-face discussions and referenda that involve pupils in exploring other young people's views on national and global issues. These are excellent opportunities in their own right but we should heed Coleman's (2005: 13) warning: 'A key message for government is that engaging young people in on-line debates and consultation is counter productive unless there is a serious and authentic commitment to listen and learn – in short to engage with them.' And, at school level, such opportunities need to be paralleled by appropriately scaled opportunities for pupils to talk about and influence teaching and learning *within* their own classrooms.

Stage 4

The next two stages are more speculative as we have only rather sparse data about what consultation might look like. Stage 4 affirms its importance for *learning*: it becomes a professional commitment of teachers and is so much a part of their regular practice that it no longer seems obtrusive, risky or even particularly adventurous. All pupils are involved, not just an elite few. Pupil–teacher relationships look very different from what we are used to and pupils and teachers, pupils and fellow-pupils, will see themselves as partners in learning. Evidence that Stage 4 is a realistic possibility comes from descriptions of the classrooms of strikingly innovative teachers who have thought deeply about young people's maturity and capabilities as well as about their rights and responsibilities. Here is a teacher who was won over by seeing the potential of consulting pupils about teaching and learning:

> I know a lot more from a different perspective, that's what I like about it. I do see myself differently now. I see myself as part of a partnership rather than having to fathom the entire process by myself from start to finish.
>
> (Boyer *et al.*, 2004: 147–8)

And here is a teacher from the TLRP Project who had a long-standing commitment to consulting pupils and taking into account their perspectives:

> For me, I suppose it's just that I've always been a teacher who has wanted to listen to students and I know from working with students that the more you talk with them and involve them, the more it changes the learning relationship. So I suppose I've decided that a quite different model is possible – which can have a huge impact upon what I want my classroom to be like. It isn't like that yet, but I know where I want to go and the sort of classroom I want to see. We've planned lessons, rewritten curriculum materials, syllabuses and specifications in a way that enables them to say, 'Well, I'm this sort of learner and this is what I enjoy. This is what will change me. We should try that this way.'
>
> (Mulliss, interviewed 2002)

Gill Mulliss's experiences confirm the possibility outlined by Maxine Greene (2000: 297) when she said that pupils' 'critical discourse on their own world is itself a way of remaking that world'.

Stage 5

This is when what happens in the classroom at Stage 4 is adopted at whole-school level. McQuillan (2005) tells the story of developments at Frontier (a pseudonym) High School where pupil voice was a central feature of the drive towards pupil empowerment. We quote the account at some length because it seems to demonstrate the importance of maintaining a coherent values-led approach across all aspects of school life:

The school sought to promote empowerment in multiple ways, much as one employs varied teaching strategies to honour different learning styles . . . Students had a voice in the classroom and could shape the curriculum and their program of study. Each had a faculty advisor and belonged to a cross-grade advisory group. They inevitably encountered opportunities to exercise power and influence.

(*Ibid*.: 662)

Frontier High's commitment to the academic, political, and social dimensions of student empowerment began when the design team created a 'vision statement that included five foundational elements'. The first entailed '*excellence in student learning* [that] will be reflected in all school policies and practices'. A second goal was to promote '*high expectations*' for all by providing support that would enable students to achieve these expectations and by creating an environment that 'encourages students to persevere in the face of difficult tasks'. Third, the school would be a '*democratic learning community*' in which everyone is a learner, everyone is a teacher, and everyone accepts responsibility for supporting, encouraging, and assuring learning by their peers. Students and staff participate in decisions about learning and the learning environment. They share in the responsibility for maintaining the school community. The fourth element, *respect for cultural diversity*, involved 'cultivating the ability of all members [of the school] to see issues and situations from many perspectives' . . . The final tenet, '*personalisation*', was defined as follows:

- students and their families are known and valued; . . .
- students' unique experiences, strengths, prior knowledge, and different rates of learning are the starting points for teaching and learning;
- the curriculum combines student interests with district goals and faculty expertise;
- students have choices in the content and pacing of their learning;
- students demonstrate what they have learned in a variety of ways including writing, art, music, movement and other forms of expression.

(*Ibid*.: 653; emphasis added)

As at Frontier, schools reaching our Stage 5 would be engaged in constructing a school-wide framework that respects pupils' capabilities;

pupil voice would be a prominent feature. Pupils would contribute widely to planning and practice, at school and classroom levels, and would feel that they could help shape procedures for governance. They would genuinely feel that school was 'theirs' and that they were valued members, actively pursuing its learning purposes. Criteria for judging achievement would broaden so that aspects of personal and social development would be valued as highly as academic achievement. Alongside or integrated with the academic agenda, the values of the citizenship agenda would be authentically enacted in the daily inter-changes of the school. Teaching would be organised rather differently and pupils would take more responsibility for making use of resources in support of their learning, with teachers acting as mentors as well as offering specialist academic courses (whether advanced courses in different subject areas or courses covering basic skills in numeracy, literacy and oracy). Teachers would have time to discuss progress with individual pupils and would provide constructive guidance on ways of improving work.

Moving to Stages 4 and 5

For Stages 4 and 5 to be a realistic possibility in more than a handful of schools, the whole apparatus for directing pedagogy and curriculum and for keeping teachers accountable within such a framework needs to be fundamentally rethought. That would also mean a loosening of the iron grip of tests and examinations. Interestingly, there are signs that some independent schools are taking a stand on this issue; Mansell and Paton, in a recent article (*The Times Educational Supplement*, 25 August 2006) quote a teacher from Bedales:

> There's a tendency to say, 'do this and do this' and you've got an A grade rather than saying the syllabus should be the minimum starting point for a process of learning . . . We do not see that as an educational process. We see that as an exercise in passing exams.

We have learned, through our work on consulting pupils and talking to their teachers, that improvement strategies designed to focus directly on test scores and examination grades may look successful as judged by short-term performance criteria but are not so successful when it comes to laying the foundations for a commitment to learning that lasts beyond schooldays and the last exam. As David Hargreaves (2003: 11) shrewdly observed, 'It is possible . . . to increase student test performance while weakening student commitment to learning.' As the teacher quoted above said, we need to value and prioritise 'the educational process' rather than strategies for ratcheting up examination grades. Teachers need to be able to use their professional expertise and judgement in working more creatively with their pupils; at present, however, as they start to develop consultation and participation practices in their classrooms they are constantly looking over their shoulders, aware of the negative power of central surveillance mechanisms, and experiencing the kind of tension between creative autonomy and compliance that Bastian *et al.* (1985: 1) described some years back: schools, they said, are caught between 'a desire . . . to serve the competitive demands of a stratified society, and a desire . . . to play a socially integrative and democratic role, serving the right of all children to develop to their fullest potential'.

Finally, if we have learned anything in the last few years about worthwhile change in schools as opposed to a quick glow enhancer it is that it takes time, commitment and a steady nerve to build and sustain a culture that reflects the school's core values and ensures that all initiatives that are introduced help to advance those values. Schools begin to falter and lose their identity when they are awash with innovations that express different values and that may even send contradictory messages to pupils – as David Hargreaves (2003: 2) well knows: 'Sadly, government and the many stakeholders in education research seem to find it exceptionally difficult to co-ordinate their innovative activities to achieve coherence within clear and shared purposes.' The coherence of new and existing innovations needs to be monitored and affirmed and their cumulative potential evaluated.

If it is to flourish in classrooms and schools, consultation needs to be recognised by different groups of researchers and by policy-makers for its capacity to strengthen pupils' commitment to learning and to contribute in realistic and exciting ways to school improvement. At present, for example, it tends to be ignored by the body of school-effectiveness researchers to whom government policy-makers like to listen. Indeed, as Corbett and Wilson have said, 'Despite . . . repeated calls for reform aimed at students, young people themselves occupy, at best, a minuscule part of the literature on the process of changing and reforming education' (quoted in McQuillan, 2005: 640). To be fair, though, the number of schools that have made pupil consultation and pupil participation the linchpin of their development efforts is probably still quite small and case-study research which can help to define the potential of an innovation in particular settings may be more appropriate than the large-scale surveys that have tended to be the hallmark of school-effectiveness research. Nevertheless, now that we understand more about what consultation can look like in practice and what it can achieve if thoughtfully developed – concerns that were central to our agenda in the TLRP Project – an imaginatively designed evaluation could help raise the profile of pupil voice among policy-makers. After all, McQuillan's (2005: 665) claim – that 'the most promising strategy for reversing [the] long-standing failings of our educational system would be to make student empowerment – in all of its dimensions – our top educational priority' – is surely worth examining.

The project's approach

> The function of research is not necessarily to map and conquer the world but to sophisticate the beholding of it.
>
> (Stake, 1995: 43)

The TLRP Project, Consulting Pupils about Teaching and Learning, consisted of a number of small, relatively self-contained enquiries which were designed and managed by different research teams within the overall framework of the project (see Chapter 1). Colleagues had different educational backgrounds and represented different disciplinary perspectives (sociology, philosophy and psychology). We tried to make use of this diversity of experience and interest to come at pupil voice from different angles and in different ways, and there was no grand design supporting a particular theoretical position. We also set up and maintained a network of interested people – mainly practitioners, but also some policy-makers and researchers, and mainly but not entirely from the UK. We launched a project newsletter, *Communicating*, as a way of keeping in touch with the members of our network and, in time, the members increasingly contributed articles to the newsletters. We also had a series of academic seminars which were a useful way of bringing together members of the core team.

The involvement of researchers from different institutions (in our case Cambridge, London, Sussex and originally Keele and Strathclyde[1]) was one of the ESRC TLRP criteria for funding – and one that made liaison difficult. Involvement in the project represented only a fraction of tenured colleagues' professional responsibilities and most of the contract researchers were also working part time on other projects. To give colleagues maximum flexibility to get on with their other work, we made sure that the constituent enquiries did not last the full three years of the project and we staggered the start and end dates.

The academic seminars (which were always preceded or followed by a team meeting) provided occasional opportunities for the team members to affirm their shared values and engage with the thinking of people outside the project team. The seminars focused on three topics that raised issues that the team saw as central to consultation:

- Seminar 1: Views of childhood;
- Seminar 2: Linguistic competence;
- Seminar 3: Democratic practice and citizenship education.

At each seminar two or three 'experts' in the field opened the discussion with short papers: Iram Siraj Blatchford and Virginia Morrow (Seminar 1); Andrew Pollard and Chris Watkins (Seminar 2); and Lynn Davies, Audrey Osler, Derry Hannam and Mike Wyness (Seminar 3).

But it was the six constituent enquiries that provided the main energy for the pursuit of our aims. Each had its own director and team. These projects ranged in duration from twelve to eighteen months and in their funding from £25,000 to £45,000. (These were relatively low sums and the overall project grant, at £400,000, was among the smallest of the ESRC TLRP grants – but it was all we had asked for!) A more rigorous project design might have included matched samples of pupils and charted their academic progress before and after consultation practices were introduced. But such a design would have required teachers either already experienced in, or specially trained in, consultation strategies and schools where the management team fully supported the work. We already knew that the system was not ready for such an approach: experience of 'authentic' pupil consultation was still thin on the ground and we needed something altogether more exploratory in order to understand what the problems and possibilities of consulting pupils about teaching and learning were. And, indeed, there were some fairly fundamental things on which the project team had to concentrate – such as identifying different strategies and forms of consultation as well as finding out how teachers reacted to what pupils said about their classes.

We wanted, in the circumstances, to provide informed guidance to teachers and school managers about how to make a start on consulting pupils but we were not interested in a simplistic 'what works' formula – we knew from previous experience that the experience of introducing consultation would be significantly affected by the values embedded in particular school and classroom regimes; teachers would need to plan their approach in the light of their understanding of the principles of consultation and their knowledge of school and classroom climates – in particular the degree of trust and mutual respect that existed between teachers and pupils. We were concerned not to simplify the nature of the challenge that consultation would present in certain contexts but rather 'to be accountable to complexity' (Lather, 2001: 202, Quinn (2003: 84) notes that Atkinson (2000: 328) argues that, 'a narrow focus on "what works" will close the door that leads to new possibilities, new strategies, new ways of reframing and reconceiving the educational enterprise'. And we were in fact very close to the stance that Bryk *et al.* took (1998: 260) when they described their earlier project:

> [W]e organized our study around articulating the logic of the reform and probing its critical assumptions. We sought to test this logic against evidence about what was actually happening in schools . . . Our work was framed around one over-arching question: 'What evidence exists that this initiative is evolving in ways that are likely to lead to major improvements in students' school experiences and learning?' At base, we have attempted to combine an empathetic orientation toward the espoused logic of the reform with an empirical perspective about its actual operations.

The project team's common ground resided first in a shared commitment to the broad principles of interactive social science: we saw ourselves as engaged in a kind of 'professional social enquiry' (Caswill and Shove, 2000: 155) that was ready to 'take account of the "ordinary knowledge" of those living in the everyday situations being studied'. Adapting a passage from Baldwin (2000: 184), we have tried to:

• start from *their* experiences;
• respect their concerns, experience and knowledge;
• listen to their views and represent them as authentically as possible;
• use research as a force for change and in ways that we believe they would welcome.

In short, the project was conceived as 'a process that could contribute to teachers' reflection, decision-making and judgements about their practice: not tell them what to do' (Ball, 2001: 266).

The team's common ground was also reflected in a commitment to explore the transformative potential of student consultation and participation. We saw school improvement as going beyond the narrow confines of the performance agenda to include pupils' progress as learners, their sense of self as learners (including their confidence, competence and commitment to learning) and the conditions of learning at classroom and school level. And in relation to our extended network of interested teachers and other professionals we supported Baldwin's (2000: 184) claim that 'engagement with the potential users of research is likely to increase both its quality and its utilisation'. Indeed, we saw teachers as the main gatekeepers of institutional change, and engagement was built through approaches that cast practitioners (and sometimes pupils too) in a partnership role where they were exploring issues alongside the research team, and through the prioritisation of the interview as the main data source so that *our* learning as a team reflected the insights and perspectives of the teachers and pupils who were working with us. An important dimension of our research-and-development approach was the sharing of data about what pupils said, generally as well as in particular contexts, about what helped them to learn and what obstructed their learning.

Our primary, and most robust, source of evidence of the impact of consultation was also the testimony of teachers and pupils. Claims that consultation was bringing about changes in thinking and practice were validated through confirmation by other members of the working group (whether teacher or pupils) and sometimes by observation. The overall picture of the power of consultation to effect desirable educational change was strengthened by the findings of other studies of pupil consultation and participation (see Chapter 13). Although these remained scarce they provided persuasive and confirming evidence of changing dispositions among pupils and their teachers; they demonstrated the potential that lies within the consultation process and the leverage for constructive innovation that can occur when teachers have access to tools and strategies and alternative ways of thinking about teaching and learning.

Note

1   While inter-institutional links were a condition of funding which we met at the time of submitting the proposal, colleagues from the universities of Keele (Kate Myers) and Strathclyde (John MacBeath) moved to the Faculty of Education at Cambridge before the project started. In 2005, after the project was 'officially' over but while the writing up was continuing, Diane Reay also moved to Cambridge.

Appendix 2

TLRP and related projects and publications

Publications from the Consulting Pupils about Teaching and Learning Project

Books

Arnot, M. and Reay, D. (forthcoming) *Social Inequalities Reformed: Consulting Pupils about Learning*, London: Routledge.

Arnot, M., McIntyre, D., Pedder, D. and Reay, D. (2004) *Consultation in the Classroom: Pupil Perspectives on Teaching and Learning*, Cambridge: Pearson.

Fielding, M. and Bragg, S. (2003) *Students as Researchers: Making a Difference*, Cambridge: Pearson.

Flutter, J. and Ruddock, J. (2004) *Consulting Pupils: What's in It for Schools?*, London: RoutledgeFalmer.

MacBeath, J., Demetriou, H., Ruddock, J. and Myers, K. (2003) *Consulting Pupils: A Toolkit for Teachers*, Cambridge: Pearson.

Ruddock, J. and Flutter, J. (2003) *How to Improve Your School: Giving Pupils a Voice*, London: Continuum Press.

Special issues of journals

Fielding, M. (ed.) (2001) *Forum*, 43, 2. Special edition on pupil voice.

Ruddock, J. (2006) *Educational Review*, 58, 2, May. Special edition on the TLRP Project: The Potential of Listening to Pupils.

Academic articles and book chapters

Arnot, M. and Reay, D. (2004) The framing of pedagogic encounters: regulating the social order in classroom learning, in J. Muller, B. Davies and A. Morais (eds) *Reading Bernstein, Researching Bernstein*, London: RoutledgeFalmer.

—— (2004) The social dynamics of classroom learning, in M. Arnot, D. McIntyre, D. Pedder and D. Reay (eds) *Consultation in the Classroom: Pupil Perspectives on Teaching and Learning*, Cambridge: Pearson.

Bragg, S. (2001) Taking a joke: learning from the voices we don't want to hear, *Forum*, 43, 2, 70–3.

—— (in press) 'It's not about systems, it's about relationships': building a listening culture in a primary school, in D. Thiessen and A. Cook-Sather (eds) *The International Handbook of Student Experience of Elementary and Secondary School*, Dordrecht: Kluwer Academic.

Fielding, M. (2001) Beyond the rhetoric of student voice: new departures or new constraints in the transformation of 21st century schooling, *Forum*, 43, 2, 100–9.

—— (2001) Students as radical agents of change, *Journal of Educational Change*, 2, 123–41.

—— (2004) New wave student voice and the renewal of civic society, *London Review of Education*, 2, 3, 197–217.

—— (2004) Transformative approaches to student voice: theoretical underpinnings, recalcitrant realities, *British Educational Research Journal*, 30, 2, 295–311.

Fielding, M. and Bragg, S. (2004) 'It's an equal thing . . . It's about achieving together': student voices and the possibility of a radical collegiality, in H. Street (ed.) *Developing Collaborative Enquiry*, London: Continuum.

Fielding, M. and Prieto, M. (2002) The central place of student voice in democratic renewal: a Chilean case study, in *Learning Democracy and Citizenship: International Experiences*, Oxford: Symposium.

Flutter, J. (2006) Comment améliorer l'enseignement et les apprentissages? Une expérience anglaise, *Revue Internationale d'Éducation, Sèvres*, 43, 91–104.

—— (2006) 'This place could help you learn': student participation in creating better school environments, *Educational Review*, 58, 2, 183–93.

MacBeath, J. (2006) Finding a voice, finding self, *Educational Review*, 58, 2, 195–207.

MacBeath, J., Myers, K. and Demetriou, H. (2001) Supporting teachers in consulting pupils about aspects of teaching and learning, and evaluating impact, *Forum*, 43, 2, 78–82.

McIntyre, D., Pedder, D. and Rudduck, J. (2005) Pupil voice: comfortable and uncomfortable learnings for teachers, *Research Papers in Education*, 20, 2, 149–68.

Pedder, D. and McIntyre, D. (2004) The impact of pupil consultation classroom practice, in M. Arnot, D. McIntyre, D. Pedder and D. Reay (eds) *Consultation in the Classroom: Pupil Perspectives on Teaching and Learning*, Cambridge: Pearson.

—— (2006) Pupil consultation and the importance of social capital, *Educational Review*, 58, 2, 145–57.

Reay, D. (2006) 'I'm not seen as one of the clever children': consulting primary school pupils about the social conditions of learning, *Educational Review*, 58, 2, 171–81.

Reay, D. and Arnot, M. (2003) Participation and control in learning: a pedagogic democratic right?, in L. Poulson and M. Wallace (eds) *Learning to Read Critically in Teaching and Learning*, London: Sage.

Rudduck, J. (2001) Students and school improvement: 'transcending the cramped conditions of the time', *Improving Schools*, 4, 2, 7–16.

—— (2002) The transformative potential of consulting young people about teaching, learning and schooling, *Scottish Educational Review*, 34, 2, 123–37.

—— (2004) Consulting pupils about teaching and learning, in *Learning Texts*, Nottingham: National College for School Leadership.

—— (2006) Student voice, student engagement and school reform, in D. Thiessen and A. Cook-Sather (eds) *International Handbook of Student Experience in Elementary and Secondary Schools*, Dordrecht: Kluwer Academic.

—— (2006) The past, the papers and the project, *Educational Review*, 58, 2, 131–43.

Rudduck, J. and Fielding, M. (2006) Student voice and the perils of popularity, *Educational Review*, 58, 2, 219–31.

Rudduck, J. and Lanskey, C. (in preparation) Leadership and student voice, in *International Encyclopaedia of Education*, 3rd edn, Amsterdam: Elsevier.

Rudduck, J. and Demetriou, H., with Pedder, D. (2003) Student perspectives and teacher practices: the transformative potential, *McGill Journal of Education*, 38, 2, 274–88.

Wyness, M. (2006) Children, young people and civic participation: regulation and local diversity, *Educational Review*, 58, 2, 209–18.

Articles in professional journals

Demetriou, H. and Rudduck, J. (2004) Pupils as researchers: the importance of using their research evidence, *Primary Leadership*, Paper 11 (National Association of Head Teachers), March, 31–4.

Demetriou, H. *et al.* (2001) Transforming our perceptions of pupils, *TLRP Newsletter*, 3, Schools edition, October.

Flutter, J. (2002) Thinking and talking about learning, *Teaching Thinking*, Spring issue, 42–6.

—— (2006) Engaging pupils as partners in learning, *Curriculum Briefing*, 4, 3, 3–7.

Mullis, G. (2002) 'Is this a good idea?' 'It's a great idea', *Communicating* (Newsletter of the Consulting Pupils about Teaching and Learning Project), 6, 2–3.

Rudduck, J. (2003) Pupil voice and citizenship education, March. Available at: <www.qca.org.uk/ages3-14/subjects/6236.html>.

Publications from linked projects

Finney, J., Hickman, R., Morrison, M., Nicholl, B. and Rudduck, J. (2005) *Rebuilding Engagement through the Arts: Responding to Disaffected Students*, Cambridge: Pearson.

Rudduck, J. and Flutter, J. (2004) *The Challenge of Year 8: Sustaining Pupils' Engagement with Learning*, Cambridge: Pearson.

Rudduck, J. and Urquhart, I. (2003) Neglected aspects of transfer and transition: gender and the pupil voice, in C. Skelton and B. Francis (eds) *Boys and Girls in the Primary School Classroom*, Maidenhead: Open University Press.

Rudduck, J., Brown, N. and Hendy, L. (2006) *Personalised Learning and Pupil Voice*, London: DfES.

Rudduck, J., Berry, M., Brown, N. and Hendy, L., with Chandler, M., Enright, P. and Godly, J. (2003) Learning about improvement by talking about improvement, *Improving Schools*, 6, 3, 246–57.

References

Abraham, J. (1989) Testing Hargreaves' and Lacey's differentiation-polarisation theory in a setted comprehensive, *British Journal of Sociology*, 40, 1, 46–81.

Amis, K. (1971) Pernicious participation, in C.B. Cox and A.E. Dyson (eds) *The Black Papers on Education*, London: Davis-Poynter.

Anderman, E.M. and Maehr, M.L. (1994) Motivation and schooling in the middle grades, *Review of Educational Research*, 64, 2, 287–301.

Arnot, M. and Reay, D. (2004a) The social dynamics of classroom learning, in M. Arnot, D. McIntyre, D. Pedder and D. Reay, *Consultation in the Classroom*, Cambridge: Pearson.

—— (2004b) Voice research, learner identities and pedagogic encounters, paper presented at the Third International Basil Bernstein Symposium, 15–18 July, Clare College, Cambridge.

Arnot, M., McIntyre, D., Pedder, D. and Reay, D. (2004) *Consultation in the Classroom: Pupil Perspectives on Teaching and Learning*, Cambridge: Pearson.

Atkinson, E. (2000) In defence of ideas, or why 'what works' is not enough, *British Journal of Sociology of Education*, 21, 3, 317–30.

—— (2003) Education, postmodernism and the organisation of consent, in J. Satterthwaite, E. Atkinson and K. Gale (eds) *Discourse, Power, Resistance: Challenging the Rhetoric of Contemporary Education*, Wiltshire: Cromwell Press.

Baldwin, S. (2000) Interactive social science in practice: new approaches to the production of knowledge and their implications, *Science and Public Policy*, 27, 3, 183–94.

Ball, S. (1981) *Beachside Comprehensive*, Cambridge: Cambridge University Press.

—— (2001) 'You've bee NERFed'. Dumbing down the academy: National Educational Research Forum: a national strategy consultation paper – a brief and bilious response, *Journal of Educational Policy*, 16, 3, 265–8.

Bastian, A., Fruchter, N., Gittell, M., Greer, C. and Haskins, K. (1985) *Choosing Equality: The Case for Democratic Schooling*, New York: New World Foundation.

Bates, R. (2002) The impact of educational research: alternative methodologies and conclusions, *Research Papers in Education*, 17, 4, 403–8.

Berliner, D.C. (1987) Ways of thinking about students and classrooms by more and less experienced teachers, in James Calderhead (ed.) *Exploring Teachers' Thinking*, London: Cassell.

Bernstein, B. (1990) *The Structuring of Pedagogic Discourse*, Volume IV, London: Routledge.

—— (1996) *Pedagogy, Symbolic Control and Identity*, London: Taylor and Francis.

Berry, R.A.W. (2006) Inclusion, power and community: teachers and students interpret the language of community in an inclusion classroom, *American Educational Research Journal*, 43, 3, 489–529.

Birkett, D. (2001) The school we'd like, *Guardian Unlimited*, 5 June. Available at: <http://education.guardian.co.uk/schools/story/0,5500,501374,00.html>.

Blishen E. (ed.) (1969) *The School that I'd Like*, Harmondsworth: Penguin Education.

Borland, M., Hill, M., Laybourn, A. and Stafford, A. (2001) *Improving Consultation with Children and Young People in Relevant Aspects of Policy-Making and Legislation in Scotland*, Edinburgh: Scottish Parliament, SP Paper 365.

Boyer, I. and Maney, B., with Kamler, B. and Comber, B. (2004) Reciprocal mentoring across generations: sustaining professional development for English teachers, *English Teaching: Practice and Critique*, 3, 2, 139–50.

Brice Heath, S. (2004) Risk, rules and roles, in A.N. Perret-Clermont, C. Pontecorvo, L.B. Resnick, T. Zittoun and B. Burge (eds) *Joining Society: Social Interaction and Learning in Adolescence and Youth*, Cambridge: Cambridge University Press.

Brown, S. and McIntyre, D. (1993) *Making Sense of Teaching*, Buckingham: Open University Press.

Bryk, A.S., Sebring, P.B., Kerbow, M.D., Rollow, S. and Easton, J.Q. (1998) *Charting Chicago School Reform*, Boulder, Col. and Oxford: Westview Press.

Caswill, C. and Shove, E. (2000) Introducing interactive social science, *Science and Public Policy*, 27, 3, 154–7.

Coleman, S. (2005) *Remixing Citizenship: Democracy and Young People's Use of the Internet*, Carnegie YPI Research Report, London: Carnegie Foundation.

Comber, B. and Kamler, B. (2004) Getting out of deficit: pedagogies or reconnection, *Teaching Education*, 15, 3, 303–20.

Cook-Sather, A. (2002) Authorising students' perspectives: toward trust, dialogue, and change in education, *Educational Researcher*, 31, 4, 3–14.

Cooper, P. and McIntyre, D. (1996) *Effective Teaching and Learning: Teachers' and Students' Perspectives*, Buckingham: Open University Press.

Corbett, D. and Wilson, B. (1995) Make a difference with, not for, students: a plea to researchers and reformers, *Educational Researcher*, 24, 5, 12–17.

Cummins, J. (1986) Empowering minority students: a framework for intervention, *Harvard Educational Review*, 56, 18–36.

Davies, L. (1984) *Pupil Power: Deviance and Gender in School*, Lewes: Falmer Press.

—— (2001) Pupil voice and the quality of teaching and learning, paper presented at the ESRC/TLRP Consulting Pupils Network Seminar 3: Pupil Voice and Democracy, Homerton College, University of Cambridge, 15 October.

Dent, H. (1930) The aim: an educated democracy, *The Nineteenth Century and After*, 107, January, 10–16.

DfES (2003) *Every Child Matters*, Green Paper, London: HMSO, Ref.: CM5860.

—— (2004) *Working Together: Giving Children and Young People a Say*, Guidance Curriculum and Standards, London: HMSO, Ref.: DfES/0134/2004.

Doyle, W. (1986) Classroom organization and management, in M.C. Wittrock (ed.) *Handbook of Research on Teaching*, 3rd edn, New York: Macmillan.

Dubberley, W. (1988) Social class and the process of schooling – a case study of a comprehensive school in a mining community, in A. Green and S. Ball (eds) *Progress and Inequality in Comprehensive Education*, London: Routledge.

Fielding, M. and Bragg, S. (2003) *Students as Researchers: Making a Difference*, Cambridge: Pearson.

Fielding, M. and McGregor, J. (2005) Deconstructing student voice: new spaces for dialogue or new opportunities for surveillance?, paper presented at the American Educational Research Association, Montreal.

Flutter, J. and Rudduck, J. (2004) *Consulting Pupils: What's in It for Schools?*, London: RoutledgeFalmer.

Fullan, M. and Stiegelbauer, S. (1991) *The New Meaning of Educational Change*, 2nd edn, New York: Teachers College Press.

Furlong, V.J. (1976) Interaction sets in the classroom: towards a study of pupil knowledge, in M. Hammersey and P. Woods (eds) *The Process of Schooling*, London: Routledge and Kegan Paul.

Gadeyne, E., Ghesquiere, P. and Onghena, P. (2006) Psychosocial educational effectiveness criteria and their relation to teaching in primary education, *School Effectiveness and School Improvement*, 17, 1, 63–85.

Gale, K. (2003) Creative pedagogies of resistance in post compulsory (teacher) education, in J. Satterthwaite, E. Atkinson and K. Gale (eds) *Discourse, Power, Resistance: Challenging the Rhetoric of Contemporary Education*, Stoke-on-Trent: Trentham.

Gillborn, D. and Mirza, H. (2000) *Educational Inequality: Mapping Race, Class and Gender*, London: Ofsted, HMSO.

Giroux, H. (1981) *Ideology, Culture and the Process of Schooling*, Lewes: Falmer Press.

Grace, G. (1995) *School Leadership: Beyond Education Management, an Essay in Policy Scholarship*, London: Falmer Press.

Greene, M. (1985) Teacher as project: choice, perspective and the public space, mimeo.

—— (2000) Lived spaces, shared spaces, public spaces, in L. Weis and M. Fine (eds) *Construction Sites: Excavating Race, Class, and Gender among Urban Youth*, New York: Teachers College Press.

Hargreaves, D.H. (1967) *Social Relations in a Secondary School*, London: Routledge and Kegan Paul.

—— (1982) *The Challenge for the Comprehensive School: Culture, Curriculum and Community*, London: Routledge and Kegan Paul.

—— (2003) From improvement to transformation, keynote lecture, International Congress for School Effectiveness and Improvement: Schooling the Knowledge Society, Sydney, 5 January.

Hendrick, H. (1997) Constructions and reconstructions of British childhood: an interpretative survey, 1800 to the present, in A. James and A. Prout (eds) *Constructing and Reconstructing Childhood*, London: Falmer Press.

Ireland, E., Kerr, D., Lopes, J. and Nelson, J., with Cleaver, E. (2006) *Active Citizenship and Young People: Opportunities, Experiences and Challenges in and beyond School*, fourth annual report of the Citizenship Education Longitudinal Study, Slough: National Foundation for Educational Research, DfES Research Brief No. RB732.

James, A. and Prout, A. (1997) Preface to the second edition, in A. James and A. Prout (eds) *Constructing and Reconstructing Childhood*, London: Falmer Press.

Jonathan, R. (1989) Choice and control in education: parental rights, individual liberties and social justice, *British Journal of Educational Studies*, 37, 321–38.

Kamler, B. and Comber, B. (2005) Turn-around pedagogies: improving the education of at-risk students, *Improving Schools*, 8, 2, 121–31.

Kane, R.G. and Maw, N. (2005) Making sense of learning at secondary school: involving students to improve teaching practice, *Cambridge Journal of Education*, 35, 3, 311–22.

Kershner, R. (1996) The meaning of 'working hard' in school, in J. Rudduck, R. Chaplain and G. Wallace (eds) *School Improvement: What Can Pupils Tell Us?*, London: David Fulton.

Lacey, C. (1970) *Hightown Grammar*, Manchester: Manchester University Press.

Lather, P. (2001) Working the ruins of feminist ethnography, *Signs*, 27, 1, 199–227.

Lave, J. and Wenger, E. (1991) *Situated Learning: Legitimate Peripheral Participation*, New York: Cambridge University Press.

MacBeath, J., Demetriou, H., Rudduck, J. and Myers, K. (2003) *Consulting Pupils: A Toolkit for Teachers*, Cambridge: Pearson.

McIntyre, D., Pedder, D. and Rudduck, J. (2005) Pupil voice: comfortable and uncomfortable learnings for teachers, *Research Papers in Education*, 20, 149–68.

McQuillan, P.J. (2005) Possibilities and pitfalls: a comparative analysis of student empowerment, *American Educational Research Journal*, 42, 4, 639–70.

Meadmore, S.D. (1993) The production of individuality through examination, *Journal of Curriculum Studies*, 14, 1, 59–73.

Measor, L. and Woods, P. (1984) *Changing Schools: Pupil Perspectives on Transfer to a Comprehensive*, Milton Keynes: Open University Press.

Meighan, R. (1977) The pupil as client: the learner's experience of schooling, *Educational Review*, 29, 123–35.

—— (1978) Editorial, *Educational Review*, 30, 2, 1.

Meikle, J. (2006) Schools poor at teaching citizenship, says Ofsted, *Guardian*, 28 September, 6.

Mitchell, C. and Sackney, L. (2000) *Profound Improvement: Building Capacity for a Learning Community*, Netherlands: Swets & Zeitlinger.

Mitra, D. (2001) Opening the floodgates: giving students a voice in school reform, *Forum*, 43, 2, 91–4.

Morgan, B. (2000) How teachers respond to and use pupil perspectives to improve teaching and learning, Master of Philosophy thesis, University of Cambridge.

—— (2007) Consulting pupils about classroom teaching and learning: policy, practice and response in one school, Doctor of Philosophy thesis, University of Cambridge.

Morrison, M. (2005) I was like listened to and it made me feel proud, in J. Finney, R. Hickman, M. Morrison, B. Nicholl and J. Rudduck, *Rebuilding Engagement through the Arts: Responding to Disaffected Students*, Cambridge: Pearson.

Morrow, V. (1994) Responsible children? Aspects of children's work and employment outside school in contemporary UK, in B. Mayall (ed.) *Children's Childhoods: Observed and Experienced*, London: Falmer Press.

Mulliss, G. (2002) 'Is this a good idea?' 'It's a great idea', *Communicating*, 6, 2–3.

Muncey, D.E. and McQuillan, P.J. (1996) Reform and resistance: an ethnographic view of the coalition of essential schools, New Haven, Conn.: Yale University Press.

Newsletters of the ESRC Consultation Network Project (2001–3) No. 2, September 2001; No. 6, September 2002; No. 8, February 2003; No. 11, November 2003.

Noyes, A. (2005) Thematic review: pupil voice: purpose, power and the possibilities for democratic schooling, *British Educational Research Journal*, 31, 4, 533–40.

Pedder, D. and McIntyre, D. (2004) The impact of pupil consultation on classroom practice, in M. Arnot, D. McIntyre, D. Pedder and D. Reay, *Consultation in the Classroom*, Cambridge: Pearson.

—— (2006) Pupil consultation: the importance of social capital, *Educational Review*, 58, 2, 145–58.

Portes, A. (1998) Social capital: its origins and applications in modern sociology, *Annual Review of Sociology*, 24, 1–24.

Prout, A. and James, A. (1997) A new paradigm for the sociology of childhood? Provenance, promise and problems, in A. James and A. Prout (eds) *Constructing and Reconstructing Childhood*, London: Falmer Press.

Quinn, J. (2003) The ethnographic self as hired hand: reflecting on researching educational partnerships, in J. Satterthwaite, E. Atkinson and K. Gale (eds) *Discourse, Power, Resistance: Challenging the Rhetoric of Contemporary Education*, Stoke-on-Trent: Trentham.

Qvortrup, J. (1997) A voice for children in statistical and social accounting: a plea for children's right to be heard, in A. James and A. Prout (eds) *Constructing and Reconstructing Childhood*, London: Falmer Press.

Rachal, J.R. (1998) We'll never turn back: adult education and the struggle for citizenship in Mississippi's Freedom Summer, *American Educational Research Journal*, 35, 2, 167–98.

Ranson, S. (2000) Recognising the pedagogy of voice in a learning community, *Educational Management and Administration*, 28, 3, 263–79.

Reay, D. and Arnot, M. (2003) Participation and control in learning: a pedagogic democratic right?, in L. Poulson and M. Wallace (eds) *Learning to Read Critically in Teaching and Learning*, London: Sage.

Rosenbaum, M. and Newell, P. (1991) *Taking Children Seriously: A Proposal for a Children's Rights Commissioner*, London: Calouste Gulbenkian Foundation.

Rudduck, J. (1999) 'Education for all', 'achievement for all' and pupils who are 'too good to drift' (the second Harold Dent Memorial Lecture), *Education Today*, 49, 2, 3–11.

Rudduck, J. and Flutter, J. (2004) *How to Improve your School: Giving Pupils a Voice*, London: Continuum Press.

Rudduck, J., Brown, N. and Hendy, L. (2006) *Personalised Learning and Pupil Voice*, London: DfES Innovations Unit.

Rudduck, J., Chaplain, R. and Wallace, G. (1996) *School Improvement: What Can Pupils Tell Us?*, London: David Fulton.

Rudduck, J., Day, J. and Wallace, G. (1996) The significance for school improvement of pupils' experiences of within-school transitions, *Curriculum*, 17, 3, 144–53.

Sarason, S.B. (1993) *The Case for Change: Rethinking the Preparation of Educators*, San Francisco, Calif.: Jossey-Bass.

Sealander, J. (2003) *The Failed Century of the Child: Governing America's Young in the Twentieth Century*, Cambridge: Cambridge University Press.

Senge, P.M., Kleiner, A., Roberts, C., Ross, R., Roth, G. and Smith, B. (1999) *The Dance of Change: The Challenges to Sustaining Momentum in Learning Organisations*, New York: Doubleday.

Sergiovanni, T. (2000) *The Lifeworld of Leadership: Creating Culture, Community, and Personal Meaning in Our Schools*, San Francisco, Calif.: Jossey-Bass.

Silva, E. (2001) Squeaky wheels and flat tires: a case study of students as reform participants, *Forum*, 43, 2, 95–9.

Stake, R.E. (1995) *The Art of Case Study Research*, London: Sage.

Tanner, R. (1987) *Double Harness*, London: Impact.

Taylor, P.H. (1962) Children's evaluations of the characteristics of the good teacher, *British Journal of Educational Psychology*, 32, 258–66.

Troman, G. (1988) Getting it right: selection and setting in a 9–13 years middle school, *British Journal of Sociology*, 9, 4, 403–22.

Turner, G. (1983) *The Social World of the Comprehensive School*, London: Croom Helm.

United Nations Convention on the Rights of the Child (1989) UN General Assembly, Resolution 44/25. Available at: <http://www.ohchr.org/english/law/crc.htm#art12>.

Wagg, S. (1996) 'Don't try to understand them': politics, childhood and the new education market, in J. Pilcher and S. Wagg (eds) *Thatcher's Children? Politics, Childhood and Society in the 1980s and 1990s*, London: Falmer Press.

Wallace, G. (1996a) Engaging with learning, in J. Rudduck, R. Chaplain and G. Wallace (eds) *School Improvement: What Can Pupils Tell Us?*, London: David Fulton.

—— (1996b) Relating to teachers, in J. Rudduck, R. Chaplain and G. Wallace (eds) *School Improvement: What Can Pupils Tell Us?*, London: David Fulton.

Wehlage, G.G., Rutter, R.A., Gregory, A., Smith, N.L. and Fernandez, R.R. (1989) *Reducing the Risk: Schools as Communities of Support*, Lewes: Falmer Press.

Weis, L. and Fine, M. (eds) (2000) *Construction Sites: Excavating Race, Class, and Gender among Urban Youth*, New York: Teachers College Press.

Wenger, E. (1998) *Communities of Practice: Learning, Meaning, and Identity*, Cambridge: Cambridge University Press.

Willis, P. (1977) *Learning to Labour*, Farnborough: Saxon House.

Woods, P. (ed.) (1980) *Pupil Strategies*, London: Croom Helm.

——. (1990) *The Happiest Days: How Pupils Cope with School*, London: Falmer Press.

—— (1993) *Critical Events in Teaching and Learning*, Lewes: Falmer Press.

Wragg, E.C. and Wood, E.K. (1984) Pupil appraisals of teaching, in E.C. Wragg (ed.) *Classroom Teaching Skills*, London: Croom Helm.

Index

ability, differences in 89–93, 102, 164–5
advocacy 176–7, 180
affirmation of teacher practices 126–7
agency, pupils' sense of 41, 70, 171–2, 186, 196
Amis, K. 159
anonymity 110, 157, 170, 173
anxiety 160–1, 165, 166–7, 178
appreciation of teachers 75–7, 171–2
Arnot, M. 18, 86, 88–90, 91, 93, 94, 96, 98–9, 100, 101
assessment of learning 91
Atkinson, E. 204
attention from teachers 100, 105, 164; ability differences and 92–3; gender differences and 94–5; unfairness in 92–3, 98–9
attitudes to learning, impact of consultation on 140–1
authenticity 35–6, 44; of teachers' responses 107–10, 116–17, 174
autonomy 69–71, 72

Baldwin, S. 205
Ball, S. 90
Bastian, A. 200
benefits of consultation 121–2, 152, 178; for pupils 121, 141–5; for teachers 145–8
Berry, R. 8, 185

Birkett, D. 142
Blishen, E. 155
boredom 78, 187; avoidance of 60–1, 72
Borland, M. 164
boys, working-class 89–90, 91, 100; friendships 98; resentment towards girls 93–4
Bragg, S. 41–2, 121, 176
Brice Heath, S. 164
Brown, N. 19, 70
Brown, S. 48–9
Bryk, A.S. 204

childhood 194
Children Act 1989 193
Children's Commissioner 5, 8, 21
citizenship education 5, 7, 21, 162; consultation and 10–12
class differences 88, 102
Coleman, S. 186
collaboration 65, 133, 147–8; peer 68–9, 76
Comber, B. 191
commitment to learning 6, 140–1, 186, 190, 195, 199–200
conditions for consultation 168–9, 178–90; in classrooms 169–74, 179; in schools 174–8, 179–80
conditions for learning, pupil difference and 89–102

confidence in teaching, and response
  to pupil ideas 133–5, 136, 137
confidentiality 110
connections 63–4, 71–2
constraints on consultation 134,
  137, 156–7, 166, 173
constructivist approach 4
consultation 4, 7, 12–14, 25–7;
  control over 31–2, 44; potential
  of 26, 105–7, 154, 195, 196,
  198–9
Consulting Pupils about Classroom
  Teaching project 20–1
contrasts, teacher criticism in terms
  of 80–2
control over learning 99–101
Cook-Sather, A. 195
Cooper, P. 14, 58, 59, 63, 65, 68
Corbett, D. 200
Cox, Ingrid 120
criticism of teachers 78–9, 80–2,
  123, 127; anxiety about 160–1,
  165
culture of resistance 101
curriculum, as constraint on
  consultation 134, 137, 156–7,
  166

Davies, L. 5, 10, 87
Denmark, pupil representation on
  school boards in 5
Dent, H. 12
dialogue, conditions for 36–7, 44
direct consultation 39, 44
discussion 69, 130–1, 132, 186
disengagement 159, 160
diversity of pupils' experiences 30,
  86–9, 101–2, 137, 161–2, 188;
  respect for 198

economy, in consultation process
  39–40, 45
educational effectiveness, and
  teacher response to ideas 124

English Secondary Students'
  Association 5
enthusiasm of teachers 50–1, 120–2,
  132, 147
ethnic differences 88
ethnographic studies 46–8, 59, 61–2,
  87–8
Every Child Matters (DfES) 5
experience, relating abstract ideas to
  66–7, 186
experiments 66, 81
expertise, and response to pupil
  ideas 133–5, 136, 137
explanation 76–7; need for clear
  62–5, 71; too much 78

fairness of teachers 47, 54, 55, 56;
  and unfairness 92–3, 98–9
feedback from consultation 6, 37,
  109, 144
Fielding, M. 17, 26, 41–2, 121, 176
Flutter, J. 19, 49–51, 58, 68, 70, 98
Freestone, Paul 120
friends, support from 96–8
Furlong, V.J. 61, 87

gender differences 88, 93–6, 102
generality, levels of, in what is
  learned 29–31
Germany, pupil representation on
  school boards in 5
Gillborn, D. 88
girls: resentment of boys' perceived
  laziness 95–6; teachers'
  favouritism for 94–5
Giroux, H. 12
government: and consultation 9–12,
  21; view of learning 188–9,
  190–1
Grace, G. 13
Greene, M. 155
group and individual perspectives
  161
group work 68–9, 187

grouping practices 189

Hargreaves, D. 154, 159, 183–4, 199–200
Hendrick, H. 194
humanity, of teachers 47, 50, 51

ideology of immaturity 13, 118
ideology of professionalism 119, 130
independence of pupils 70, 71, 76
informal consultation 27–9, 43
interactionist studies 86–8
interactive learning 186–7
interpersonal dimensions of learning 184–6
interviews 39, 40, 104–5
Ireland, E. 11

Jonathan, R. 191
justice, of teachers 47, 50, 51

Kamber, B. 191
Kershner, R. 57
key informants 112–13, 122, 165, 170

Lacey, C. 86
learning 198; consultation helping 113–15, 116, 117, 186–9; control over 99–101; government strategies for improving 188–9; interest in 61–2; interpersonal/personal dimensions 183–6; meaningful 61–5; pupil perspectives 58–73
Learning about Improvement project 19, 49–51, 70, 121
learning community 177, 198
learning from consultation 34, 43; generalised 29–30; open-ended 31–2; personal 30
learning group dynamics 89–101, 187–8

lessons, acceptability of commenting on 163–4, 167

MacBeath, J. 16, 39–40, 45, 121
McGregor, J. 26
McIntyre, D. 14, 16, 19, 36–7, 48–9, 58–9, 63, 65, 68, 70, 71
McQuillan, P.J. 9, 195–6, 197–8, 201
Mansell, W. 199
meaningfulness 62–5, 71–2; instrumental 63; personal 63, 64
Measor, L. 87
mediated consultation 39, 44
Meighan, R. 4
Meikle, J. 11
membership, pupils' sense of 141–2, 145, 151, 185, 190, 196
methods of consultation 16–17, 38–42
Mirza, H. 88
Mitchell, C. 165, 177
mixed-ability classes 90
modifications to teaching 79–80
Morgan, B. 20–1, 104–5
motivation: for consultation 168–9; for learning 48, 52–3, 91, 140, 141, 171
Mulliss, G. 104, 120, 142, 175–6, 197
Muncey, D.E. 195

National Curriculum, obligations to 134, 137
National Federation for Educational Research 11–12
National Union of Secondary School Students 4–5
Netherlands, pupil representation on school boards in 5
Newell, D. 190–1
Noyes, A. 25, 36

Ofsted 26; feedback from pupils 5–6, 21
on-line debates 196

pace of learning 100–1
parents: help with schoolwork 91–2; support for consultation 158–9, 178
participation 7–9, 184; active 65–6, 72, 73
Paton, G. 199
Pedder, D. 86, 97, 150
peer-group culture 98–9; pressure of 99, 110, 164, 190
peer-group relationships, and conditions for learning 96–9
performance agenda 188–9, 191, 199–200
performance review 26–7
personal and social development 6, 158, 199
personalised learning 21, 30, 184, 198
Personalised Learning and Pupil Voice project 20, 52–4, 184
planning of consultation 38, 43, 133–4
Portes, A. 150
posters 128
power, in consultation process 39–40, 45
practical work 77, 132–3
practicality of pupil ideas 125, 132–3, 135
professionalism of teachers 119, 130
prompted consultation 39, 44
pupil ideas: accepted and developed by teachers 128–9, 136–7; criteria for teachers to act on 124–9, 138; differences in teachers' attitudes to 129–36
pupil voice 11–12, 17–18, 75; diversity of interest in 3–6, 21; on learning activities 59–71;

research into 192–3, 194–6; stages in development of 192–9; on teacher–pupil relationships 51–4, 55–6; on teachers 47–51, 107–10, 116–17, 141; validity of 124–5
pupils 184; acting as researchers 17, 31, 41–2, 143–4; attitude to consultation 75, 104–13, 114–15, 116; impact of consultation on 140–5, 150–1; lower-achieving 91, 92, 96, 100, 143, 159–60, 164; preferred identities 87, 89, 187–8; whom to consult 32–4, 42
Pupils' Experiences of Teaching and Learning 19

qualities of teachers 48–51
questionnaires 104–5, 173; alternatives to 112–13; closed-choice 31, 39; pupil perceptions of 110–11, 117; teachers' responses to 107–8, 109
Quinn, J. 204
Qvortrup, J. 194

Rachal, J.R. 174
Ranson, S. 162
reassurance for teachers 26, 75–6, 83, 123, 160
Reay, D. 86, 88–90, 91, 93, 94, 96, 98–9, 100, 101
reciprocity 54, 150, 184, 185
recognition 171–3, 179, 184–5
reflection 142–3, 145–6, 173–4, 186
representativeness of pupil ideas 125–6
researchers 4, 31; pupils as 17, 31, 41–2, 143–4; use of to interview pupils 40–1
reservations about consultation: pupils' 163–5, 167; teachers' 156–63, 165–6

respect: mutual 53–4, 55, 149, 150, 169–70, 179, 185–6; for pupils 50, 51, 69–70, 146, 149, 185, 190; for teachers 75–6, 115
rights of young people 4–5, 6
role play 66, 67
Rosenbaum, M. 190–1
Rudduck, J. 14, 19, 20, 49–51, 58, 68, 70, 98

Sackney, L. 165, 177
Sarason, S.B. 168
scepticism of teachers 131–2, 135, 159
school boards, pupil representation on 5
school councils 21, 120, 178
school culture 177, 195, 200
school improvement 191, 195, 199–200, 205; consultation and 9–10
school self-review 156
schools: influence on motivation to learn 189–91; support for consultation in 157–8, 161, 166–7, 174–8, 179–80
schoolwork, pupils' attitudes to 47–8, 62
Sealander, J. 193, 194
self-esteem 145, 152, 184, 189–90, 196
Senge, P.M. 165
senior management, support for consultation 104, 158, 176, 177, 178–9, 180
sense of humour, teachers' 53
sense of self 144–5
sensitivity of teachers 50, 51, 57; and insensitivity 90
social conditions of learning 18–19, 30, 137
spidergrams 66, 81, 128
storytelling 63, 67
strategies for consultation 35–8, 43

student empowerment 9, 197–8
subcultures 86, 87, 90
Sweden, pupil representation on school boards in 5

Tanner, R. 155
teacher–pupil relationships 35, 43, 111, 117, 185–6, 196–7; impact of consultation on 149–50, 152; pupil perspectives on 51–4, 55–6
teachers 7, 13, 58; appreciation of 75–7, 171–2; attitudes to consultation 118–22, 156–63, 165–6, 200; consultation strategies 35–8; differences in attitudes to pupil ideas 129–36, 138; impact of consultation on 145–8, 151, 160; information about pupils 119, 136; lack of support for 157–9; pupil attitudes to, after consultation 114–15, 116–17; pupil perspectives on 48–51, 107–10, 141; reliance on for help with schoolwork 57, 91, 100–1; responses to pupils' ideas 16, 107–10, 122–36, 137, 161, 187; undermining of friendship support 97–8
Teachers' and Pupils' Perceptions of Effective Classroom Learning 19
Teaching and Learning Research Programme (TLRP) 4; Consulting Pupils about Teaching and Learning Project 14–21, 202–5
teaching assistants 177
teaching practices: affirmation of 126–7; alternative ideas 82–3; contrasts in 81–2, 83; ideas for modifying 79–80; unhelpful 78–9, 83–4, 127
tedium see boredom
time, constraints of on consultation 9, 35, 38, 134, 156–7, 173

TLRP *see* Teaching and Learning Research Programme
togetherness 68–9
transformation 154–5
trust 110; mutual 36–7, 43, 55, 163, 166, 169–70, 179, 185–6; in pupils 70, 76, 93–4, 146, 149, 150, 185; in schools 91, 175; in teachers 43, 54, 150, 164

understanding 62, 77; methods of achieving 62–7
United Nations Convention on the Rights of the Child 5, 9, 21, 193

visual stimuli 63, 66, 67, 81

Wagg, S. 4–5

Wallace, G. 57, 63
whole-class discussion 130–1, 132
whole-school strategies 43, 45, 178–9, 197–8
Wilson, B. 200
Woods, P. 3–4, 46–7, 48, 59, 61, 62, 63, 87–8
working-class pupils: control of own learning 100–1, 102; cultural gaps with school 91, 100; sense of teacher unfairness 92–3, 98–9; *see also* boys, working-class
Working Together (DfES) 8
written evaluations 112, 157, 164, 173

Youth Parliament 5

LB 1033 .R83 2007

Rudduck, Jean.

Improving learning through consulting pupils